PROGRAMMING ENVIRONMENTS FOR PARALLEL COMPUTING

★
WITHDRAWN
FROM
LIBRARY STOCK
★
UNIVERSITY OF STRATHCLYDE

Books are to be returned on or before
the last date below.

- 7 JUL 1994

LIBREX –

IFIP Transactions A: Computer Science and Technology

International Federation for Information Processing

Technical Committees:

SOFTWARE: THEORY AND PRACTICE (TC2)
EDUCATION (TC3)
SYSTEM MODELLING AND OPTIMIZATION (TC7)
INFORMATION SYSTEMS (TC8)
RELATIONSHIP BETWEEN COMPUTERS AND SOCIETY (TC9)
COMPUTER SYSTEMS TECHNOLOGY (TC10)
SECURITY AND PROTECTION IN INFORMATION PROCESSING SYSTEMS (TC11)
ARTIFICIAL INTELLIGENCE (TC12)
HUMAN-COMPUTER INTERACTION (TC13)
FOUNDATIONS OF COMPUTER SCIENCE (SG14)

IFIP Transactions Abstracted/Indexed in:
INSPEC Information Services

#26217009

A-11

PROGRAMMING ENVIRONMENTS FOR PARALLEL COMPUTING

Proceedings of the IFIP WG 10.3 Workshop on
Programming Environments for Parallel Computing
Edinburgh, Scotland, 6-8 April, 1992

Edited by

NIGEL TOPHAM
ROLAND IBBETT
University of Edinburgh
Edinburgh, Scotland

THOMAS BEMMERL
Institut für Informatik
TU München
Munich, Germany

1992

NORTH-HOLLAND
AMSTERDAM • LONDON • NEW YORK • TOKYO

ELSEVIER SCIENCE PUBLISHERS B.V.
Sara Burgerhartstraat 25
P.O. Box 211, 1000 AE Amsterdam, The Netherlands

ISBN: 0 444 89764 X
ISSN: 0926-5473

© 1992 IFIP. All rights reserved.
No part of this publication may be reproduced, stored in a retrieval system or transmitted in any form or by any means, electronic, mechanical, photocopying, recording or otherwise, without the prior written permission of the publisher, Elsevier Science Publishers B.V., Copyright & Permissions Department, P.O. Box 521, 1000 AM Amsterdam, The Netherlands.

Special regulations for readers in the U.S.A. - This publication has been registered with the Copyright Clearance Center Inc. (CCC), Salem, Massachusetts. Information can be obtained from the CCC about conditions under which photocopies of parts of this publication may be made in the U.S.A. All other copyright questions, including photocopying outside of the U.S.A., should be referred to the publisher, Elsevier Science Publishers B.V., unless otherwise specified.

No responsibility is assumed by the publisher or by IFIP for any injury and/or damage to persons or property as a matter of products liability, negligence or otherwise, or from any use or operation of any methods, products, instructions or ideas contained in the material herein.

pp. 161- 170, 193-214: Copyright not transferred.

This book is printed on acid-free paper.

Printed in The Netherlands

D 005.275 IFI

Preface

This publication is based on the proceedings of the International Federation for Information Processing (IFIP) Working Group 10.3 Conference on Programming Environments for Parallel Computing which took place at the Edinburgh Parallel Computing Centre (EPCC), Edinburgh, Scotland, in April 1992. The conference was co-sponsored by the Parallel Processing special interest group (PPSIG) of the British Computer Society (BCS) and by PARS of the German Computer Society GI (Gesellschaft für Informatik).

The charter of the IFIP Working Group 10.3 is to develop innovation in digital systems, having one or more computing elements, in order to improve the quality of attributes such as cost, reliability, performance, programmability, extensibility and function. Such innovation is to be sought by considering the interrelation of Software, Firmware and Hardware in specification, design and implementation.

Although parallel architectures were considered pure research vehicles some years ago, this situation has changed dramatically in recent times. Commercial parallel systems are available from a wide variety of vendors, each competing for market shares. The 1990's seem set to become the decade of parallel and distributed computing. However, the experience of many users, porting commercial and scientific software to parallel machines, has highlighted a clear need for good programming environments. The subject of this working conference, "Programming Environments for Parallel Computing", was targetted at bringing together researchers who share the goal of making parallel programming easier and more accessible.

The papers within these proceedings cover five main areas: programming environments, visualisation and monitoring systems, programming models for parallel systems, the construction of parallel applications, and toolkits and debuggers for parallel systems.

In the area of environments Magee and Dulay describe a system called *MP*, and Schäfers *et al.* describe a graphical programming environment.

The area of visualisation and monitoring saw the majority of submissions, and this is reflected in the balance of contributions in these proceedings. Sistare *et al.* describe the *PRISM* system from Thinking Machines Corporation, Dauphin *et al.* discuss the validation of parallel programs using program models and event traces, and there are papers from van Reik and Tourancheau, Glendenning *et al.*, and Zabala and Taylor describing a variety of generic visualisation and monitoring systems. Bemmerl *et al.* describe the adaptation of a portable performance measurement system to a multi-transputer monitoring system.

Four papers discuss the subject of programming models for parallel systems. Szafron *et al.* describe the *Enterprise* parallel programming model. Mallon and Dew present a method of interprocessor communication using shared objects. Orlando and Vanneschi describe a system called *SYMPLE* – a CSP-like model for performing static optimisations. Giloi *et al.* describe a *virtual processor* model for massively parallel systems.

A number of papers on constructing parallel applications were presented at the conference, and these concentrate primarily on ways to help the programmer develop scalable applications. In this area we have contributions from Kitajima and Plateau who describe a system called *ALPES*, from Dobson and Wellings who describe a system for building scalable parallel applications, and from Decker and Rehmann who describe an application development environment called *ADE*.

In the area of tools and toolkits for parallel processing there is a paper by Gannon *et al.* which describes the *SIGMA II* program analysis and restructuring library, and a paper by Tatemura *et al.* describing a debugger, called *HyperDEBU*, for parallel logic programs.

A total of forty papers were submitted, and each was evaluated by at least three international programme committee members. Seventeen papers were finally selected by the programme committee for publication, representing academic and industrial research groups from Canada, France, Germany, Italy, Japan, Switzerland, the UK and the USA.

A major event within the conference was the demonstration of many of the research prototype tools described in these proceedings. The whole area is essentially practical – the tools and environments being most useful when they are widely disseminated, enabling researchers to use them and learn from them. The conference concluded with a panel discussion which reviewed the state-of-the-art and gave directions for future research.

Thomas Bemmerl
Roland Ibbett
programme co-chairmen

Nigel Topham
co-editor

Table of Contents

Acknowledgements

The Working Conference on Programming Environments for Parallel Computing was organised by Edinburgh Parallel Computing Centre, with support from UnivEd Technologies Ltd, on behalf of the sponsors, IFIP WG 10.3 and co-sponsors, GI/ITG-PARS and BCS PPSIG. The success of any conference depends on the quality of the papers, the enthusiasm of the participants and the work of the organising committee. It is therefore a pleasure to thank all those involved in the PEPC Conference for their contributions to its success.

Roland Ibbett

organising committee chairman

PROGRAMMING ENVIRONMENTS FOR PARALLEL COMPUTING
N. Topham, R. Ibbett and T. Bemmerl (Editors)
Elsevier Science Publishers B.V. (North-Holland)

© 1992 IFIP. All rights reserved.

MP: A Programming Environment for Multicomputers

Jeff Magee and Naranker Dulay

Department of Computing,
Imperial College of Science, Technology and Medicine,
180 Queen's Gate, London SW7 2BZ, UK.
Email: jnm@uk.ac.ic.doc

Abstract

MP is a programming environment for message passing parallel computers. Programs are constructed in MP from hierarchically structured configurations of process types. These process configurations are described in the Darwin configuration language. Processes are programmed in a conventional sequential language augmented with message passing primitives. In contrast to many environments, MP fully type checks communication in parallel programs. The environment facilitates the reuse of both process types and process configurations by means of generic structures described in Darwin. Executable binary programs developed in MP are independent of the number of processors and interconnect topology of the target multicomputer. The paper outlines program development in the MP environment by means of an example program to compute the transitive closure of a graph (Warshall's algorithm). MP is currently targeted at developing programs for transputer based multicomputers.

Keyword Codes: D.2.6; D.1.3
Keywords: Software Engineering, Programming Environments;
Programming Techniques, Concurrent

1. Introduction

Successful developments in computing are generally evolutionary rather than revolutionary. Evolution here means that a new tool or technique must provide a development path which permits users to incrementally upgrade their existing software base to utilise that tool or technique. In the context of parallel programming this means that the environment must allow users to capitalise on their existing base of sequential programs. Two approaches can be taken to providing this upgrade path - *implicit* and *explicit* parallelism. The implicit approach involves the use of automatic parallelising compilers to detect and exploit parallelism in an existing sequential code. The explicit approach involves restructuring the sequential code into a parallel form while retaining most of the sequential code in processes which execute in the parallel framework. These approaches are most usefully viewed as complementary rather than competitive in providing an upgrade path from sequential to parallel code. Automatic or more accurately semi-automatic, approaches have proved successful for scientific array calculations[1,2,3] while the explicit approach yields greater benefit for less regularly structured problems[4,5].

MP supports explicit parallelism. Its novelty lies in the explicit description, in the Darwin language[6], of the parallel structure or framework in which sequential processes execute. These Darwin structures can be generic allowing a user to select an appropriate structure from a library rather than programming his own. Darwin supports hierarchic structuring of programs where components may be composed from sub-component types which may themselves be either Darwin structures or sequential processes. Further, Darwin supports the description of dynamic structures which change as program execution progresses. Processes in MP are programmed in a sequential programming language extended with message passing primitives. To date, extensions for Pascal, C and C++ have been implemented. The approach is to preprocess programs in the extended language to the original language. In contrast to commercially available systems such as CSTools[7] and Express[8], we have chosen to "deeply" embed MP message passing. For example, the message passing primitives extend the basic data types and type constructors provided by the host language. Our desire is to retain for parallel programming the advantages that the language type system gives to sequential programming. However, we retain the benefit of reusing existing sequential routines written in that language.

When a user of a sequential programming environment develops a program for a particular processor architecture / Operating system his expectation is that the developed binary program will execute unmodified on different computers which have that basic architecture/ OS combination. Current development environments for distributed memory multicomputers do not always meet this expectation since recompilation (and sometimes source program modification) is required to cater for different numbers of processors and different interconnect topologies. MP targets development at the virtual machine architecture of Figure 1. Neither the number of processors nor the interconnect topology is "hardwired" into a program.

Programs developed in MP are thus intended to execute on message passing machines with *Pmax* identical processing elements. Each processing element consists of a CPU, local memory and an interface to the communication network. Processing elements can support many independent threads of execution (processes). Pairs of processes may directly communicate with each other whether they are resident on the same processor or on different processors. The communication network is thus assumed to support full interconnection between any two processes wherever they are located. While future generations of parallel machines should implement this directly, it is currently the responsibility of the MP runtime system.

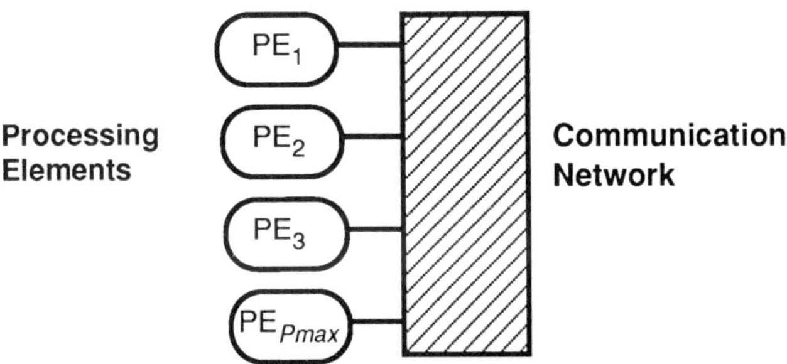

Figure 1 - Message Passing Parallel Machine

Currently, MP is targeted at developing programs for transputer based multicomputers - in our case a Meiko Computing Surface. However, application level source programs may be written with no knowledge of the transputer architecture and may be compiled to execute on networks of Unix based workstations. Source program portability between distributed memory parallel computers is thus an objective of MP, although this goal has not yet been substantiated except for the limited case mentioned above.

Section 2 of the paper outlines program development in MP through the example of Warshall's algorithm. The MP communication primitives and the Darwin configuration language are overviewed in sufficient detail to make the example comprehensible. A more complete exposition of Darwin and the MP communication primitives may be found in [6] and [9] respectively. Section 3 describes the implementation aspects of MP concerned with parallel execution and presents some performance data. Finally, section 4 discusses MP in relation to other programming environments and draws some conclusions.

2. Programming in MP

The structure of an MP parallel program is described in terms of the set of component types used to construct that program, the set of instances of these types and the interconnections between instances. This structure is programmed in the Darwin language as shown in Figure 2 for a simple producer-consumer program. Darwin has been developed as part of the ESPPRIT II funded REX project [10].

The basic structuring entity in Darwin is the component. Components may be parameterised with the basic types `int`, `real` and `string`. Components are composed from other component types. The specific types used to construct a component are declared by:

use <*list of component types*> .

In the example, the component `prodcons` is constructed from the component types `consumer` and `producer`.

Instances of these component types are declared by:

inst *<instance name>* : *<component type>* (*<parameters>*).

or sometimes to avoid inventing an unnecessary name for a single instance:

inst *<component type>* (*<parameters>*)

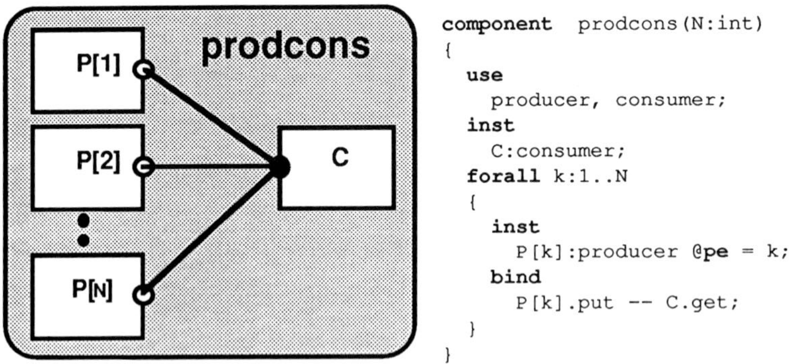

Figure 2 - Darwin Producer-Consumer program

Instance declaration is analogous to the declaration of variables in conventional sequential programming languages. The example declares one instance `C` of the consumer component type and using the replicator **`forall`**, a set of instances `P[k]` of producer where `k` ranges from 1 to `N`. These component types do not require actual parameters. The annotation `@pe=k` specifies the location on the virtual machine of Figure 1 at which instance `P[k]` should be executed (i.e PE_k). Instances declared without a location annotation are colocated with their enclosing component. The toplevel component is by default allocated to PE_1. Instances may be annotated with properties other than location e.g. priority.

Connections between instances are declared by:

bind *<instance>.<service required>* -- *<instance>.<service provided>*.

In the example, a connection is made from each `producer` instance `P[k].put` to the `consumer` instance `C.get`. Darwin is purely a structuring language, it is not concerned with how bindings are used for communication. If parameter passing was used to effect binding (as for example in Occam 2[11]) this separation of concerns would not be possible since communication entities (for example channels) would need to be declared at the same scope level as components to allow the full range of structures to be defined.

Components in Darwin may be constructed from other component types, as above, or they may be sequential processes. In the following we use Pascal to program process types. Figure 3 gives the programs for the `producer` and `consumer` process types of Figure 2.

```
process producer;
require put;
var
  put: @port(integer,real);
  i:integer;
begin
  for i:=1 to 100 do
    put ! (i, sqrt(i));
end.
```

```
process consumer;
provide get;
var
  get: port(integer,real);
  i:integer; r:real;
begin
  loop
    get ? (i, r);
    writeln(i,r);
  end;
end.
```

Figure 3 - MP-Pascal Producer and Consumer Process programs

Services in MP are provided via ports which are queues of messages. For example, the `consumer` process of Figure 3 queues messages consisting of an integer value and real value. Messages are transferred from the port into the local variables of a processes via the receive operation. In this case the operation is `get?(i,r)`. The compiler or preprocessor ensures that the types of variables mentioned in a receive operation are compatible with the port on which the operation is performed. Ports are accessed remotely by remote references. A remote reference type is declared by prefixing the port declaration with an @ symbol. In the example, the variable `put` holds a reference value which refers to a port to which messages consisting of an integer and a real value can be sent. Messages are sent to a remote port by performing a send operation on a remote port reference. In the example, the send operation is `put!(i,sqrt(i))`. The send operation is synchronous in that it blocks until the message has been received. Consequently, the port message queue may actually be implemented as a queue of blocked processes. Again, the compiler checks that the values sent are compatible with the declared port reference type.

The effect of a bind declaration in Darwin is to assign the port reference value **provided** by one process into the port reference variable **required** by another process. These bindings are typed checked by the Darwin compiler using structural type descriptions supplied by process compilers.

Remote references may refer to port structures (ie records and arrays) as well as to single ports. As a notational convenience for the common case of a remote reference referring to a single port, the type may be declared as `->datatype` instead of `@port(datatype)`. In contrast to the channels of Occam 2[11] remote references may be sent in messages to allow more complex communication protocols to be constructed from the basic primitives[9]. MP also provides a guarded command construct similar to that of Ada[12] and Occam although this is not used in the following example.

Warshall's Algorithm

To illustrate some of the more powerful features of the MP programming environment we develop a parallel algorithm for computing the transitive closure of a directed graph (Warshall's Algorithm). The following common constant and type declarations will be used:

```
const   Maxsize = 512;
type    boolvec = packed array[1..Maxsize] of boolean;
            boolmat = packed array[1..Maxsize] of
                    record C:boolvec end;
```

A reasonably efficient sequential implementation of the algorithm, which avoids unnecessary stride calculations, is given in Figure 4. The transitive closure is computed in place from the initial adjacency matrix `R` describing the directed graph. The initial value of `R` is read from a file by the procedure `readmat` and the final value output by the procedure `writemat`.

```
procedure transclos(size:integer);
var
  n,i,j:integer; R:boolmat; T:boolvec;
begin
  readmat(R,1,size);
  for n:=1 to size do
  begin
    T:=R[n].C;
    for i:=1 to size do
      with R[i] do
        if C[n] then
          for j:=1 to size do C[j]:=C[j] or T[j];
  end;
  writemat(R,1,size);
end;
```

Figure 4 - Warshall's Algorithm (sequential)

The simplest way to parallelise the program of Figure 4 is to use a data parallel approach such that the rows of the adjacency matrix `R` are divided among the available processors. Each iteration of the outer loop of the program (index `n`) requires that a value for `T = R[n].C` be communicated to each processor. Apart from this data dependence each processor can compute its slice of the matrix independently. However, the input of the adjacency matrix and subsequent output must be synchronised such that each processor reads and subsequently writes the appropriate part of the matrix.

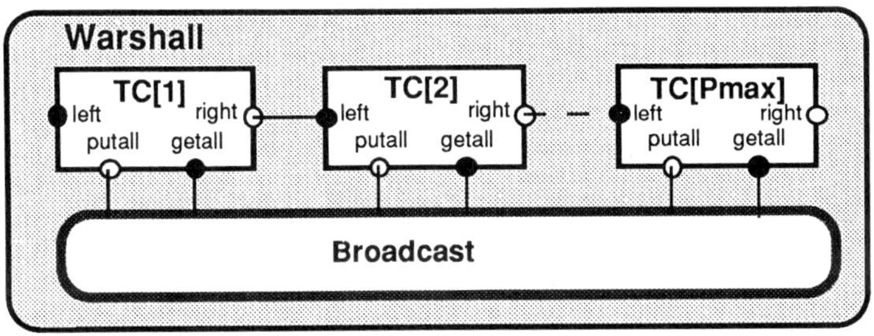


```
process transclos(size:integer);
 provide left, getall;
 require right,putall;
 use spmd: slice,this,Pmax;
 var
   left:port(); right:->void;
   getall:port(boolvec); putall:->boolvec;
   n,i,j,first,last:integer; R:boolmat; T:boolvec;
begin
  slice(1,size,first,last);
  if this <>1 then left?();
  readmat(R,first,last);
  if this<>Pmax then right!();
  for n:=1 to size do
  begin
    if Pmax=1 then  T:=R[n].C else
    begin
      if (n>=first) and (n<=last) then putall!(R[n].C:size);
      getall?(T:size);
    end;
    for i:=first to last do
      with R[i] do
       if C[n] then
         for j:=1 to size do C[j]:=C[j] or T[j];
  end;
  if this <>1 then left?();
  writemat(R,first,last);
  if this<>Pmax then right!(signal) else halt;
end.
```

Figure 5 - Warshall's Algorithm (parallel)

Figure 5 gives the parallel version of the procedure `transclos` together with a diagram of the configuration in which it is intended to run. Input and output is serialised by passing a synchronisation message (containing no data) from left to right between the instances `TC[1]` to `TC[Pmax]` of the process `transclos`. The entire parallel program terminates when the last instance has output (**`halt`**). Processes which complete without calling **`halt`** do not cause the program to terminate - they are merely made permanently inactive and their storage released. The routine `slice` imported from the definitions unit `spmd` computes the `first` and `last` index that a process should be concerned with given the total range. The detail of allocating only the storage required for this slice has been omitted in the interests of brevity. Thus each instance has the full matrix although it only uses a subrange of the rows. The imported variable `this` and `Pmax` hold respectively, the number of the processing element that the instance is running on and the total number of processing elements.

The boolean vector `T` is broadcast by an instance to all other instances including itself when the value of `n` lies within its slice of the matrix. The broadcast message is sent to the port reference `putall` and received from the port `getall`. The `:size` part of the send and receive operations indicate that only `size` elements of the vector are sent and received. The message passing operations directly implemented by MP are either one-to-one or many-to-one as described earlier. Broadcast operations must therefore be constructed from these basic primitives.

```
component bnode(p1:int)
{
   provide  inn; require left,right;
}

component bintree(n:int; p1:int; use bnode)
{
  provide inn; require out[n];
  when n==1
    bind inn--out[0];
  when n>1
  {
    inst
      root: bnode(p1);
      left: bintree(n/2,p1,bnode);
      right:bintree(n/2 + n%2,p1,bnode) @pe = this + n/2;
    bind
      inn -- root.inn;
      root.left -- left.inn;
      root.right -- right.inn;
    forall i:0..n/2 -1
      bind left.out[i] -- out[i];
    forall i:0..n/2 +n%2 -1
      bind right.out[i] -- out[i+n/2];
  }
}
```

Figure 6 - Binary Tree in Darwin

A naive implementation would merely use a single broadcast process which received a message and then sent it to the broadcast participants. This would take O(n) time for n participants. A more satisfactory approach is to use a binary tree to implement the broadcast, resulting in $O(\log_2 n)$ time. In Darwin this can be simply accomplished using the generic binary tree structure shown in Figure 6. This is an example of a recursive configuration. Note that the program computes a balanced tree for any number of outputs `out[0]..out[n-1]`. The annotation associated with the right subtree (i.e. `@pe=this+n/2`) allocates nodes at a particular depth of the tree to different processors, ensuring parallel execution. The keyword **`this`** denotes the processing element at which the enclosing component is instantiated. The nodes of the tree are described by the skeletal component program bnode. The binary tree may be instantiated with any process or Darwin component type which conforms to this skeleton. To implement a broadcast operation using this generic component it is only necessary to define a process type which inputs a message and then sends out two copies as shown in Figure 7.

```
process split(size:integer);
 provide  inn; require left,right;
 var
  inn:port(boolvec); left,right:->boolvec; B:boolvec;
begin
  loop
    inn?(B:size);
    conjoin left!(B:size) & right!(B:size);
  end;
end.
```

Figure 7 - Split process

The program uses the MP **conjoin** operation to start the send operations in parallel. The **conjoin** statement terminates when all its communication operations (which can be sends or receives) complete. Its use here ensures that the underlying transputer DMA hardware is fully utilised such that data transfer can proceed in parallel. Given the process of figure 7 we can now define the structure of the overall parallel Warshall program as shown in Figure 8. Note that a single binary tree is used for broadcast, rather than multiple trees each rooted at an TC instance. The single tree ensures that each TC instance receives broadcast messages in the correct order.

```
component warshall (size:int)
{
  use transclos,bintree,split;
  inst
    broadcast:bintree(Pmax, size, split);
  forall i:1.. Pmax
  {
    inst
      TC[i]:transclos(size) @pe = i;
    bind
      TC[i].putall -- broadcast.inn;
      broadcast.out[i-1] -- TC[i].getall;
      TC[i].right -- TC[i % Pmax +1].left;
  }
}
```

Figure 8 - Structure of Parallel Warshall in Darwin

The program works for any matrix size up to 512 and any number of processing elements. In its construction we have reused a standard Darwin generic component bintree. In fact, the entire warshall component could be made generic and parameterised with the transclos process type if it was felt that a range of algorithms would conform to this structure. The reuse of process and component types in MP is facilitated by the fact that they specify not only the services they require but also the services they provide. We term this property *context independence* since processes and components may be programmed, compiled and tested independently of the larger environment in which they will eventually execute. The next section explains how the Warshall program is executed in the MP environment and presents some performance results from its execution. Although we have used an example where the structure is determined at program initialisation time, Darwin includes configuration operations which can be invoked by processes to dynamically change the structure.

3. The MP execution environment

Currently, MP is targeted at developing parallel programs for a Meiko Computing Surface consisting of 32 T800 transputers each with 4 Megabytes of RAM. The machine is hosted by a SPARC based Unix workstation. The machine is statically configurable in that its constituent transputers can be interconnected to form different physical topologies within the constraint of four links per transputer. MP uses Darwin to describe the desired physical topology as shown in Figure 9 for a torus.

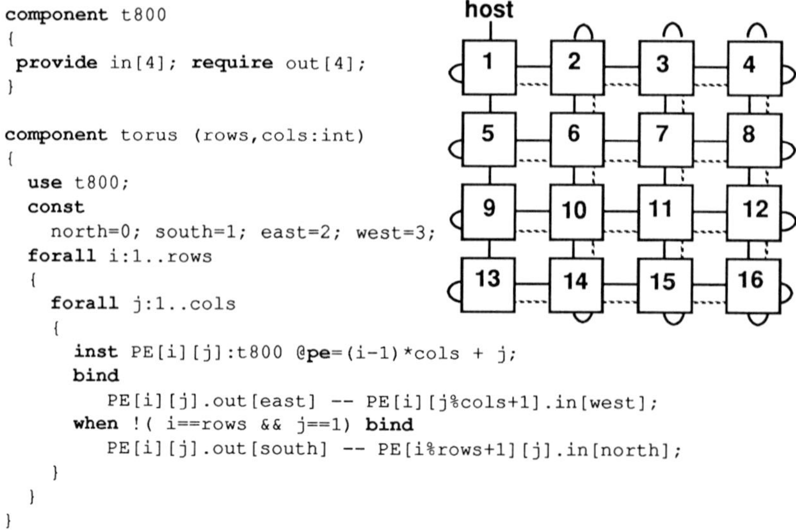


```
component t800
{
 provide in[4]; require out[4];
}

component torus (rows,cols:int)
{
  use t800;
  const
    north=0; south=1; east=2; west=3;
  forall i:1..rows
  {
    forall j:1..cols
    {
      inst PE[i][j]:t800 @pe=(i-1)*cols + j;
      bind
         PE[i][j].out[east] -- PE[i][j%cols+1].in[west];
      when !( i==rows && j==1) bind
         PE[i][j].out[south] -- PE[i%rows+1][j].in[north];
    }
  }
}
```

Figure 9 - Torus physical structure in Darwin

The torus is incomplete since link 0 of transputer 1 is used in the Meiko Surface for communication with the host. Since transputer links are bidirectional, in the interests of brevity, if a connection is specified in one direction in Darwin, the underlying runtime system for the hardware description assumes the reverse direction connection is also being made. In general, users select a physical configuration from a library rather than writing their own. The objective is to relieve the programmer of the burden of physical configuration while retaining the ability to "handcraft" special purpose configurations for performance reasons.

The Darwin language compiler translates Darwin programs into C. In the case of physical configurations, this C program together with its Darwin runtime support executes on the host and computes a "flat" graph in which the vertices are transputers and the edges are communication links. This graph is used to configure the Meiko Surface. The program then computes a minimum spanning tree over the graph and uses it to bootstrap the Meiko with the parallel program. The physical graph is also loaded into the machine to enable the runtime system to compute routing tables. When the bootstrap is complete, the host program acts as a server for I/O operations from the Meiko. To execute the example program of the previous section for an input matrix of size 128 by 128 on a 4 by 4 torus the user would type the following command on the Unix host:

```
torus 4 4 warshall 128
```

Since parallel programs developed in MP are completely independent of the physical interconnection topology, the user may just as simply execute the program on a ternary tree of 16 processors with the command:

```
tree 16 warshall 128
```

The Darwin logical configuration program computes a "flat" graph in which the vertices are process instances and the edges port reference to port bindings. The configuration program executes at each processor and instantiates the processes which are located at that processor. Since each processor knows the complete program graph, inter process bindings can be computed without remote communication. After the initial program has been instantiated, instances and bindings resulting from configuration operations are created by servers running in each processor.

Remote references are represented at runtime by the triple:

```
<pe_id, proc_id, offset>
```

where `pe_id` is the processing element number, `proc_id` is the process instance identifier and `offset` is the offset from the base address of the data segment of that process. The pair `<pe_id,proc_id>` provide a unique identifier for each process instance in a program. Process instance identifiers within a processing element are allocated cyclically over a large range to enable the detection of invalid references. A reference becomes invalid when the process instance to which it refers has terminated and its data segment released. Currently, a remote reference is represented in store by two 32 bit words. References with `pe_id =0` are used to communicate with the I/O server running on the host computer.

Ports are implemented using a seven word control block which includes a transputer channel word for data transfer and head and tail pointers to the queue of processes awaiting access to the channel word. A count of the waiting processes is also maintained. The remaining words are required by the implementation of the guarded command statement. Figure 10 summarises the performance of the MP message passing primitives. The communication times are independent of the number of remote reference variables bound to a port. In this, MP differs from its predecessor Tonic[13] where communication time was proportional to the fan-in factor. MP uses a queuing mechanism for fan-in where Tonic used the transputer ALT construct.

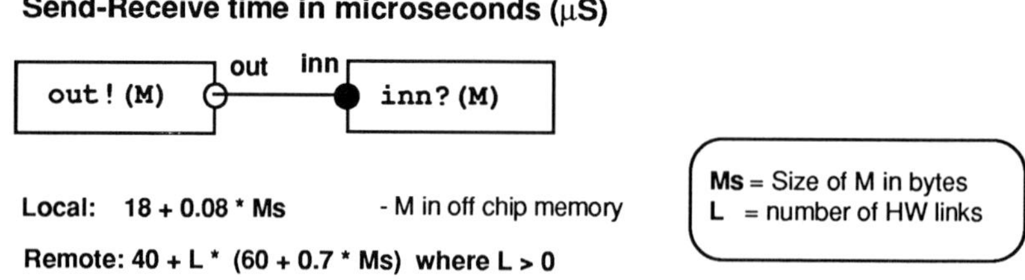

Figure 10 - Message Passing Performance

Figure 11 shows the results of running the `warshall` program using the `torus` with parameters (1,1), (2,2), (4,2), (4,4) and (8,4). The times of Figure 11 are for computation only (i.e. I/O time omitted). Speedup is calculated as the runtime for one processor divided by the runtime for **n** processors. This is reasonable since the parallel program (Figure 5) only adds the test `Pmax=1` to the sequential algorithm (Figure 4) when it executes on one processor. The input graph is in each case fully connected, such that each vertex has an edge to every other vertex, to ensure that `size` cubed iterations are performed. The absolute run times and speedups can be compared with those reported in [3] for the same algorithm with the same input assumptions written in Dataparallel C. For example, they report for `warshall 512` running on a 32 processor Intel IPSC/2 - runtime 22.6 seconds, speedup 21.3 and for a 32-processor NCube 3200 - runtime 31.8 seconds, speedup 30.6.

Processors	1	2	4	8	16	32
warshall 128						
Time(secs)	9.17	4.6	2.4	1.3	0.79	0.64
Speedup	1.0	2.0	3.9	7.0	11.7	14.2
warshall 256						
Time(secs)	72.98	36.6	18.45	9.51	5.1	3.17
Speedup	1.0	2.0	4.0	7.7	14.3	23.0
warshall 512						
Time(secs)	582.4	292	146.2	74	38.06	21
Speedup	1.0	2.0	4.0	7.9	15.3	27.8

Figure 11 - Performance of Parallel Warshall

MP does not currently provide an interactive debugger, however, it does support comprehensive error reporting which notifies the user of the processor number, process instance, process type and source line number where an error occurred. A performance monitoring utility is provided which can be included into a program by the following Darwin declaration:

```
use perfmon;
inst perfmon("ReportFileName", level_of_detail);
```

Figure 12 is an example performance report for the execution `torus 3 3 warshall 256` with an input graph of the form:

$V_1 \rightarrow V_2 \rightarrow \ldots\ldots\ldots \rightarrow V_{256}$ where V is a vertex and $\rightarrow$ denotes an edge.

```
***** Performance Monitor ****
Execution Time: 9115.200 ms
Maximum Dilation: 2
Average Dilation: 1.06
Per Processor
Pno :      1    2    3    4    5    6    7    8    9
No:        6    2    3    2    4    2    3    3    2
Kb:      407  393  394  393  395  393  376  394  393
Load:   0.94 0.83 0.73 0.63 0.50 0.39 0.29 0.18 0.07
L0:        2   28   29  316  285   29  287    .    .
L1:      369    .  258   28  256    2    .   29   31
L2:      315    2  344  542  258  258  258  258    2
L3:      572  600    2   30    2  258    .  514  258
```

Figure 12 - Performance Report

`Execution time` gives the total runtime of the program including elaboration, input and output. `Maximum Dilation` is the maximal distance in terms of hardware links between any two processes which are directly connected in the logical Darwin program. That and `Average Dilation` give a measure of how well the the logical configuration maps to the selected physical configuration. The numbers listed under the `Per Processor` heading are, respectively, processor number (`Pno`), number of process instances (`No`), memory used in Kilobytes (`Kb`), processor load (`Load`), and number of messages sent to a link (`L0,L1,L2,L3`). The load on each processor is calculated as the (total time - idle time) / totaltime. Idle time is computed by an idle process supplied by the `perfmon` component. Note that for this input graph, the load is not evenly distributed across the processors as it is for the fully connected graph used to produce the performance results of Figure 11. The difference in load is due to the `if C[N] then ..` statement in the program of Figure 5 which short circuits `size` iterations if `C[N]` is false. The inefficient use of processing resource for this particular input highlights one of the problems with supporting only a data parallel approach. The performance monitor may also be used to produce a traffic matrix for a particular program execution. In the future, it is planned to extend the monitor to produce data periodically and on demand and to integrate its output with a general purpose graphical configuration display tool.

4. Discussion & Conclusion

The MP system has been developed from our experience with the Conic environment for writing distributed programs for networked workstations[14]. A version of the Conic system for transputers named Tonic[13] has been in use by students and outside users for well over a year. Some of their experiences are reported by a group at Glasgow University in [15]. The MP environment has been available and in use by students within the authors' research section since September 1991 and has recently been made available for undergraduate teaching. While MP inherits from Conic the concept of a separate configuration language and context independent components[16], it significantly extends the facilities offered in Conic in a number of ways. The most important of these extensions are firstly the provision of generic components and secondly the ability to accommodate more dynamic structures through the ability of processes to pass remote references in messages and to invoke configuration operations. In Conic, the allocation of components to processors was not orthogonal to the logical program structure as it is in MP. Configuration changes were offered as a management facility rather than as a programmed function.

The Conic and Tonic systems were restricted to a particular sequential programming language while MP offers a range of programming languages. Although the Darwin compiler type checks bindings it does this in terms of a common structural type representation provided by the sequential language preprocessors. Darwin is thus largely independent of the sequential programming language since it does not need to interpret or manipulate these type representations. It merely needs to be able to perform compatibility tests. Freeing Darwin from the datatyping system significantly simplifies and optimises the implementation of generic components. Commercial environments such as CStools[7] offer no facilities for ensuring message compatibility between senders and receivers.

The use of generic components together with the context independent property of ordinary components and processes simplifies the task of parallel programming by capturing commonly used functions, paradigms and structures as library components. Generic components describe not only a logical interconnection structure but also information on how that structure should be mapped to the physical machine. It is possible, for example, to capture much of the functionality of a Single Program Multiple Data (SPMD) system such as EXPRESS[8] as a set of generic components[9]. However, it is likely that EXPRESS programs which used only the built in high level global communication operations such as *exbroadcast, excombine* and *exsync* would be simpler than their MP equivalent. The advantage of MP is realised when a programmer wishes to define his own global communication operations. Further, MP can be used to capture parallel programming paradigms such as supervisor-worker and divide and conquer which do not conform to the SPMD model.

The use of a configuration language naturally poses the question as to whether the activity of configuration programming would be better accomplished using a graphics based tool. Our experience with ConicDraw[17], a visual programming tool for Conic, suggests that graphic representations are valuable as an aid to comprehension and as a framework to meaningfully display status and performance data on executing programs. However, visual programming of large regular graph structures is a tedious activity best left to the concise descriptions afforded by a textually based configuration language. The developers of the Poker environment, a visual programming environment for distributed memory parallel programs, have also met this problem[5]. However, Poker does not have a textually based configuration language. Our current approach in the REX[10] project is to develop a graphics based tool in which the textual description can be generated from a graphic description and vice-versa. Each component of a program may thus be designed and viewed in whichever representation a developer is most comfortable with.

In conclusion, we believe that parallel programming is a solution to be exploited and not a problem to be overcome. Parallel programs for distributed memory machines have an enforced modularity which is compatible with good software engineering practice. The configuration programming paradigm supported by MP has many of the advantages of Object Oriented programming without sharing its problems with distribution[18]. In MP, our goal has been to provide parallel programmers with equivalent facilities to those found in sequential environments and in addition to free them from some of the concerns of the underlying hardware while retaining the benefits of efficient execution. After all, the primary objective of parallel programming is execution speed. Our future work will be concerned with validating the MP approach by application to large scale examples and extending the environment to relieve programmers of some of the burden of allocation.

Acknowledgements

The authors would like to acknowledge discussions with our colleagues in the Parallel and Distributed Systems Group during the formulation of these ideas. We gratefully acknowledge the SERC under grant GR/G31079, and the CEC in the REX Project (2080) for their financial support.

References

[1] H. Zima, H.Bast, and H. Gerndt, "SUPERB: A tool for semi-automatic MIMD-SIMD parallelization", Parallel Computing, Vol 6, pp. 1-18, 1988.

[2] K. Ikudome, G. Fox, A. Kolawa and J. .W. Flower, "An automatic and symbolic parallelization system for distributed memory architectures", Proc. 5th Distributed Memory Computing Conference, Charleston, S. Corolina, April 1990.

[3] P.J. Hatcher, M.J. Quinn, A.J. Lapadula, B.K. Seevers, R.J. Seevers, R.J. Anderson and R.R. Jones, "Data-Parallel Programming on MIMD Computers", IEEE Trans. on Parallel and Distributed Systems", PDS-2(3), July 1991, pp 377-383.

[4] D. Gelernter, "Generative communication in Linda", ACM TOPLAS 7(1) Jan 1985, pp80-112.

[5] D. Notkin, L. Snyder, D. Socha et al., " Experiences with Poker", Proc. of ACM/SIGPLAN PPEALS, pp 10-20, July 1988.

[6] J. Magee, N. Dulay and J. Kramer, "Structuring Parallel and Distributed Programs", Proceedings of IEE International Workshop on Configuring Distributed Systems, Imperial College, March 1992.

[7] Meiko Ltd, "CS Tools Documentation Guide", 650 Aztec West, Bristol, 1989.

[8] Para Soft Corporation, "EXPRESS user manual", 1989.

[9] J. Magee, N. Dulay and J. Kramer, "Constructive Communication in MP", Dept. of Computing, Imperial College, Research Report 92/4, Feb 1992.

[10] REX Technical Annexe (1989), ESPRIT Project 2080, European Economic Commission.

[11] Inmos Ltd, "OCCAM 2 reference manual", Prentice Hall, 1988.

[12] Department of Defense, U.S., "Reference manual for the Ada programming language", ANSI/MIL-STD-1815A, DoD, Washington, D.C., Jan 1983.

[13] J.N. Magee and N. Dulay, " A Configuration Approach to Parallel Programming", PARLE 91, Vol II, LNCS 506, pp 313-330.

[14] Magee, J., Kramer, J., and Sloman, M. (1989). "Constructing Distributed Systems in Conic" IEEE Transactions on Software Engineering, SE-15 (6).

[15] Y. Mather, P.J Gawthrop, D.W. Roberts, "Distributed Real time control using Tonic",presented at Transputer Applications conference TA91.

[16] Kramer, J., and Magee, J.(1985). "Dynamic Configuration for Distributed Systems", IEEE Transactions on Software Engineering, SE-11 (4), 424-436.

[17] Kramer, J., Magee, J., and Ng, K. (1989). "Graphical Configuration Programming", IEEE Computer, 22(10), 53-65.

[18] Kramer,J., Magee, J., Sloman, M.S., and Dulay, N. "Configuring Object Based Distributed Programs in REX", To be Published in IEE Software Engineering Journal , Special Issue on Object Oriented Systems, March 1992

PROGRAMMING ENVIRONMENTS FOR PARALLEL COMPUTING
N. Topham, R. Ibbett and T. Bemmerl (Editors)
Elsevier Science Publishers B.V. (North-Holland)

© 1992 IFIP. All rights reserved.

SIGMA II: A Tool Kit for Building Parallelizing Compilers and Performance Analysis Systems

Dennis Gannon, Jenq Kuen Lee, Bruce Shei, Sekhar Sarukkai, Srinivas Narayana, Neelakantan Sundaresan [a]
Daya Atapattu[b]
Francois Bodin[c]

[a] Department of Computer Science, Indiana University, U.S.A

[b] SCA New Haven, Connecticut, U.S.A

[c]IRISA & University of Rennes, France

Abstract
SIGMA II is a system for building program transformation tools. Its intended use is for building source to source program parallelization restructurers and performance analysis instrumentation tools for application written in FORTRAN, FORTRAN90, C, C++ and certain extensions of these languages including PCF FORTRAN, Cedar FORTRAN, and pC++. SIGMA II contains an interprocedural analysis system and symbolic data dependence procedures. The interface to SIGMA is through a system of over 100 functions which provide the tool builder with complete access to the syntax and semantics of user programs. In addition to supporting language extensions, SIGMA II supports an extensive FORTRAN and C annotation system to aid in allowing users to place assertions in the code that can direct the parallelization processes.

Keyword Codes:
D.2.6; D.3.0; D.1.0
Keywords:
Software Engineering, Programming Environments;
Programming Languages, General;
Programming Techniques, General

1. Introduction

Parallel computation research is still far from the long sought objective of automatic parallelization of real applications for large, scalable high performance systems. The best results have been achieved with applications written with explicitly parallel programming languages and they are only obtained after extensive performance "tuning". Because of this fact, parallel programming tool design research is an active and flourishing area and there is constant need to re-invent many important but basic components of the program analysis process. For example, FORTRAN 90 is now a standard, but very few tool builders have been able to incorporate it into their environment even though the technology to do so is conventional and the required data dependence analysis techniques are well known. Furthermore, few existing restructuring systems have been able to exploit interprocedural analysis for multi-source file applications.

A more fundamental problem is that many good ideas for new tools go unexplored because of the large start-up cost of building a conventional source code analyzer. Rapid prototyping of new tools is almost impossible without a stable infrastructure of supporting components.

SIGMA II has been designed to fill this gap by providing a tool kit for analyzing and restructuring application programs intended for use on scalable parallel systems. Its intended use is for building end-user tools to aid in the process of program parallelization and performance analysis. Simply put, SIGMA II is a data base for accessing and manipulating program control and data dependence information. The interface to the end-user tool consists of over 100 C functions that can be used to access and modify the data base.

Support for multiple source languages is supported in SIGMA II. Input to the analysis data base can be either FORTRAN77, FORTRAN90, (some support for PCF FORTRAN is also provided), C, C++ and pC++ (which is extension to C++ for a variation on data parallel programming we call "object parallel" computation [9]). While this does not cover all the languages used for parallel programming, it does cover the majority of areas where large applications exist.

While there is little support for extensions to standard languages, SIGMA II provides support for a very powerful annotation and directive system that lets users add source code comments that can be passed to the tool. These annotations can be used for data distribution directives, program instrumentation commands or restructuring directives.

The functions provided by the data base can be used by the end-user tool in one of three ways.

- *Extracting syntactic information.* This includes symbol and type table information, program control flow structure, user annotation and directive information, and access to the complete parse tree of the application.

- *Extracting semantic information.* This includes interprocedural definition and use summaries for each function and procedure, data dependence analysis and scalar propagation and symbolic analysis and simplification of scalar expressions.

- *Restructuring* the program by modifying the data base contents and to generating (unparsing) new versions of the source code based on the modifications.

Sigma was originally designed as the back end to an interactive restructuring system that was part of the Faust Parallel Programming Project [6] at CSRD. As this project evolved it was clear that the tools in Sigma could be used in may other parts of the Faust project as well as several other projects at other institutions. In 1989, it was decided to encapsulate the internal mechanisms and data structures and provide a simple interface to the data base for other projects. This redesign has taken two years and the complete system is now ending an alpha test phase and is ready for a public beta test release. Sigma II has run on machines from Sun, NeXT, Dec, IBM, SGI, Stardent, BBN and Alliant and it should work on any machine that supports "old style" K&R C .

Of course, SIGMA is not the only tool kit of its type. Delta is a system developed at CSRD for prototyping restructuring systems [10] and Tiny [15] from OGI has been widely used as a testbed for dependence analysis testing and transformations systems. Paraphrase II from CSRD [11], Parascope from Rice [5], PTRAN from IBM [1], Pat from Georgia Tech [2], Superb from Vienna, and PIPS from Paris [7] and many others are all powerful restructuring systems that could be packaged as at tool kit like SIGMA.

The types of systems that Sigma II has been used for include

1. The Faust interactive restructurer [6].
2. The Sigmacs program parallelization system [14].
3. The SIEVE parallel performance analysis tool [13].
4. An annotation driven program instrumentation tool (at Indiana University).
5. An interactive program control flow graph browser (at CSRD).
6. An interactive parallel program performance prediction tool [3]
7. The pC++ "object parallel" programming language compiler [9].
8. The PARTI Distributed Memory Compiler from ICASE [12].

Other projects that are using Sigma II that are currently in development include the computation steering group at CSRD, the code optimization and restructuring group at University of Rennes. Other projects at Indiana, Illinois and Cornell are currently using the system and several other sites in the U.S. and Europe are evaluating it.

In this paper we will describe the architecture of the data base and illustrate the process of building tools with it. We will discuss two applications in some detail.

2. The SIGMA Architecture

The *SIGMA* systems consists of two basic components:

1. A set of parsers one each for FORTRAN, C and pC++ that translate the source code into a special internal form.
2. A library of data base utilities for extracting and modifying information stored in the internal form generated by the parsers.

Parallel programming tools are designed to work with user application program which are often very large and exist as multiple source files. In Sigma terms, each application program defines a *project* which consists of a set of source files, a set of dependence files and a project file. The source files are either FORTRAN, C or pC++ and any needed header files. For each source file there is a corresponding dependence file generated by the parser. (The convention is that source files end in ".f" or ".c" and the corresponding dependence file ends in ".dep" with the same root name.) The project file is an ascii file containing a list of all the associated dependence files in the project. (The project file usually has a ".proj" suffix and the dependence files are listed one per line.)

The dependence file for each source file contains a complete parse tree and symbol table for the program fragment in that file. In addition it contains a first-pass analysis of the interprocedural flow for the functions and subroutines in that module. In the following paragraphs we outline the structure of the dependence file and list the functions used to access this information.

2.1. The Data Base Structure

Because we are working with a system for imperative style languages, the internal structure has been designed to closely match language features most often found within this class. Consequently, certain features of some advanced programming languages cannot be well supported with our structures. For example, first class functions, closures and continuations would not be well suited to the style of our design. Our approach was originally designed by Piyush Mehrotra for a Pascal like language and was then extended for the language Kali. [8]. It was only later that we realized that the extensions to Fortran and C++ were rather straight forward.

In the Sigma model, each program is a collection of graphs and tables corresponding to a collection of source files. Each graph is a structured parse tree for the program. The nodes correspond roughly to FORTRAN statements and the tree structure is based on control constructs. The children of a statement are called the *control children* of a node which is known as the *control parent.* (This is a slight abuse of the term control parent because the presence of "goto" statements can imply that the true control flow graph may look very different from this tree.) The root of the graph is called the *global node* for the file. The nodes with control children correspond to

- a global node for each file,
- subroutine or function headers,
- looping constructs (*DO* in FORTRAN and *do*, *for* and *while* in C),
- conditionals ($if - then - else$ and *switch*),
- structural "control" in pC++ consisting of *struct*, *class*, *collection*.

Because of pure conditionals like $IF - then - else$ each set of control nodes has two sets of children, the *false branch* and the *true branch*, but for most control nodes the *false branch* is empty.

In the data base each statement, expression, symbol table and type table entry is identified with an integer. This *node id* is the principle means of access to the information stored in a node. Each statement node has several potential attributes including

- the type of the node which identifies the statement type,
- the name and line number of the source file containing this statement,
- the identifier of the control parent of this node,

- a symbol reference such as a do loop parameter in FORTRAN or a subroutine name in a call statement,
- a list of data dependencies associated with the statement,
- user defined properties (described later),
- the comments that precede the statement (and the associated program annotations),
- two or three expressions associated with the node (see the next section for details),
- and the list of control children of the node.

Each of these attributes can be accessed for a given statement by one of the data base functions. From the point of view of the control structure, we are only concerned with the identifier of the node, the type, and the control children. If we use the notation *N[type]* to refer to the node id and its type, then to describe the control children of a node we can use a LISP style s-expression to describe the tree as

```
( N[type]  (true-subtree) (false-subtree)).
```

To illustrate this structure consider the following simple example where the source code has been numbered with the node identifiers on the left.

```
1        program test
2        real x(100)
3        integer i
4        do i = 1, 10
5               x(i) = 1.0
        enddo
        end
  c
8        subroutine foo(x, y)
9        real x, y
10       if(x.gt.y) then
11              x = 0.0
        else
13              y = x+1
        endif
15       return
        end
```

The graph for this program fragment, illustrated in figure 1, can be described as follows.

```
( 0[GLOBAL]
    ((1[PROG_HEDR]
                ( 2[VAR_DECL]  3[VAR_DECL]
                 (4[FOR_NODE] (5[ASSIGN_STAT]  6[CONTROL_END]) NULL )
```

```
                  7[CONTROL_END])
    NULL)
     (8[PROC_HEDR]
                ( 9[VAR_DECL]
                 (10[IF_NODE] ( 11[ASSIGN_NODE] 12[CONTROL_END])
                              ( 13[ASSIGN_NODE] 14[CONTROL_END]))
                  15[RETURN_STAT]
                  16[CONTROL_END])
            NULL)
   NULL
)
```

(Notice that each basic block is terminated by a special node of type CONTROL_END.)

The data type used by Sigma II to communicate the structure of programs in the data base to the end-user applications is called an *ELIST* which is a Lisp style s-expression. All the library functions access the data base and return values which are either integers or pointers to *ELIST* values. To illustrate how the library works, consider the function *SiControlChildren(node)* which returns the *ELIST* of nodes immediately controlled by the node given as the argument. For the program above we have

```
SiControlChildren(1)  returns ( (2 3 4 7)  () )
SiControlChildren(4)  returns ( (5 6) () )
SiControlChildren(10) returns ( (11 12) (13 14) )
```

Given a node identifier, one can retrieve any information associated with the node such as its type and the source text form. For example, for the statement with identifier 5 in the program above, we have

```
SiStmtType(5)         returns ASSIGN_STAT
SiStmtUnparse(5)      returns ( "x(i) = 1.0" )
```

To manipulate *ELIST* structures we have standard lisp like function *SiECar()*,*SiECdr()*, *SiECons()*, *SiECadr()*, *SiEAppend()*, etc.

Each program statement in the data base can have as many as three algebraic expressions associated with it and each expression is represented by an *ELIST*. For example, a *Do* loop statement has a low bound expression, an upper bound expression and an increment expression. An assignment statement has two expressions corresponding to the left hand side (*lhs*) and the right hand side (*rhs*). For example, consider the statement

```
x(i+1) = y + z(i,j).
```

In this case, the expression appears as binary trees of expression node ids as follows.

```
lhs =  (1[ARRAY_REF:x]
        (2[PLUS_OP] 3[VAR_REF:i]  4[CONST_VAL])
        NULL)
rhs =  (5[PLUS_OP]
        6[VAR_REF:y]
```

```
(7[ARRAY_REF:z]
   (8[EXPR_LIST]
    9[VAR_REF:i]
    (10[EXPR_LIST] 11[VAR_REF:j] NULL))
    NULL)
)
```

There are many functions that manipulate expressions and data dependence information. To illustrate the types of functions available to the tool builder, a few of these functions are listed in the table below. The complete list of functions and their definitions is given in the SIGMA documentation.

Function	Result
int SiOpenProject(proj_name, proj_file)	Open the named project data base
int SiSelectFile(file_name)	select a source file within a project.
ELIST SiGetProcList(proj_name)	the list of subroutines and function
ELIST SiGetFileList(proj_name)	the list of source files
ELIST SiGetGlobalDecl(proj_name)	the list of global declarations
int SiStmtAtLine(line_no)	the id of the statement at a give source line
ELIST SiUnparseBlock(int id)	unparse a block of code controlled by stmt id
int SiCopyStmt(int id)	make a copy of a statement
int SiGetStmtSymbol(int id)	for example, the iteration variable in a loop
ELIST SiGetBothSides(int id)	the lhs and rhs expression identifiers
ELIST SiExpandChildren(int id)	the complete parse tree controlled by id
int SiNewStmt(type, symbol, exp1, exp2, exp3)	create a new statement
int SiMakeNewSubroutine(name)	create a new subroutine
int SiNewLoop(ELIST e)	a new loop with properties and body listed in e
int SiInsertStatments(stmt, ELIST e)	insert a list of statements at a given point
ELIST SiFindLabelRefs(scope_id, label_id)	find statements referring to label
ELIST SiVarsUsedInStmt(id)	variables used a given statement
ELIST SiVarsModifiedInStmt(id)	variables modified in a given statement
ELIST SiReachingDefs(stmt)	the set of reaching definitions
ELIST SiWhereDefined(var)	the list of stmts where a variable is modified
ELIST SiGetSubscript(int stmt_id, int expr)	a table of subscript coefficients
ELIST SiLoopBounds (loop_id)	the bounds of a loop
ELIST SiGetECarriedDeps(loop_id)	the loop carried data dependencies
ELIST SiModInRoutine(routine_call_id)	the side effects of a call
int SiNewExpr (type, lchild, rchild)	create a new expression node
int SiNewSymbolRef(type, symb, expr)	create a new variable reference
int SiReplaceExpr(old_exp, new_exp)	to modify an expression in a stmt
int SiReplaceVar (expr1, id, expr2)	to substitute one variable with another
int SiVarType (id)	the type table entry for a variable
int SiNewVarInt (type,scope,name)	create a new variable

In addition to the data base of statement and expression trees, Sigma contains a full symbol table that is indexed by the id and the name of the variable. A type table is also provided.

2.1.1. Interprocedural and Data Dependence Analysis

The interprocedural analysis supported by SIGMA II is based on the needs of the data dependence system which, in turn, is focused on loop level parallelization. What the interprocedural analysis system does can be summarized as follows. For each subroutine and function, a list of all the data structures, visible outside the routine that are used or modified by a call to that routine, is built. These lists are described in terms of the formal parameters, common block variables and global variables in the computation. Array accesses are simplified into array section descriptions to make these lists as short as possible. For example the subroutine

```
subroutine Foo(A, B, n, m)
real A(n,m), B(100)
common /xxx/ k, C(100)
do i = 1, n
   do j = 10, m-10
       A(i,j+1) = A(i,i) - 3.8*B(j)+C(k)
   enddo
   B(C(i)) = 0.0
enddo
C(1:5) = B(4:8)+B(6:11)
return
end
```

will have the following summary associated with it.

```
USED:  B(10:m-10), B(4:11), C(k), C(1:n), A(1:n, 1:n), k, n, m
MODIFIED: A(1:n, 11:m-9),  B(1:100), C(1:5)
```

This example illustrates several limitations of the analysis. First observe that the diagonal access *A(i,i)* has been approximated by *A(1:n,1:n)*. This is because rectangular regions are used to approximate array references and the analysis is always conservative. The second approximation involves the reference *B(C(i))* which is approximated by *B(1:100)* because the range of values stored in C is not known. (In a future release of the system we plan to use a more symbolic analysis which will represent these regions as *(A(i,i), i=1:n)* and *B(C(1:n))*.)

The first pass of the system that generates the *".dep"* files each routine is analyzed without regard to function or subroutine calls. A second pass in the global analysis uses an iterative scheme to merge regions from called procedures into the regions defined by each calling procedure.

At the point of a call to a subroutine a library function *SiGetCallInfo()* can be used to express the side effects of the call in terms of the actual parameters at the call site. For example

```
real X(10000), Y(100,100)
...
call Foo(X, Y(1,s+1), s, t)
```

will return an expression list values of the form

```
MODIFIED: X(10*s+1 : s*(t-9)), Y(1:100,s+1), C(1:5).
```

A similar value is returned listing uses of data structures in the call.

Once the global side effect information has been propagated to each call site in the program data dependencies can be computed. The dependence analysis is done upon demand on a subroutine by subroutine basis. Distance vectors are computed whenever possible and scalar propagation and some pseudo induction variable detection is also done. The current dependence analysis in SIGMA is viewed as a default system, because many users of the tool kit are interested in testing their own dependence analysis algorithms. (Indeed, there are many new papers on dependence testing in the literature and the algorithms used in SIGMA are not at the state of the art.) What SIGMA provides is full access to interprocedural summaries as described above and special functions for parsing complex subscript expressions into coefficient tables to simplify the work of a full dependence analysis system. In addition a full set of symbolic algebra procedures is available to aid in this task.

3. Building Tools with Sigma II

Most of the tools that are built with the Sigma tool kit have a similar structure. An initialization procedure that opens the data base and, if needed, does the interprocedural flow analysis is followed by a loop that cycles through the functions and subroutines in the project and invokes the kernel of the tool for each routine. For example, if the tool takes the name of the project from the command line, the main program takes the form shown below.

```
main(argc, argv)
int argc;
char **argv;
{
   ELIST aSubroutine, enames, /* names of the subroutines */
         procs;               /* id of the surbroutines   */
   char *filename;

   if (SiOpenProject(argv[0]) < 0)
   {
      printf("*** could not open project %s\n", argv[0]);
      exit(0);
   }
   if (SiDoGlobalAnalysis() != 0)
   {
      printf("global analysis failed\n");
      exit(0);
    }
    /* now get the list of all subroutine node ids */
    procs = SiGetProcIdList(proj_name);
    /* also get a list of all the names of subroutines in this project */
    enames =  SiGetProcNameList(proj_name);
```

```
    /* for each subroutine on the procedure list explore the  */
    /* control flow graph.  first select the correct source file */
    for (; procs; procs = SiECdr(procs))
    {
       aSubroutine = SiECar(procs);
       /* extract the file name */
       filename = SiECadr(SiECar(enames));
       SiSelectFile(filename);
       /* Invoke the the control traversal for this procedure */
       CONTROL_TRAVERSAL(aSubroutine);
       enames = SiECdr(enames);
    }
 }
```

The *for* loop in this program is the one that cycles through the list of subroutines and functions in the application that has been loaded into the data base. The variable *procs* is an EList of the statement identifiers for each subroutine or function header. The identifier of an object such as a statement is only unique up to source file (because of separate compilation). Hence before any operation is done on the data base, the source file must be specified to set the context. The second list *enames* is a list of lists of the form

```
( (subroutine-name filename line-number) ...... )
```

and so to extract the file name the function *SiECadr()* is applied to the first term on the list.

The typical control traversal template takes the form shown below. For each control statement in the subroutine or function there is a loop with a switch statement and an action to take for each statement type. If another control node is encountered in the switch the control traversal is called recursively.

```
CONTROL_TRAVERSAL_TEMPLATE( statement_id, ....)
{
   ELIST children, branch;
   int child_stmt;

   /* extract the control children of this statement */
   children = SiControlChildren(statement_id);
   /* children is a list of the form ( (true branch) (false branch) ) */
   /* first traverse the true branch then the false branch */
   while (children)
   {
      branch = (ELIST) SiECar(children);
      /* loop through each child statement on the branch */
      while (branch)
      {
```

```
        child_stmt = (int) SiECar(branch);
        switch (SiStmtType(child_stmt ))
        {
           /* for each type of program statement we may do */
           /* a different operation.  For children that    */
           /* are control statements, we can call the      */
           /* CONTROL_TRAVERSAL_TEMPLATE recursively       */
        }
        branch = SiECdr(branch);
     } /* go to next stmt on branch  */
     children = SiECdr(children); /*is there another branch? */
  }
}
```

For well structured programs, this control traversal is nothing more than a depth first traversal of the control dependence tree.

Tools that use Sigma either extract information from the program data base to be used in some other context such as performance analysis and prediction, or they use Sigma to modify or restructure the users application. In the latter case the control traversal routine is usually designed to modify the data base which is then "unparsed" into the new program structure and written to a file.

4. Example: Program Restructuring

Consider the problem of building a source-to-source program transformation system to help in vectorizing and parallelizing applications. There are many standard transformations that one would like to support in such a system. Examples include loop distribution, loop unrolling, loop merging, loop interchange, loop blocking (strip mining), vectorization, scalar expansion, loop parallelization, variable copy localization, etc. To illustrate how this could be written with Sigma II, we will illustrate the construction of simple versions of two of these transformations.

4.1. Loop Interchange

If we have two loops, $L1$ and $L2$ which have the following properties:

1. $L2$ is perfectly nested inside $L1$, i.e. $L2$ is the entire body of $L1$,

2. the induction variable for $L1$ does not appear in the loop bounds for $L2$ and

3. either $L1$ or $L2$ has no loop carried data dependencies, i.e. there are no memory locations that are used or modified by one iteration of the loop that are modified or used by a later iteration,

then the two loops may be interchanged. (The third condition is more restrictive than is really needed, but the most general condition requires a more complete discussion of dependence distance vectors than is necessary to make our point.) To accomplish this task we write a C function that takes the identifier of the outer loop and returns -1 if any of the conditions fail and returns the identifier of the new outer loop after the interchange, if the test passed.

```
int LoopInterchange(int L1)
{
   ELIST body1, body2, bounds2, cntl_end;
   int L2, induct_var1, bounds2;

   if (SiStmtType(L1) != FOR_NODE)
      return -1;
   body1 = SiECar(SiControlChildren(L1));
   L2 = SiECar(body1);
   /* body1 should be ( L2[FOR_NODE]  x[CONTROL_END] ) */
   if (SiStmtType(L2) != FOR_NODE ||
       SiStmtType(SiECadr(body1)) != CONTROL_END)
      /* violates rule 1 */
      return -1;
   cntl_end = SiECdr(body1);
   if (SiGetECarriedDeps(L1) != NULL && SiGetECarriedDeps(L2) != NULL)
      /* violates rule 3 */
      return -1;
   induct_var1 = SiGetStmtSymbol(L1);
   bounds2 = SiGetLoopBounds(L2);
   if (ReferenceFound(induct_var1, bounds2))
      /* violates rule 2 */
      return -1;
   body2 = SiECar(SiControlChildren(L2));
   SiReplaceStmt(L1, L2);
   SiSetControlChildren(L1, body2, NULL);
   SiSetControlChildren(L2, SiEAppend(SiENumber(L1), cntl_end), NULL);
   return L2;
}

int ReferenceFound(int name, ELIST e)
{
   if (e == NULL)
      return 0;
   if (SiReferenceFound(name, SiECar(e))
      return 1;
   return ReferenceFound(name, SiECdr(e));
}
```

In this routine the function *SiSetControlChildren()* is used to make the loop $L1$ have the original body of $L2$ and to make $L2$ have the body given by the expression

```
( ( L1[FOR_NODE]  x[CONTROL_END] ) () ).
```

SiSetControlChildren takes three arguments: the target control node and the "true" and the "false" branches of control to be set.

Also the function *ReferenceFound()* which goes down a list of expressions, in our case the lower bound, upper bound and increment for the loop, and checks for an occurrence of the variable in the expression.

4.2. Scalar Expansion

Scalar expansion is a technique for eliminating loop carried data dependencies that are caused by scalar variables that are reused in the body of a loop. For example in the code fragment

```
do i = 1, 100
   a = x(i) + 3.14
   y(i) = a*a
enddo
```

uses the scalar a as a temporary and there is no recurrence that prohibits parallelization of the loop. Scalar expansion can be applied to a to convert it into an array and modify the code to the form below.

```
real aTmp(1:100)
do i = 1, 100
   aTmp(i) = x(i) + 3.14
   y(i) = aTmp(i)*aTmp(i)
enddo
a = aTmp(100)
```

With the code in this new form, loop distribution and vectorization can be applied to parallelize the loop. In its full generality, scalar expansion can be applied to any scalars including those that are used to forward a value from one iteration to the next, but here we treat only the case where the scalar is not involved in any loop carried flow dependencies. We describe a simple function that takes a loop and a scalar variable as input and introduces a temporary array equal to the size of the loop bounds and modifies the loop appropriately.

The task is relatively simple and involves creating a new array type and a new variable in the symbol table and replacing occurrences of the old variable with the new variable. SIGMA expression manipulation functions can do most of the work. We need the following functions from the SIGMA library,

- **SiVarName(v)** which returns the string associated with a variable v.
- **SiLoopBounds(L)** which returns a triple

  ```
  (lower upper stride)
  ```

  representing the loop bounds.

- **SiNewExpr(type, left, right)** which creates a new expression of type *type* with left and right operands given by *left* and *right*.
- **SiMakeArrayType(basetype, dimension, range_expression)** which adds an entry to the type table that can be used to define an array of dimension *dimension* whose sizes in each dimension are given by the expression *range_expression* and which is of base type *basetype*.
- **SiNewVar(type, scope, newname)** which generates a declaration for a new variable of name *newname* and of type *type* in the scope containing *scope*.
- **SiNewSymbolRef(type, variable, subscript)** which generates an expression that is a reference to a *variable* as either an array reference with a *subscript* or a standard variable reference with no subscript.
- **SiWhereDefined(var)** builds a list of pairs of the form

  ```
  ((statement-id  expression-id) ....)
  ```

  which are the points, i.e. statement and expression, at which the variable *var* is assigned a value. **SiWhereUsed()** is the same but it looks for places where the value is used.
- **SiControlledBy(stmt1, stmt2)** is a predicate which is true if statement *stmt2* is a control ancestor of statement *stmt1*.
- **SiReplaceVar(inExpression, var, newExpression)** looks for references to the variable *var* in expression *inExpression*. These references are replaced with the expression *newExpression*.

The code for this transformation is shown below.

```
expand_scalar(int L, int v)
{
   /* L is the ID of the Loop and          */
   /* v is the ID of the scalar variable */
   char *newname;
   ELIST s, bounds,  refs;
   int i, type, bnd_expr, it_var, array_var, array_ref, subscript;
   int it_ref, inStatement, inExpression;

   /* create the new variable name from the original+"Tmp"      */
   s = SiVarName(v);
   newname = (char *) malloc((i = strlen(SiECar(s)))+4);
   strcpy(newname[i], "Tmp");

   /* build a "type" for the array.                             */
```

```
   bounds = SiLoopBounds(L);
   /* create an expression of the form lowbound:highbound      */
   bnd_expr = SiNewExpr(DDOT, SiECar(bounds), SiECadr(bounds));
   type     = SiMakeArrayType(TYPE_FLOAT,  1,  bnd_expr);

   /* allocate a symbol table entry and make a declaration at  */
   /* scope containing statment L                              */
   array_var = SiNewVar(type, L, newname);

   /* now make a reference of the form aTmp[i].  First get     */
   /* the induction variable and make a reference to it        */
   it_var    = SiGetStmtSymbol(L);
   it_ref    = SiNewSymbolRef(VAR_REF, itvar, -1);
   subscript = SiNewExpr(EXPR_LIST, it_ref, NULL);
   array_ref = SiNewSymbolRef(ARRAY_REF, array_var, subscript);

   /*search for the definitions and uses of the variable v.    */
   refs = SiEAppend(SiWhereDefined(var), SiWhereUsed(var));

   /* for each reference, check to see that it is in the loop L*/
   /* and make the substitution for the array_ref expression   */
   for (;refs; refs = SiECdr(refs))
   {
      inStatement  = SiECar(SiECar(refs));
      inExpression = SiECadr(SiECar(refs));
      if (SiControlledBy(inStatement, L))
         SiReplaceVar(inExpression, v, SiCopyExpr(array_ref));
   }
   return array_var;
}
```

5. Example: Program Annotations and Instrumentation

One approach to designing performance analysis tools is to make them execution history event driven. This means the application is modified so that it leaves a record, i.e. an **event trace file**, which documents all the major control flow paths the program followed during the execution as well as any other actions, such as major data structure modifications, that are of interest in the performance analysis.

One difficulty in building an instrumentation tool of this type is that, if one were to instrument every control branch, every loop entry and exit and every variable reference, the trace file is too large and the performance is severely degraded. A minimal instrumentation is to add an instrumentation function call for each subroutine entry and exit. In addition, one can allow selected loop and variable reference instrumentation by having the user add source code annotations before loops that are to be monitored and special annotations to indicate where a variable is to be traced.

SIGMA has a general annotation system based on source code comment lines. These annotations take the form

```
C$annotate[ IfDefined(<keyword>), <expression_list> ]
```

where the *IfDefined()* clause is optional and allow tools to selectively look only for certain types of annotation. The argument *keyword* is any string such as "INSTRUMENT" and *expression_list* is a list of any expressions valid in a simple grammar. Rather than describe the detailed grammar here, we will illustrate the concepts with a few examples.

In some cases the annotations can describe assertions to aid in restructuring. For example, to assert that a vector of integers P is a permutation one can write

```
C$annotate[  ForAll( i, j, ((P(i) = P(j)) => (i = j))
C                           && in( P(i), [1:size(P)]) ].
```

where the *ForAll* operator defines a sequence of unbound variables defining a local scope followed by an expression involving these variables and program variables as defined by the scope that contains the annotation. An alternative formulation of this assertion would be

```
C$annotate[  P(1:size(P)) = 1:size(P) ].
```

Another class of assertions is the set of directives which can be used to express directions to the restructuring system about how and where certain restructuring operations should be done. For example, suppose there are two do loops labeled 110 and 111. To interchanges the loops with labels 110 and 111 followed by strip mining the loop labeled 111 into chunks of size n/p, one could write,

```
C$annotate[ Perform(Interchange(110, 111), Block(111, n/p)) ]
```

If our case, we are interested in performance analysis instrumentation. Among the things we are interested in are inserting events that record access to certain data structures. For example, the annotation

```
C$annotate[ IfDef(INSTRUMENT), RecordEvent(A_ARRAY_UPDATE,,A(i,j), i,j) ]
```

might be used to record that array A at location (i, j) has been modified at this point in the execution. Both the location and the value have been recorded. (ARRAY_UPDATE is a symbolic name for a user defined constant which can be specified at the top of the file with

```
C$annotate[ Define(ARRAY_UPDATE, 22) ]
```

Pointwise information is often too detailed and slows down the computation too much. Another variation would be to record that a particular row $A(i, 1:n)$ of the matrix has been updated. This can be done with

```
C$annotate[ IfDef(INSTRUMENT), RecordEvent(A_ROW_UPDATE, i, 1, n) ]
```

The important thing to note is that RecordEvent simply dictates that certain tuples of values shall be dumped in the trace buffer along with the timestamp and processor number that executed the code. It is up to the performance analysis tool to understand the meaning of each record in the trace file.

Data structures are not the only thing one may wish to annotate. In order to replay execution, one also needs control flow information. This can be accomplished with simple events which establish that a given control path is being followed. For example, the annotation

```
C$annotate[ IfDef(INSTRUMENT), RecordEvent(TRACE_CONTROL) ]
```

can be put at the top of a block by the user to indicate that each loop entry and control branch should be instrumented within the following block.

Other than a few operators such as *ForAll* which define scopes for symbolic names, the semantics of an annotation are defined by the tool builder. Each annotation is embedded in a comment statement and each comment statement is attached to the following line of non-comment source code. The library functions that extracts an annotation is

```
SiGetAnnotation(char * keyword, int statement_id)
```

which checks to see if the given statement has an annotation that matches the keyword. (If keyword is NULL, then any annotation will match.) The function returns the expression in the annotation as the id of the parsed expression. In this way the tool can treat the expression as any other expression in the program and all the SIGMA expression manipulation functions apply to it.

To illustrate the application of this concept, consider the task of implementing the *TRACE_CONTROL* directive above. We will modify the control traversal template so that each time a control statement like a *Do* loop or *if* statement is encountered we check for an annotation like the one above. If one is found we extract the argument of the *RecordEvent* function. and if it is *TRACE_CONTROL*, we will turn on a flag which cause the correct flow monitoring code to be inserted in the program. In the code below, we illustrate by inserting *LOOP_ENTRY* and *LOOP_EXIT* events around all *do* loops contained within the block that has been annotated.

```
Instrumentation_Traversal( int statement_id, int trace_on)
{
   ELIST children, branch;
   int child_stmt, AnnotationId, ArgumentId;

   /* detect block level instrumentation */
   if ((AnnotationId = SiGetAnnotation("INSTRUMENT", statement_id)) &&
       (SiExprType(AnnotationId) == FUNC_CALL) &&
       (strcmp(SiECar(SiVarName(SiVarId(AnnotationId))),
              "RecordEvent") == 0))
   {
      ArgumentId = SiECar(SiGetLRChild(AnnotationId));
      switch ((int) SiECar(SiGetConstVal(ArgumentId)))
```

```
      {
         case TRACE_CONTROL: trace_on = 1; break;
              /* .....  other block level instrumentation cases  .... */
      }
   }
   if (SiStmtType(statement_id) == FOR_NODE && trace_on)
      generate_loop_entry(statement_id);

   children = SiControlChildren(statement_id);
   while (children)
   {
      branch = (ELIST) SiECar(children);
      while (branch)
      {
         child_stmt = (int) SiECar(branch);
         switch (SiStmtType(child_stmt))
         {
            /* check each statement in the block for special  */
            /* statement level annotations and call           */
            /* Instrumentation_Traversal recursively for loops*/
            /* and conditions and other control statements.   */
         }
         branch = SiECdr(branch);
      } /* go to next stmt on branch  */
      children = SiECdr(children); /*is there another branch? */
   }

   if (SiStmtType(statement_id) == FOR_NODE && trace_on)
      generate_loop_exit(statement_id);
}
```

6. Conclusion

SIGMA II has proven to be of substantial value in the construction of a number of parallel programming tools. By providing a toolkit which provides researchers an easy way to access FORTRAN90, C and C++ application syntax and semantics, we feel new ideas can be more quickly tested and production systems can be more easily built.

The complete source code, documentation and example applications are available by anonymous FTP from cica.indiana.edu as a compressed tar file. However, it must be stated that the system is still evolving. Our FORTRAN90 front end has not been extensively tested because, at the time of this writing, there are still not very many programs that use the full set of features of FORTRAN90 (such as modules, operator overloading and pointers.) As our test set becomes larger, we will eliminate existing bugs. Another area where SIGMA II is still very weak is in the analysis of C programs that use dynamic data structures and pointers. This topic is still an area of active research but we plan to provide much more support in this area within the next year.

7. Acknowledgements

The authors are indebted to Craig Chase at Cornell, Joel Saltz at ICASE, David Jablonowski and David Hammerslag at CSRD for their patience with early versions of this system and for many important debugging and optimization suggestions.

1 Allen, F., Burke, M., Charles, P., Cytron, R., and Ferrante, J. *"An overview of the PTRAN analysis system for multiprocessing"* In Proceedings of the 1987 International Conference on Supercomputing (Athens, Greece, 1987).

2 Appelbe, B., Smith, K., and McDowell, C. *"Pat: A parallel-programming toolkit"* IEEE Software 6, 4 (July 1989), 29–38.

3 Daya Atapattu, *"Performance Prediction of Supercomputer Programs"* Ph.D. Thesis, Indiana University, 1991 (Feb. expected), Computer Science Department, Indiana University, Bloomington, Indiana.

4 Atapattu, D., and Gannon, D. *"Building analytical models into an interactive performance prediction tool"* In Proceedings of Supercomputing '89 (Reno, Neveda, Nov. 1989), IEEE Computer Sciety and ACM SIGARCH, pp. 521-530.

5 Balasundaram, V., Kennedy, K., Kremer, U., McKinley, K., and Subhlok, J. *"The ParaScope editor: An interactive parallel programming tool"* In Proceedings of Supercomputing '89 (Reno, Neveda, Nov. 1989), IEEE Computer Sciety and ACM SIGARCH, pp. 540–550.

6 Guarna, Jr., V. A., Gannon, D., Jablonowski, D., Malony, A. D., and Gaur, Y. *"Faust: An integrated environment for parallel programming"* IEEE Software 6, 4 (July 1989), 20–27.

7 Irigoin, F., Jouvelot, P., Triolet, R., *"Overview of the PIPS project"* International Workshop on Compilers for Parallel Computers, Paris, Dec. 1990.

8 Koelbel, C., Mehrotra, P., Van Rosendale, J., *"Supporting Shared Data Structures on Distributed Memory Architectures"* 2nd ACM SIGPLAN Symposium on Principles and Practices of Parallel Programming. March 1990, pp. 177-186.

9 Lee, J. K., Gannon, D., *"Object Oriented Parallel Programming, Experiments and Results"* In Proceedings of Supercomputing '91 (Albuquerque, Nov. 1991), IEEE Computer Sciety and ACM SIGARCH, pp. 273-282.

10 Padua, D., *"The Delta program manipulation system, preliminary design"* Technical Report no. 880. Center for Supercomputer Research and Development, University of Illinois at Urbana-Champaign. June 1989.

11 Polychronopoulos, C., Girkar, M., Haghighat, M., et al. *"The Structure of Parafrase-2: An Advanced Parallelizing Compiler for C and Fortran"* Languages and Compilers for Parallel Computing, Gelernter, D., Nicolau, A., Padua, D., ed. pp 423-453. MIT Press, 1990.

12 Saltz, J., Crowley, K., Michandaney, R, Berryman, S., *"Run-time scheduling and execution of loops on message passing machines"* Journal of Parallel and Distributed Computing, 8:303-312.

13 Sarukkai, S., Gannon, D., *"Parallel Program Visualization Using SIEVE.1"* Technical Report, Center For Innovative Computer Applications, Indiana University, Nov. 1991.

14 Shei, B., Gannon, D., *"Sigmacs: A Programmable Program Restructuring Tool"* 1990 Workshop on Compilers for Parallel Systems, Aug. 1990, Irvine, Ca. MIT Press (to appear).

15 Wolfe, M., *"The Tiny Loop Restructuring Research Tool"* Procedings of International Conference On Parallel Processing, 1991.

16 Zima, H., Bast, H., Gerndt, M., *"Superb: A tool for semi-automatic MIMD/SIMD parallelization"* Parallel Computing, 6:1-18, 1988.

PROGRAMMING ENVIRONMENTS FOR PARALLEL COMPUTING
N. Topham, R. Ibbett and T. Bemmerl (Editors)
Elsevier Science Publishers B.V. (North-Holland)

© 1992 IFIP. All rights reserved.

Data Visualization and Performance Analysis in the Prism Programming Environment

Steve Sistare, Don Allen, Rich Bowker,
Karen Jourdenais, Josh Simons, Rich Title

Abstract

The Prism programming environment is a graphical environment to support the development of programs that run on a massively parallel architecture; namely, the Connection Machine system. Such programs have traditionally been difficult to debug because of limited interactive access to the massive quantities of data being computed. Prism overcomes the data bottleneck with integrated visualizers that can present program data graphically in a non-invasive, flexible, and interactive manner. After debugging is complete, it can be difficult to obtain peak performance from massively parallel programs because of a lack of precise knowledge as to where computational resources are consumed. Prism allows users to monitor, in a minimally invasive manner, the utilization of many different resources down to the source-line level of detail. Such utilizations are presented to the user in an easy-to-read histogram format.

Keyword Codes: D.2.2; D.2.5; D.2.6
Keywords: Tools and Techniques, Testing and Debugging, Programming Environments

1. Introduction

Massively parallel machines have acquired a reputation for being difficult to program, but this is largely an artifact of the lack of programming tools such as those described in [8] [12] [14] [15] [16] [19] that are available on serial machines. Indeed, the data-parallel programming model is conceptually simple and elegant, and can be a pleasure to work with when supported by tools such as those supplied by Prism.

Prism provides the user with an integrated set of tools to develop, debug, and tune the performance of massively parallel applications. These tools are accessible through an easy-to-use point-and-click interface based on OSF/Motif.

Prism offers debugging features like those found in **dbx**, but in a graphical setting. In addition, Prism functionality goes beyond **dbx** in a number of ways. Data visualization is viewed as an integral part of the debugging process, not separated from it. Therefore, Prism's visualization was designed to be easy and efficient to use while debugging. Arbitrary language expressions involving parallel data may be visualized at any time during

---

Contact information: Thinking Machines Corporation, 245 First St., Cambridge, Mass 02142. Email: allen@think.com, bowker@think.com, karen@think.com, simons@think.com, sistare@think.com, title@think.com

program execution without requiring program modification. Program data may be viewed under a number of compact yet expressive graphical representations, which allows the user to spot flaws in large data sets at a glance. Of course, Prism can also be used as a tool to view perfectly correct application data in a non-invasive manner.

Prism's performance-analysis features enable the user to find out where and how the program is spending its time. Prism goes beyond standard profilers such as **prof** and **gprof** in two important respects: (1) Performance data is broken down according to what Connection Machine or front-end resource is being used, and (2) the resolution goes down to the source-line level. This allows the user to see, for example, exactly where inter-processor communication is taking place and at what cost – an important measure on a data-parallel machine.

At this point the reader may want to refer to Figure 1, which shows a screen with some windows from the Prism environment. In the center is the main window, with the top-level pull-down menus, the source window, and the commands area. Surrounding that are various optional pop-up windows: a help window in the upper left, several visualizers into the array a in the lower left, and some performance histograms on the right. Data visualization and performance analysis are discussed in detail in sections 4 and 5, but first a brief introduction to Prism's user interface and debugging functionality is given.

2. User Interface

Prism's user interface runs under the X Window System and is based on the Motif widget set. The interface is designed to be easy to learn, and once learned, fast and efficient to use.

Pull-down menus, buttons, and dialog boxes make most of the functionality of Prism easily and obviously available to the user. The appearance of dialog boxes is standardized as much as possible to increase user familiarity with the interface. For example, most dialogs have apply, close, and help buttons. Standard keyboard accelerators can activate the close or help buttons in any dialog at the touch of a key.

A comprehensive on-line-help system provides nicely formatted documentation on all aspects of using Prism. In addition, context-sensitive help is available in all dialogs and pull-down menus, via a help button in the former and a help menu option in the latter. Help screens contain links to related help topics for further information. The structure of the help database forms a general graph which is specified by a simple grammar in a help description file. Each help button points to a graph node, which contains the name of a dvi-format file, generated by LaTeX, containing the help for the node. Prism interprets the dvi file and thus generates high-quality output. Finally, integration of Thinking Machines' WAIS database searching and text retrieval software into Prism provides users with a powerful capability for on-line searching of the entire Connection Machine documentation set.

Prism provides a number of shortcuts that increase the speed of use of the interface. Pull-down menu items may be copied to a region where they become buttons that perform the same action. Some users prefer a command-line interface over a graphical one, so commands can be typed in a text region that maintains a history of commands and Prism output. A number of actions that apply to program entities, such as printing a

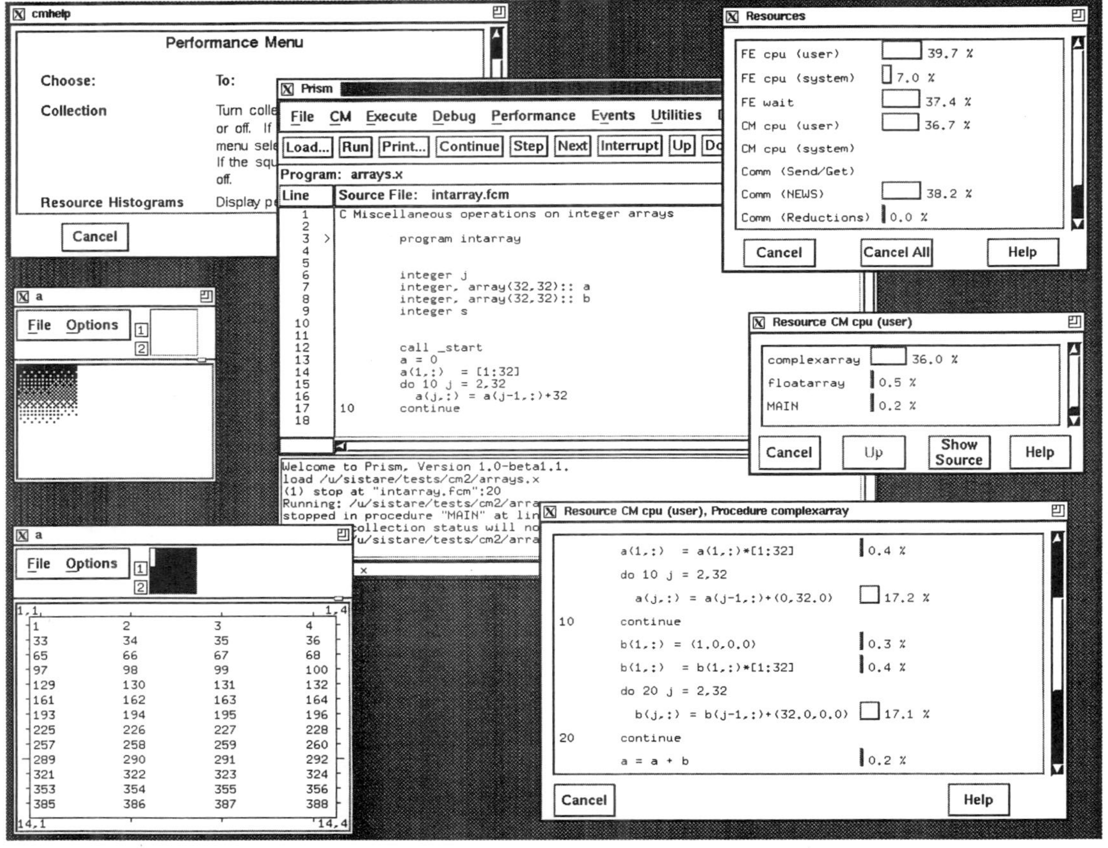

Figure 1. The Prism programming environment

variable or listing a function, can be rapidly performed by interacting with the source region, which displays the source code for the current function or file. The user simply selects some text in the region, such as a variable name, and then chooses a pop-up-menu option to apply to the selected entity.

Lastly, Prism allows interesting and useful graphical interactions with some of the underlying debugger functionality. The Where, File, and Function dialogs display lists of stack frames (i.e., function invocations), available source files, and available functions, respectively (see Figure 2). If the user clicks on any list item, the source region displays the source code for that item, and if the item is in the Where or Function list, the default scope for variable lookups is set to the chosen function. Prism events (see below) may be created and modified using the event table dialog, which allows complete generality in specifying event descriptions.

3. Debugging Data-Parallel Programs

The data-parallel languages for the Connection Machine include CM Fortran and C*. These are extensions of the Fortran and C languages that provide for the manipulation of arrays in parallel. Since these languages still have essentially a single control flow, it is relatively straightforward to extend existing debugging paradigms (such as provided by **dbx**) to programs written in these languages. Therefore, we chose **dbx** as the base for Prism's debugging features.

We first extended dbx's expression parser to handle CM Fortran (Fortran 90) and C* expressions. The results of these expressions may be printed out in the commands window or may be fed to a visualizer. To evaluate parallel expressions, Prism needs to be able to fetch parallel data from the Connection Machine. It does so by using the "call" command mechanism to call runtime routines that are linked with the user program. These routines copy data from the nodes of the Connection Machine to the address space of the front-end user process. Prism then uses the standard UNIX ptrace mechanism to copy the data into its own address space. In this way, Prism can retrieve parallel CM Fortran arrays or C* parallel variables. The compilers are responsible for linking in the correct machine-specific data-fetching routines when an executable is built, which makes Prism independent of the Connection Machine target system. In fact, the same version of Prism itself is used on both the CM-2 and the CM-5.

Another area where dbx's capabilities were extended is in Prism's *event description table*. The idea is to generalize and enhance the **dbx stop**, **trace**, **when**, and **display** capabilities. A Prism event description consists of a trigger condition, and actions to be performed. Examples of trigger conditions include whenever the program reaches a certain point (standard breakpoints), whenever a condition becomes true, or whenever the value of a variable changes. Actions can be arbitrary Prism commands, such as **print**. For example, by setting up an event that triggers on every line, whose action is to update a visualizer for the array x, it is possible to watch the array x change as the program runs. A user may also control whether execution is stopped at an event or continues, and whether or not an event is triggered silently. Events may be created by typing the appropriate dbx-like command or by entering fields in the event table dialog, shown in Figure 3. In either case, events may subsequently be modified using the dialog.

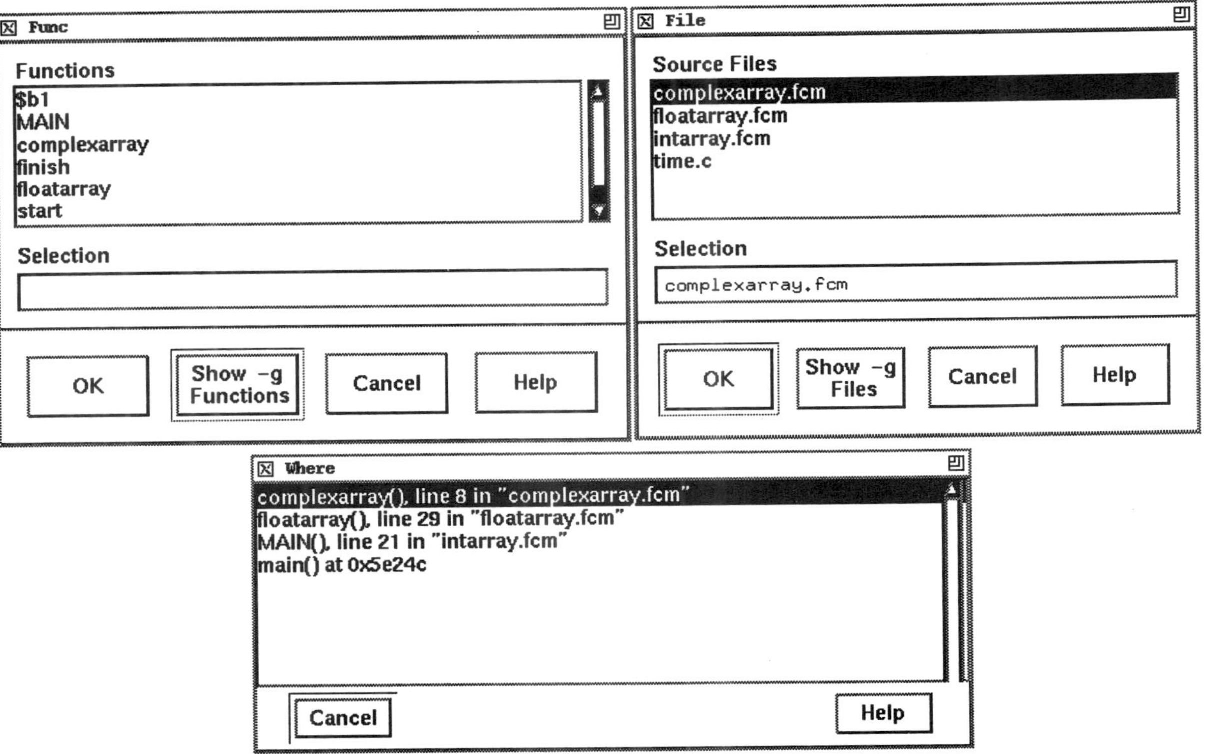
Func
Functions
$b1
MAIN
complexarray
finish
floatarray
start
Selection
OK
Show -g Functions
Cancel
Help
File
Source Files
complexarray.fcm
floatarray.fcm
intarray.fcm
time.c
Selection
complexarray.fcm
OK
Show -g Files
Cancel
Help
Where
complexarray(), line 8 in "complexarray.fcm"
floatarray(), line 29 in "floatarray.fcm"
MAIN(), line 21 in "intarray.fcm"
main() at 0x5e24c
Cancel
Help

Figure 2.

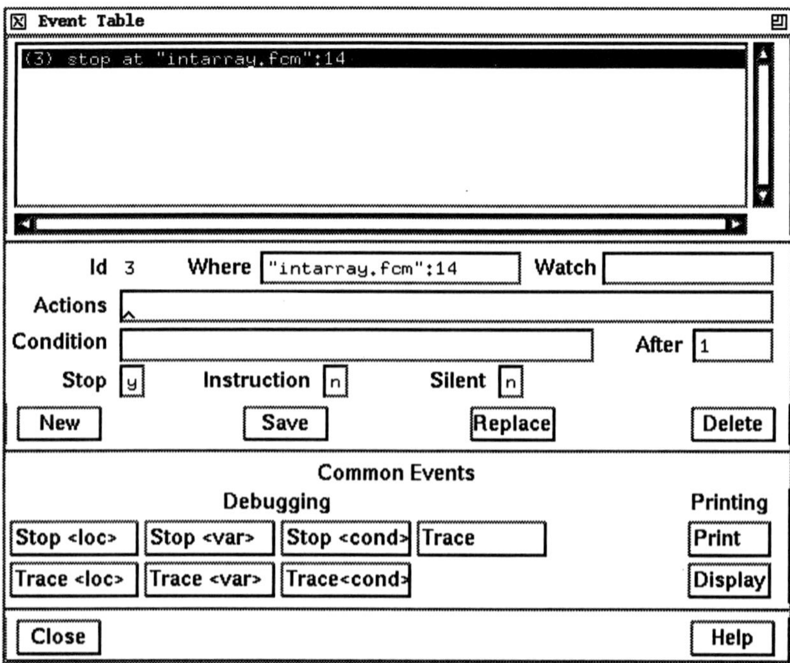

Figure 3. The event-description table.

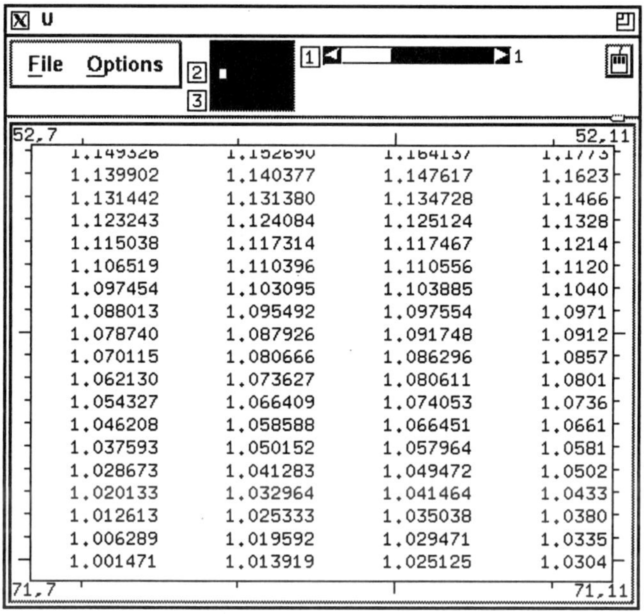

File Options

52,7 52,11

1.149326	1.152690	1.164137	1.1773
1.139902	1.140377	1.147617	1.1623
1.131442	1.131380	1.134728	1.1466
1.123243	1.124084	1.125124	1.1328
1.115038	1.117314	1.117467	1.1214
1.106519	1.110396	1.110556	1.1120
1.097454	1.103095	1.103885	1.1040
1.088013	1.095492	1.097554	1.0971
1.078740	1.087926	1.091748	1.0912
1.070115	1.080666	1.086296	1.0857
1.062130	1.073627	1.080611	1.0801
1.054327	1.066409	1.074053	1.0736
1.046208	1.058588	1.066451	1.0661
1.037593	1.050152	1.057964	1.0581
1.028673	1.041283	1.049472	1.0502
1.020133	1.032964	1.041464	1.0433
1.012613	1.025333	1.035038	1.0380
1.006289	1.019592	1.029471	1.0335
1.001471	1.013919	1.025125	1.0304

71,7 71,11

Figure 4. A three-dimensional visualizer.

4. Data Visualization

Prism currently provides a tightly integrated capability for the visualization of parallel and serial data. A separate window, called a visualizer, may be created for each variable or expression to be visualized. Visualizers give the user an efficient means to navigate through and interpret the large amounts of data that are typically found in massively parallel programs.

Visualizers are designed to view multi-dimensional arrays of data. Any variable or expression of type array may be viewed, whether the data resides on the CM or the front end. Data is fetched using the mechanism described in Section 3, so programs do *not* have to be modified to display a visualizer. The user simply runs a program to a breakpoint and enters an expression to be visualized. The visualizer displays one section of a two-dimensional slice of data, and the user may pan around in this slice using simple graphical gestures. A ruler may be enabled that shows the coordinates of the array elements at the four corners of the visualizer window. For higher-dimensional data, sliders are provided for varying the coordinates of axes that are orthogonal to the displayed slice. Assignments of array axes to the sliders and the two window dimensions are shown by small text fields

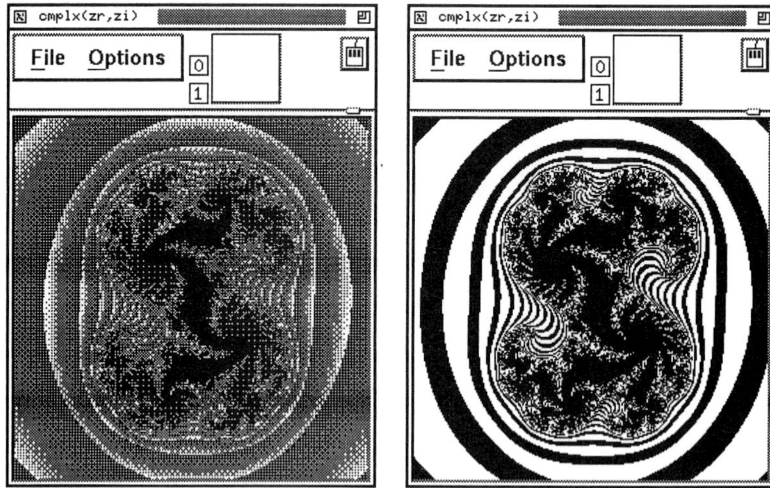

Figure 5. Visualizing the complex basis of a julia set. A dithered representation is chosen on the left, while a threshold is applied on the right.

---

that can be edited to change the displayed layout, allowing arbitrary slices of data to be displayed.

Referring to Figure 4, we see a typical visualizer. Axis 1 has been assigned to the slider, and axes 2 and 3 have been assigned to the rows and columns of the visualizer. The black box in the upper middle is referred to as the data navigator and represents the entire slice of data that may be viewed. The white tab in the navigator represents the portion of the slice being viewed in the main window below. The user may either click on this tab with the mouse and drag it to effect panning in the data slice or click anywhere in the data navigator to zoom to that location in the slice. Alternatively, the user may click on and drag the data region itself for finer control over panning.

The data in Figure 4 is shown in a numeric format. Though this may seem little different from the **dbx** print command, the data navigation capabilities offered by Prism make visualization using text vastly superior to dumping a potentially huge array to a terminal, because the user may easily view any portion of the data without sorting through pages of output. However, other graphical representations are also available. The representation may be easily changed at any time by selecting a new one from a pre-defined list under the visualizer's options menu.

One such representation maps each data element to a colored pixel based on the value of the element. By default, a spectral color map is used, with the smallest value in the data set mapped to blue and the largest value mapped to red. Values between are stretched

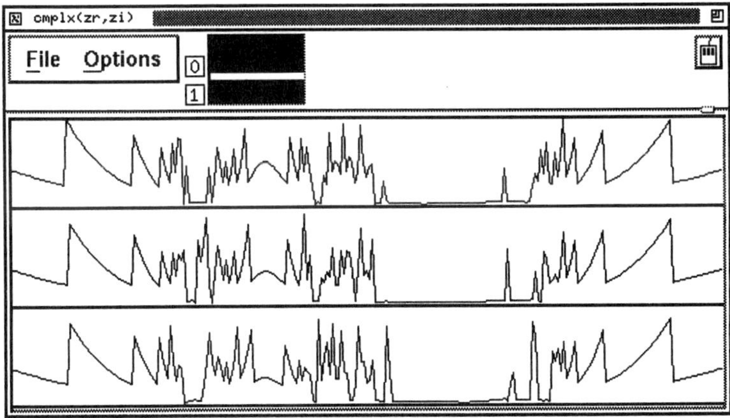

Figure 6. The rows of the julia set are plotted.

linearly across the colormap. The user may also pin down the values that map to blue and red, allowing different ranges of the data set to be emphasized. On a black and white display, values are mapped in a similar fashion to intensity, and the result is dithered to produce black and white pixels. An example of the dithered representation may be seen in Figure 5a, in which the magnitude of the complex basis of a julia set [11] is being visualized. The colors present in the color-mapped equivalent of this visualizer are striking, but unfortunately they cannot be reproduced here. The julia set was computed by a C* program on a 256 by 256 grid, and its 65536 data elements may be copied from the CM to Prism and visualized in a few seconds.

Several additional representations are available, including threshold, graph, surface, and vector. The threshold representation compares each data element to a threshold value, which can either be the mean of the data set or a value supplied by the user. Values above the threshold are mapped to a white pixel, and all others map to black. The representation of the julia set of Figure 5a has been changed to threshold to produce Figure 5b. The graph representation creates separate plots of each row of the data slice and stacks them on top of each other, as shown in Figure 6. The surface visualizer is the three-dimensional extension of the graph visualizer; the data slice is treated as a height field whose surface is rendered as a series of contours. Hidden lines are removed using a horizon algorithm like that found in [23]. This algorithm is fast and efficient in both memory and time; the surface in Figure 7 took just a few seconds to render on the SparcStation front end machine. In this figure, the julia set rises out of a ground plane that is tilted 45 degrees from the viewer (note that the iteration count at each element of the julia set is being visualized here rather than the complex basis magnitude). Points at

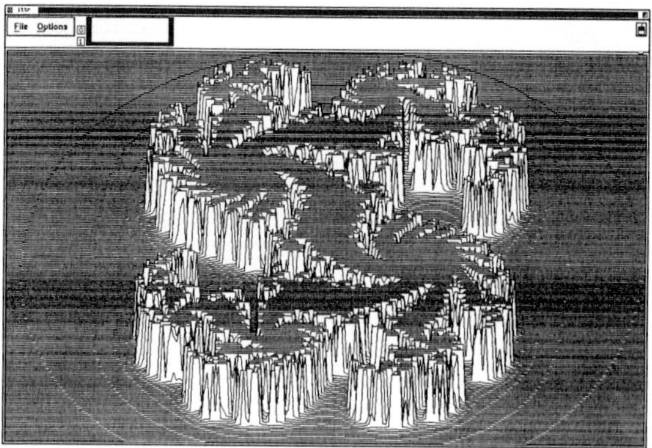

Figure 7. Surface rendering of julia set with hidden lines removed.

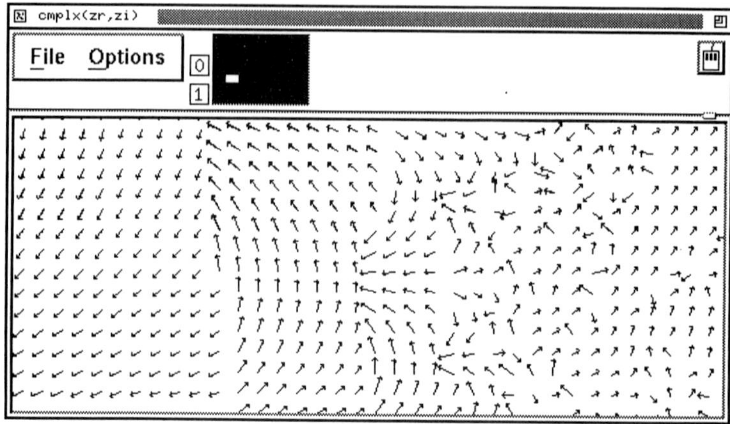

Figure 8. The magnitude and direction of a portion of the complex basis for the julia set is shown.

the top of the window are in general further from the viewer than points at the bottom. As with any visualizer, the user may pan through the data, and this may be done fairly rapidly because only the regions that panning exposes are re-rendered.

The final representation to be discussed is the vector representation, appropriate for visualizing vector-valued data such as Fortran's complex data type. For programs that compute vectors but do so by storing the real and imaginary components in separate variables, Prism provides the cmplx intrinsic to build a complex data element. Though this is a standard Fortran intrinsic, it may be used while debugging programs in any of Prism's supported languages. A vector visualizer of the complex basis of the julia set is shown in Figure 8.

The graphical representations allow large amounts of data to be viewed at once and and give an excellent picture of the behavior of the underlying variable or expression. As compared to the numeric format, however, they give an inexact indication of the value of each array element. To maximize the usefulness of the graphical representations, Prism provides a point-and-click operation to query the value of any element.

The built-in visualizers provided by Prism give the user fast and effective means to view large aggregates of data. Though implemented here in a data-parallel framework, they are independent of the programming model and machine architecture used to compute the data. They simply require that some means is available for collecting the data from the processing nodes and passing it to Prism.

5. Performance Analysis

While data-parallel programs share important characteristics with their sequential counterparts, i.e., sequential or pseudo-parallel control flow, their ambitious performance goals, combined with the added complexity of inter-processor communication and large data sets, make comprehensive performance tools an absolute necessity.

In Prism, we have begun to implement such a suite of performance-analysis tools. Our initial work focuses on providing Connection Machine users with an understanding of where and how their data-parallel programs are spending their time. The CM Fortran and C* compilers accept a command line option that, when specified, inserts timer calls at the start and end of front-end procedures, and around code blocks that are executed in a data-parallel fashion on the Connection Machine. These code blocks are categorized by function, which includes inter-processor communication, global reduction, general computation on the processor nodes, and several others. The timing results and their categories (also referred to as *resources*), are stored into a call-graph database that is built in the user process's address space as execution proceeds.

5.1. Timing Algorithm

The method used to time code blocks that run on the Connection Machine 2 is non-obvious due to the architectural decoupling of the CM-2 and its front end. The front-end pushes instructions down a FIFO queue that is read by the CM; thus, assuming a synchronization point is not reached, the front end can get ahead of the CM. Sampling of the front-end program counter is therefore ineffective in determining where the CM is spending its time. A timer running on the front-end would be similarly useless. Therefore, timers that run on the CM must be used, so start-timer and stop-timer calls are pushed down the FIFO around code blocks of interest. However, reading the resulting time poses a different problem. A read-timer request must be sent down the FIFO, and the front end must wait for the result to be sent back. The FIFO empties while the front end is waiting instead of being continually refilled as it normally would. While individual code blocks can be accurately timed in this manner, the performance characteristics of the program as a whole are drastically altered.

The solution lies in the use of multiple timers and the fact that a stop-timer request can be issued without requiring the front end to wait. The Connection Machine supports a number of virtual timers – currently 64. As each code block is executed, a timer is allocated for the block and associated with it. A start timer command is pushed down the FIFO, followed by a command to execute the code block, followed by a stop timer command. However, the timer *is not yet read.* Future invocations of this code block start and stop the same timer. It is only when a code block needs a timer but none are available that all timers are read, written into the call-graph database, and returned to the timer allocation pool. In addition, all unread timers are flushed when a program terminates. It may seem that just as many reads are being performed as before, and that they are simply being deferred, but that is not true due to locality of execution. Within loops, for example, the same timers will be started and stopped many times without being read.

This solution works very well in practice and allows the FIFO to behave essentially as if timing were not being done.

5.2. Overhead

The overhead incurred while profiling a program consists of extra cpu time consumed by the timer calls as well as extra memory consumed by the call-graph database. The instructions to make the timer calls also take some extra memory, but this is insignificant. The timers that measure CM-based resources run on the CM itself, and are fast – they may be started or stopped in 10 microseconds. The operations that they time typically take much longer. Thus, we have seen programs compiled under profiling take less than 5% longer than non-profiled programs.

However, even if a program has been compiled with the profiling option, the timers may be conditionally disabled at run time. When the user program starts, a global flag is set if a particular environment variable is defined, and timers are called based on the setting of the global. By not defining the environment variable, essentially all of the overhead associated with profiling – timer execution time and database memory – may be eliminated. All that remains is the time to conduct a flag test and instruction branch at every timer instance. This time is utterly dwarfed by the computations being performed on the Connection Machine. Thus, as a practical matter, all programs may be compiled with profiling by default, and timing data is only collected when the user toggles it on from Prism.

5.3. Displaying Histograms

When the program completes its execution, control passes to Prism, which copies the call-graph database into its own address space. The data may then be presented to the user as a series of histograms. The top-level histogram, seen in the upper left of Figure 9, shows the time taken by each resource for the program as a whole. The histogram bars are

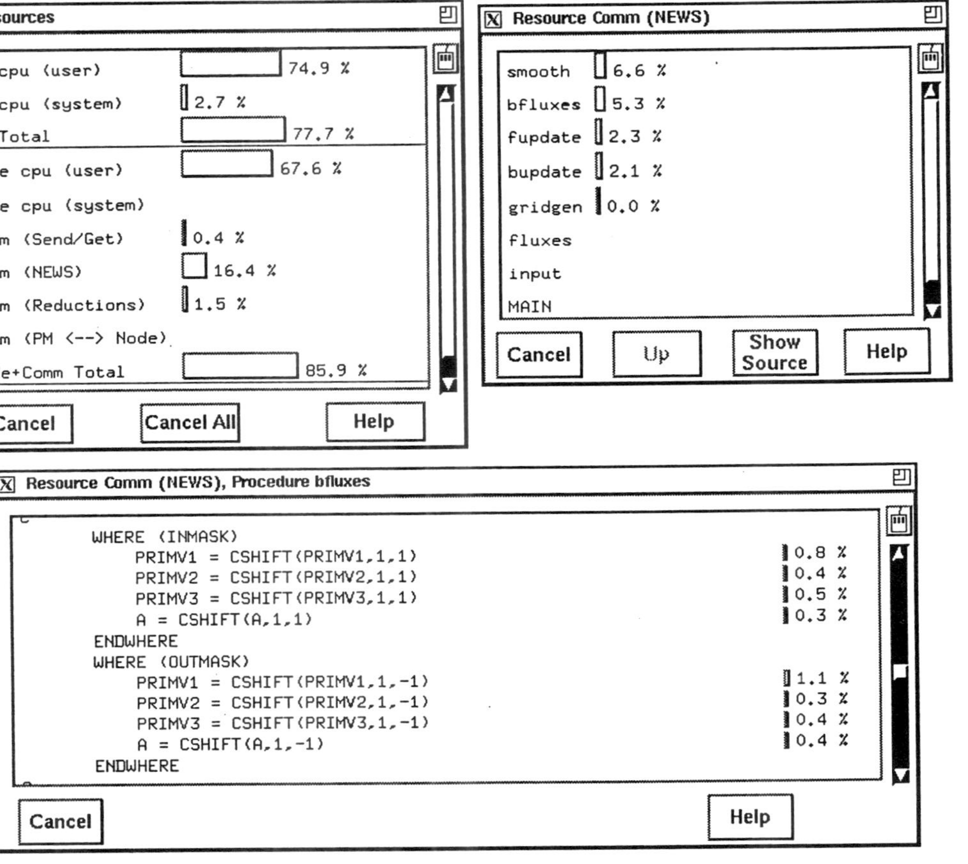

Figure 9. Performance histograms.

mouse-sensitive, and clicking on a bar opens up a new histogram like the one in the upper right of the figure, which lists the usage of nearest-neighbor (NEWS) communication in each of the procedures of the program. This procedure histogram is shown in flat mode, meaning that the time shown is spent within each procedure and not its descendents. Call-graph mode is also available in which a parent procedure is shown with a listing of its children, and histogram bars represent the time for the labeled procedure and its descendants *from that point in the call graph.* The parent procedure may be clicked on to move up in the call graph, and a child may be clicked on to move down. Finally, the user may click on any of the procedure histogram bars to show the time spent at each source line of the procedure for the chosen resource (see the third window in Figure 9). The hierarchical nature of the displays ensures that the user can easily identify the most heavily utilized resource, and, by navigating about the call graph using point-and-click gestures, home in on the places in the source code that are the major contributors to that utilization.

We feel that providing integrated profiling of a program's use of all the resources available to it represents an important advance over profiling tools that provide information about processor utilization only. It is important that performance analysis tools permit the user to easily understand where the leverage is; this is not possible without an understanding of a program's usage of all parts of the computing system that can contribute to execution time.

6. MIMD Support

To date, our efforts have been primarily focused on providing facilities for debugging data-parallel programs, since the data-parallel model is the only programming model supported on the CM-2 and is a heavily used model on the CM-5. However, the CM-5 also allows multiple threads of control communicating via message passing, and programs using this model must be supported in Prism.

Prism currently supports the MIMD model by offering a command-line interface to a separate node-level debugger. This interface runs in a separate window, providing visibility and control of what is going on in the processing nodes, while Prism remains active and can be used on the code that runs on the scalar front-end machine.

A full description of the MIMD debugging commands is outside the scope of this paper, but briefly, they provide dbx-like debugging of processor nodes. The user can switch debugging context among the nodes, and capabilities are also provided for iterating any command across all nodes or sets of nodes.

7. Future Directions

Future plans for Prism include building on its existing functionality as well as adding completely new tools. New graphical representation formats will be made available for Prism's integrated visualizers. In addition, we plan to study the visualization of data that is not explicitly present in the variables of a user program, such as communication patterns and memory layouts. Lastly, Prism will be able to gather data from the user program and export it to external visualization systems such as AVS. The external system will complement Prism's visualization capabilities by offering complete generality in defining visualizations.

In the area of performance analysis, we will be looking at additional tools to analyze MIMD programs. Additional support will also be available for debugging such programs. In particular, we want to provide a graphical interface to the present MIMD functionality and investigate alternate paradigms for MIMD parallel debugging. This entire area is a fruitful one for further research.

Lastly, Prism will provide an interface to automatic and interactive tools for translating Fortran 77 code to efficient Fortran 90 code. Users will be able to debug the resulting program at the source level in either language.

8. Conclusion

Prism is an easy-to-use environment that enables Connection Machine programmers to be at least as productive as their counterparts on serial machines. Prism's debugging features, which include convenient access to large amounts of data via visualizers, give programmers powerful methods for diagnosing program defects. The performance-analysis tool provides resource utilization information that is even more detailed than that provided by tools on serial machines, and does so with very little impact on a program's performance characteristics. Finally, the individual capabilities offered by Prism are integrated in a coherent fashion which makes the whole more valuable than the sum of its parts.

1 Aral, Gertner, Schaffer, "Efficient Debugging Primitives for Multiprocessors", *SIGPLAN notices*, May 1989, p.87.

2 Cleveland, L., "A Program-Understanding Support Environment", *IBM Systems Journal*, no. 2 1989.

3 Cooper, Kennedy, Torczon, "The Impact of Interprocedural Analysis and Optimization on the Design of a Software Development Environment", *SIGPLAN notices*, July 1985, p. 107.

4 Cooper, Kennedy, Torczen, Weingarten, Wolcott, "Editing and Compiling Whole Programs", *SIGPLAN notices*, January 1987, p. 92.

5 Cooper, Kennedy et al., "A Practical Environment for Scientific Programming", *IEEE Computer*, 20(11), November 1987.

6 Fisher, G., "A Graphical Multilanguage Applications Environment", *IEEE Transactions on Software Engineering*, June 1988, p. 774.

7 Frederick Brooks, "No Silver Bullet", *IEEE Computer*, 20(4), April 1987.

8 Goldberg and Robson, *Smalltalk-80: The Language and it's Implementation*, Addison-Wesley 1983.

9 Haberman and Notkin, "Gandalf: Software Development Environments", *IEEE Transactions on Software Engineering*, December 1986, p. 1117.

10 Leblang and Chase, "Computer-Aided Software Engineering in a Distributed Workstation Environment", *SIGPLAN notices*, May 1984, p. 104.

11 Mandelbrot, B.B., *The Fractal Geometry of Nature*, Freeman, San Francisco, 1982.

12 Mitchell, C., "Engineering VAX ADA for a Multi-language Programming Environment", *SIGPLAN notices*, January 1987, p. 49.

13 Pazel, P., "DS-Viewer - An interactive graphical data structure presentation facility", *IBM Systems Journal* no. 2, 1989.

14 "Saber-C Reference Manual", Saber Software (now Centerline Software), Inc., Cambridge, MA.

15 Sweet, R., "The Mesa Programming Environment", *SIGPLAN notices*, July 1985, p. 216.

16 Swinehart, Zellweger, Hagmann, "The Structure of Cedar", *SIGPLAN notices*, July 1985, p. 230.

17 Taylor, Selby, Young, Belz, Clarke, Weleden, Osterweil, and Wolf, "Foundations for the Arcadia Environment Architecture", *SIGPLAN notices*, February 1989.

18 Teitelbaum and Reps, "The Cornell Program Synthesizer: A Syntax-Directed Programming Environment", *CACM*, September 1981, p. 563.

19 Teitelman and Masinter, "The Interlisp Programming Environment", *IEEE Computing*, April 1981, p. 25-34.

20 Teitelman, W., "A Tour of Cedar", *IEEE Transactions on Software Engineering*, 11(3) 1985.

21 Toomey, Plachy, Scarborough, Sahulka, Shaw, Shannon, "IBM Parallel Fortran", *IBM Systems Journal* no. 4, 1988.

22 Wheeler and Canek, "Introduction to Systems Application Architecture", *IEEE Computer*, 20(11), November 1987.

23 Wright, T., "A Two-Space Solution to the Hidden-Line Problem for Plotting Functions of Two Variables", *IEEE Transactions on Computers*, January 1973.

PROGRAMMING ENVIRONMENTS FOR PARALLEL COMPUTING
N. Topham, R. Ibbett and T. Bemmerl (Editors)
Elsevier Science Publishers B.V. (North-Holland)

© 1992 IFIP. All rights reserved.

A Graphical Programming Environment for Parallel Embedded Systems

Lorenz Schäfers, Christian Scheidler[a]
Ottmar Krämer-Fuhrmann[b]

[a] Daimler-Benz AG, Systems Engineering Research, Alt-Moabit 91b, D-1000 Berlin 21
ljs@b21.uucp, scheid@b21.uucp

[b] GMD, German National Research Center for Computer Science, Schloss Birlinghoven, D-5205 Sankt Augustin
ok@gmdzi.de

Abstract

This paper describes a graphical programming environment for parallel embedded systems with real-time requirements. It comprises tools for design, animation and optimization of parallel programs. A design-tool allows the hardware independent specification of process nets and their mapping onto a specific target system. Animation and optimization features are provided by a visualization-tool and a performance-tool. Whereas the visualization-tool shows the system's behaviour from the view of the application software, the performance-tool animates the behaviour of the underlying hardware. Runtime information is provided by a software monitor. In an initial step transputer based systems are targeted.

Keyword Codes: D.2.6; C.1.2
Keywords: Programming Environments; Multiple Data Stream Architectures (Multiprocessors)

1. Introduction

Parallel computers, quite apart from technological developments, offer a long term possibility to improve the performance of computer systems. The technical know-how necessary for the realization of parallel processing systems is already available. This fact manifests itself in the steadily rising number of parallel systems being used in research and industry.

Current difficulties with parallel computing lie on the software side, as opposed to hardware. A particularly suitable quote is "It appears to be easier to build parallel computers than to use them" [18].

The programming environment TRAPPER (TRAffonic Parallel Programming EnviRonment) is an effort to cope with these difficulties. TRAPPER is under development within the Daimler-Benz research program TRAFFONIC™, which addresses the use of electronics in traffic systems. In one of the TRAFFONIC projects, a parallel processor is developed which can be embedded into vehicles, and which can be used for various automotive applications. The machine is based on INMOS T9000 and C104 technology, which enables parallel processing with virtual fully-connected networks. The tools which are developed in the context of TRAPPER will be used on this parallel processor.

The TRAFFONIC parallel processor is intended for use as a universal development platform in a broad spectrum of high-tech applications which cover the range from image- and signal processing to control systems and artificial intelligence. Autonomous vehicle guidance using image-processing was chosen as a demonstrator.

TRAPPER is based on the programming model of communicating sequential processes (CSP) [6]. This model is characterized by a high measure of flexibility, as the processes can execute both different and identical sub-tasks. The programming model is suited to a large class of industrial applications, such as those referred above. For example, an image-processing system consists, in general of cascaded processing blocks, which execute various operations on the image data, thus lending itself straightforward to the CSP model.The communicating processes model is also used in real-time applications in control systems engineering.

2. Overview

TRAPPER comprises different tools for the various phases of the software development cycle.

The *design-tool* contains a graphical editor which allows the hardware independent specification of process graphs. Each process is an independent, sequential task having access to local memory only. Processes can communicate with each other by message passing constructs. Furthermore, the design-tool allows the user to specify the configuration of the hardware system and determines the mapping of the process graph onto the hardware. The mapping is expressed in the configuration language NDL (network description language) and written into the configuration file.

A *monitoring-tool* collects runtime information about CPU- and link-load or scheduling information. A library allows the user to define software events, which will be monitored likewise. All events are time stamped automatically and are stored in monitor files.

Two different tools allow the visualization of the program execution. The *visualization-tool* enables program animation, i.e. the graphical display of execution phases, variable contents and application specific information. It is therefore useful during the debugging phase. The *performance-tool* displays information about the hardware, i.e. load characteristics and scheduling information. It is especially suited during the optimization phase. Both tools allow not only on-line animation but also off-line animation, with stepping and backtracing facilities. Furthermore, they support the snapshot concept, which displays actual system states, as well as the visualization of dependencies between events on a time scale.

The TRAPPER programming environment is based on the GRACIA project of the German National Research Center for Computer Science (GMD). GRACIA is a programming environment for the design and animation of parallel programs for MIMD type systems [9]. The main emphasis of this environment is to support *scientific supercomputing* on a variety of systems, so that programs developed with GRACIA can run on different architectures.

By contrast, the objective of the TRAPPER project is to realize an integrated environment for the design, animation and optimization of parallel programs for *embedded systems* with real-time requirements.

TRAPPER extends GRACIA on various fronts:

– It provides a tool for monitoring and optimizing performance for the target hardware.

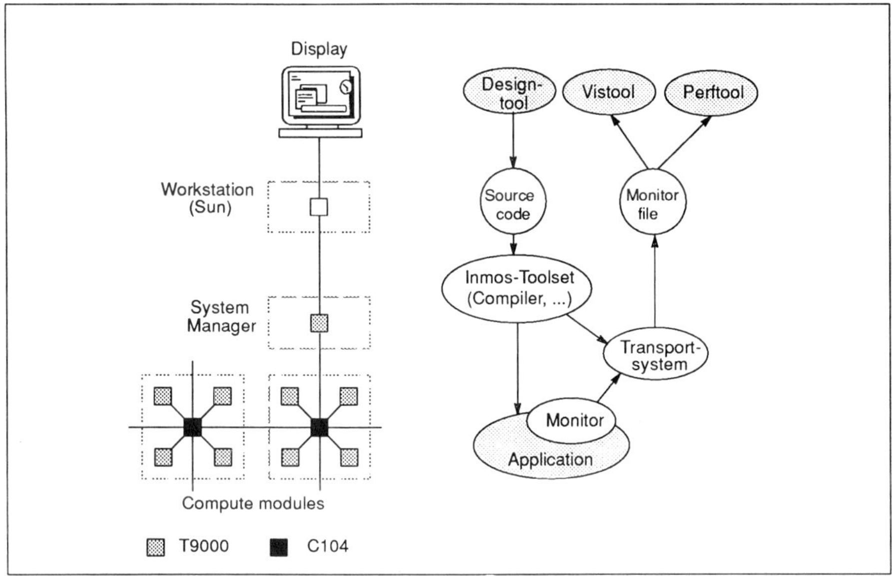

Figure 1. TRAFFONIC hardware and TRAPPER software overview

- It allows graphical configuration of the target hardware including peripheral devices such as A/D, D/A, frame grabber, CAN (Controller Area Network) etc..
- It enhances software and hardware visualization capabilities, e.g. allows time-axis's based visualization of the inter process communication and the performance.

The tools are implemented in C++, using the InterViews [13] toolset, which is based on the XWindow system.

The TRAFFONIC hardware is based on the latest T9000 technology. Four nodes are placed on a board. Arbitrary communication patterns between processors are enabled by the C104 communication chip. Peripheral boards realize the interface to a video system and the CAN. The TRAFFONIC system has a hardware driven central clock, which is important for the monitoring, i.e. time-stamped events.

Figure 1 shows an overview over the TRAFFONIC hardware and the TRAPPER software system. Program development for the TRAFFONIC system is done on UNIX workstations and is supported by the design-tool of the TRAPPER programming environment. The compilers can run either as cross-compiler on the workstation, or directly on the Transputer system. Monitoring of hard- and software-events is done by the monitor-system. A transport system sends its results to the workstation, where they can be observed and analysed by the visualization- and performance-tool.

The outline of this paper is as follows. The following four chapters describe the TRAPPER tools in more detail. Chapter 3 describes the design-tool with its configuration facilities. The monitoring system is explained in chapter 4. Chapters 5 and 6 describe the software and hardware animation systems, respectively (visualization- and performance-tool).

3. The Design-Tool

In the *design phase* the user develops the application independently from the target hardware. The *parallel* structure of the application (process graph) is developed *graphically*, using a graphic editor, whereas the *sequential* components (process code) are developed in *textual* form using a standard text editor. Similar approaches have also been made by [1][15][17].

The *configuration phase* forms the link to the specific parallel hardware. The process graph is mapped onto the parallel hardware using the software configurator. In this way every process of the process graph is allocated to a node of the parallel system.

From the given data (process graph, process code, software and monitor configuration data) the generator creates files which contain

- the source program in C-code, and
- the configuration specification in Inmos 'Network Description Language' (NDL).

These files are processed further by standard tools from Inmos (ICC-Toolset) [8].

3.1. The process graph

The user develops the process graph using the graphic editor. The user-interface of the graphic editor is based on ideas from object-oriented graphic editors.

Large process graphs can be designed *hierarchically* as a composition of *subsystems*. A subsystem is a graphical building block and can be viewed as a black box, which contains a subgraph of the process graph. A subsystem itself can contain other subsystems.

A process graph can be either designed top-down or bottom-up:

- Using the top-down approach the application engineer describes the system as a composition of subsystems. Subsystems are split until they can be described as a composition of sequential processes.
- Using the bottom-up approach the application engineer first describes the sequential processes. Processes are then assembled to form subsystems.

A sample process graph is given in figure 2. Boxes represent processes, edges are for communication channels.

The most important, regular process topologies (ring, lattice, torus, k-tree) are embedded in the tools as *graphical libraries*, and do not need to be generated anew for each application. The process graphs are stored in the graphical library in a parameterised form. The pre-defined topologies are displayed as *icons*. The user selects the desired topology by clicking on an icon with the mouse. The graphical library can be extended by the user. The new process graphs generated in this fashion can also be stored as icons.

The process graph produced by the graphic editor can be used as software documentation. This achieves consistency between software and documentation.

3.2. The process code

Once the process graph has been produced, the static process structure of the application is described. The runtime behaviour of the application is not defined by the process graph alone, as this contains no information about the behaviour during runtime of the process.

The runtime behaviour of the processes is described in a textual form. Any programming language, which supports a message-based communication concept, can be used (ANSI-C with Inmos communication library, OCCAM, Par.C, ...).

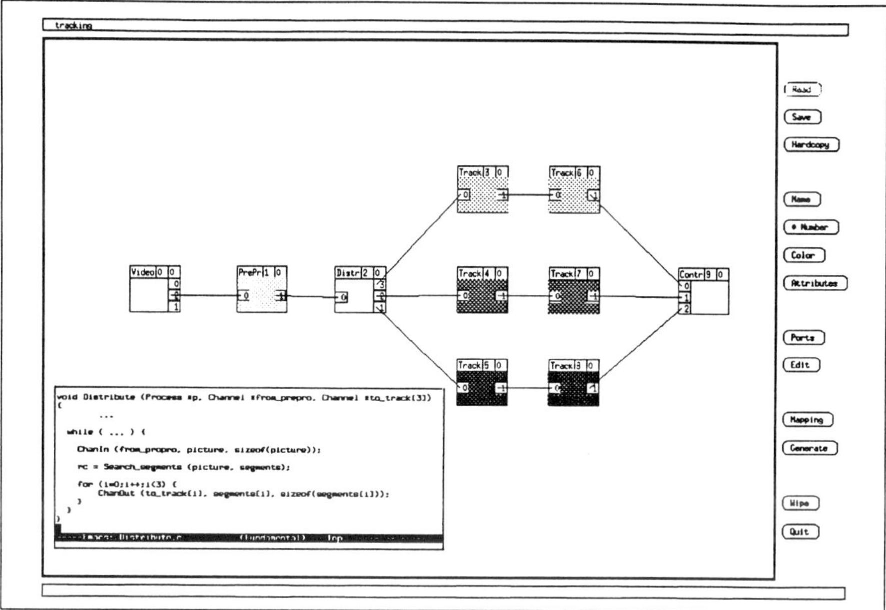

Figure 2. Sample process graph of the design-tool

The user selects an arbitrary process with the mouse, and activates a standard text-editor such as vi or emacs available in UNIX. The user then writes the sequential process code with the text editor. In figure 2, the code of one process is being edited in a separate window.

Duplicate processes, which all execute the same code, are only edited once. This is the same principle as the class concept of object-oriented programming languages. Processes which execute the same code can be interpreted as *instances* of a *process class*.

Each process gets attributes that can be changed, e.g. to be edited or not. This ensures that certain processes are not altered. They can then be stored as finished process building blocks. This enables reusability at the process level.

To provide real-time support, processes can be annotated with timing constraints, which are automatically checked during runtime.

Furthermore, the design-tool offers the possibility to deliver the development environment with pre-programmed building-blocks suited to particular types of applications.

3.3. Configuration of the process-graph

In the *configuration phase* the process graph is mapped onto the target hardware. The application engineer can either select a pre-defined hardware topology or design a new topology with the help of the graphic-editor. The design-tool supports both manual and automatic software configuration.

Manual configuration of the software makes sense for small systems. These systems are typical for the current transputer systems in vehicles.

For the manual configuration, the process graph is used as a graphic user-interface. The user uses the mouse to allocate a colour to each process which is associated with a given processor. In a second window, the design-tool displays the hardware topology graphically.

The manual configuration of parallel systems with large numbers of nodes is impractical. An automatic configuration of the software has advantages, but the fundamental optimization problem (graph-partitioning) belongs to the class of NP-complete problems. This means that in practice only sub-optimal solutions can be found. The quality of such a heuristic solution is highly dependent on the quality of the input data (processor load, communication load).

The solution of the heuristic mapping is displayed in the process graph by colouring the nodes. Each colour is associated with a unique processor. For large systems numbers are used instead.

The mapping found by the design-tool is a suggestion. The user may accept this suggestion and end the configuration phase, or manually modify the mapping by re-colouring of nodes.

On completion of the configuration phase the parallel program is in an usable state, i.e. it can be compiled, loaded and executed. If the user is then interested in observing the system behaviour with the visualization- and performance-tools, the monitor system has to be configured.

4. The Monitor

The monitor provides runtime information as input for the visualization-tool and the performance-tool. The former needs information about the state of the application, the latter needs information about the state of the underlying hardware.

Monitoring tools can be realized as hardware, software or hybrid monitors. Each of them has advantages and disadvantages that are the subject of current research projects [1][4][7][21].

4.1. Software monitoring

Within TRAPPER, a software monitor is used. A software monitor is a piece of code that is part of the system software, part of the application or is an independent process. It runs together with the application software on the target node. Software monitors have the advantage that they do not need extra hardware and are thus more flexible. Portability can be achieved across different target systems.

The main disadvantage of a software monitor is intrusion. The effect of intrusion is twofold:

- An application running together with monitor generally consumes more CPU time than one without monitor. This fact becomes especially crucial in real-time applications. These form an important class of applications for TRAPPER. In time-critical applications an activation of the monitor may lead to a violation of timing constraints.
- Interference of the monitor may also change the behaviour of the parallel application. In that respect, parallel systems differ from sequential systems substantially. Intrusion of the monitor means that the parallel application behaves differently when the monitor is switched on. System behaviour becomes non-reproducible.

There exists no generally satisfactory solution to these problems. To cope with the first problem, we chose a pragmatic approach by making the monitoring overhead controllable by the user. This is achieved by configuring the monitor with respect to the granularity of observation. There is a direct relation between the level of detail in observation and the resulting costs. The more details the user wants to monitor, the more processor time has to be spent.

Using software monitoring does not provide a solution to the second problem since even a slight degree of intrusion may change the application's behaviour.

4.2. Implementation

One of the goals of TRAPPER is to provide portability over a large range of parallel systems. To achieve this, implementation of the system must not rely on the underlying hardware. We carefully chose appropriate abstraction levels for implementation of the different monitor parts. The following section first introduces events as the basic concept and subsequently details the monitor's implementation and its level of abstraction.

Monitoring is based on *events*. Informally, an event depicts a state change of the hardware or the software. Each event that shall be monitored causes an event message to be constructed. The event message describes the event. In particular, it contains a time stamp for use by the visualization- and the performance-tool. This is facilitated using a global clock (cf. chapter 2). This solution was adopted in order to alleviate problems which arise from using local clocks [10]. In this context, configuration of the monitor means the specification of those events that are to be recognized.

First of all, application specific events are considered. TRAPPER classifies them into data, execution and parallel events. A *data event* occurs each time a value is assigned to a variable. An *execution event* occurs, when a process reaches a certain program statement. The statement must be defined by the user prior to program execution. Normally, the user associates a certain meaning with such an event, therefore it it also referred to as *user defined event*. *Parallel events* comprise sending and receiving of messages within the model of communicating sequential processes.

All these application specific events are generated using *source code instrumentation*, which is a *language dependent* technique.

Monitoring of the hardware has to provide load characteristics and scheduling information. As a starting point, RTSM (real-time system manager) is used as operating system of the TRAFFONIC parallel processor. RTSM allows for monitoring of CPU load and link load of the transputer. TRAPPER uses these monitoring capabilities. They are *operating system dependent*. Slight modifications are necessary for other operating systems, that support load monitoring. Evaluation of VRTX as a standard real-time operating system to be used together with TRAPPER is in progress.

Lastly, a "spy" is used to gain scheduling information of the transputer. Monitoring with a spy is realized by a process, which manipulates the process queue ("ready queue") of the transputer [14]. When the spy process is active, it records information about the next process to be executed. It then alters the queue links and thus is executed again, as soon as the next application process is de-scheduled. Monitoring using the spy is strongly *hardware dependent*.

The events are forwarded to the host by a subsystem of the monitor called *transport system*. The transport system can operate in synchronous and asynchronous mode. In synchronous mode the events are steadily passed on to the host, whereas in asynchronous mode they are buffered at the target nodes. Buffering is especially suitable for short monitoring periods and/or rarely occuring events. It can minimize network intrusion to zero. On the host, data is either directly used as input to the visualization- and performance-tool (on-line animation) or written into a script file for off-line animation.

5. The Visualization-Tool

The visualization-tool allows the observation of the behaviour of the parallel software system. It is integrated with the performance-tool in TRAPPER, in such a way that a consistent view on the states of hardware and software components is offered.

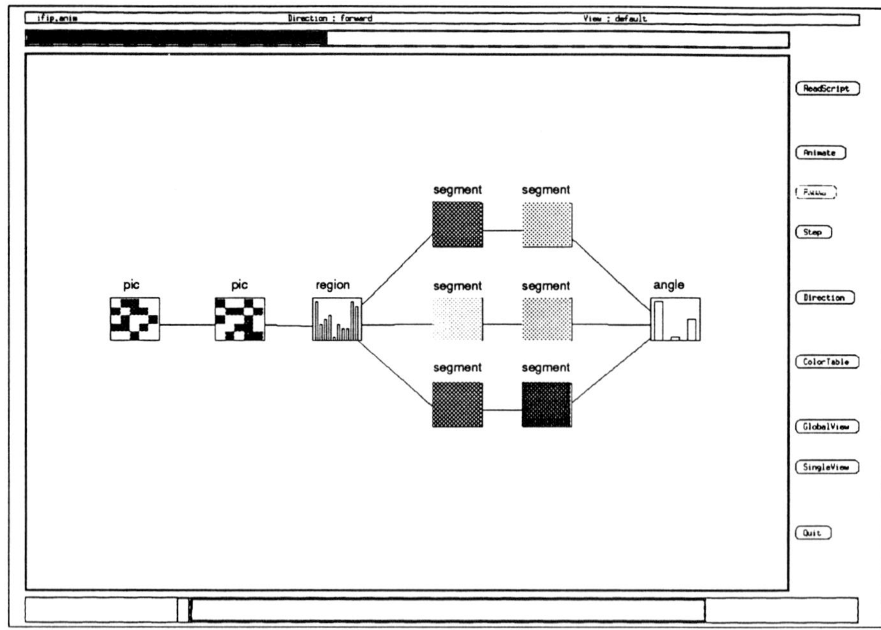

Figure 3. Sample view of the visualization-tool

The visualization-tool supports the programmer in the analysis of the parallel algorithm by displaying runtime data of the application. This helps the user to understand the dynamics of distributed systems, gives debugging information, allows the detection of errors (i.e. deadlocks by the visualization of cycles of outstanding communication requests) and gives important information for code optimization [2][19].

The visualization-system can be driven in two modes, depending on how it is coupled with the application. A direct coupling during runtime enables on-line animation, so that the events are displayed immediately on the workstation. This mode makes sense when the event frequency is low enough for the graphical display system to be observable by a human user. In most real-time applications, an off-line animation is preferable. In this mode, the events are collected in an intermediate file which is read by the animation system. This decoupling of the animation from the execution allows the observation of the software events with a selectable time behaviour. Additional features, like single stepping and backtracing are offered by TRAPPER, so that the programmer can drive the animation to the interesting program phases.

The visualization-system has two different views, one which is based on the process graph and a second one which is based on the time scale. The process graph animation shows a snapshot of the application, i.e. a consistent view at the current time. Each process and communication link displays information about its actual state, i.e. variable contents, subroutine being executed or outstanding communication operations. The second view is oriented on a time scale and shows state changes for a set of processes. With this animation the duration of program phases and data dependencies between different processes are visualized.

The snapshot animation is based on the process graph which is specified by the programmer in the design phase. This concept has the advantage that visualization is performed on exactly the same representation (i.e. the process graph) which the user used to design the application. All events visualized change the process graph, in which process boxes are used to display information about processes and links are used to display communication information. The programmer can select between a variety of different animation features:

- colouring of nodes or edges,
- textures on nodes or edges,
- changing the line width or drawing arrows on the edges,
- displaying plots, histograms or rastered squares in the process boxes,
- progression of the time.

A sample view of the visualization tool is given in figure 3. Variables are visualized as rastered squares (pic), histograms (region, angle) and coloured nodes (segment).

The time scale animation shows the same events in relation to a time scale. For a set of processes which can be selected interactively by the user, the states are displayed either as a moving curve or by a coloured time bar. This animation represents communication operations also as arrows between processes at different time instants. This feature allows a very detailed insight to the cooperation of distributed processes and therefore enables the programmer to debug and optimize his program.

6. The Performance-Tool

The performance-tool supports the user in the optimization phase, which completes the software development after the design and debugging phases. It visualizes and quantifies the load of the hardware resources. The software developer gets hints on possible bottlenecks that are due to load imbalances. Relevant work in this area is described in [5][11][12][16].

Use of the performance-tool is tightly coupled to the use of the visualization-tool. Whereas the visualization-tool shows the system's behaviour from the view of the application software, the performance tool animates the behaviour of the underlying hardware. An important task of the performance-tool is then to find a relation between the behaviour of the hardware and the software, e.g. to relate a non-satisfactory CPU load and a specific code segment which causes it. Using this information, the user may locate sources of insufficient program performance and thus improve the performance of the application.

The performance-tool visualizes the states of the hardware. Resources to be shown are CPU load, link load and the scheduling on the processor. Moreover, there are performance statistics and critical path analysis [20]. It is also possible to simultaneously present graphs from the performance-tool and the visualization-tool. These features are especially suited to find the code segments that need improvement.

Like the visualization-tool, the performance-tool offers two different views: the first is based on the hardware graph, which has been designed using the design-tool, the second is based on graphs with time scale.

Within the hardware graph the CPU load and link load are shown by colouring the node symbols and link symbols. Besides, exact values are given in a pop-up window by clicking on a single

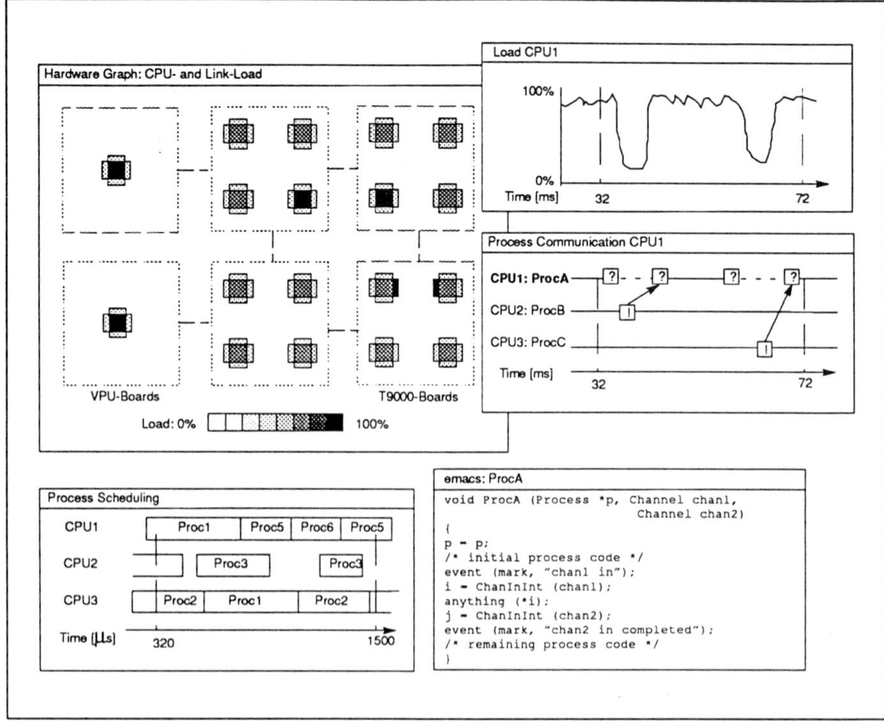

Figure 4. Sample View of the Performance-Tool

symbol with the mouse. Animation of the hardware graph shows the whole parallel machine and gives a first, rough impression of its behaviour.

A more detailed insight can be gained with animations based on graphs with time scale. Each graph then shows the behaviour of a selected resource in its temporal course. Included are visualization of CPU load, link load, scheduling information (Gantt chart) and critical path analysis. An additional feature is the simultaneous view of CPU load and process communication. This enables the user to associate an insufficient CPU load with specific communication events. This is the case, if a process is waiting for communication and there is no other process waiting to be scheduled on that node.

Figure 4 shows an example. The upper right window outlines the load on CPU 1. The middle right window shows the communication behaviour of process A that is running on that node. A communicates with B and C that are located on other nodes. Waiting for messages within A influences the load of CPU 1. The dotted vertical lines are caused by "marker routines" inserted into the application by the user. They help to identify the piece of code just executing. The corresponding source code is displayed in the lower right window. On the left, there is the hardware graph with its coloured boxes for nodes and the attached links. The lower left window shows a scheduling diagram.

Another feature of the performance tool is to provide performance statistics. They include runtime, CPU utilization, communication overhead, speedup, efficiency and granularity of the application. They are available for each node and the system as a whole. They serve to value the optimality of the application.

The performance-tool can be driven in on-line and off-line mode, like the visualization-tool.

7. Conclusion and future work

In the previous chapters we described in detail an integrated environment with tools for design, animation and optimization of parallel programs. A prototype version of TRAPPER with limited functionality is currently used in various departments of the Daimler-Benz company and at the GMD on T8xx based systems.

The widespread use of parallel machines results in increasing demands for such tools. In that context, our further research in the area of tools will address all components of the TRAPPER system:

- A library of predefined algorithms from specific application classes, e.g. image- and signal-processing, and control, shall be added to the design-tool. Thus, the user will no longer need to re-program them. The performance behaviour of these algorithms as a function of the number of nodes will help the user to appropriately allocate available resources.
- There is work in progress at the GMD to configure other parallel architectures of the MIMD class than Transputer based machines. They include the Alliant FX Series, the Intel iPSC, and the Connection Machine CM-5.
- Furthermore, a simulation-tool is planned to be incorporated into TRAPPER, thereby enabling the user to study the runtime behaviour of the application on different simulated hardware platforms. This enhancement will help in rapid prototyping.
- Concerning the monitor, evaluation of its overhead has to be worked out as the next step.
- The visualization- and the performance-tool will be enhanced further. A debugger will be integrated to the visualization-tool and the performance-tool will provide other forms of support for performance-tuning, e.g. phase behaviour analysis [16].

Acknowledgement

The authors would like to thank Dimitris Gerogiannis for reviewing a draft of the paper and his suggestions that improved its clarity.

References

[1] Thomas Bemmerl and Arndt Bode. "*An Integrated Environment for Programming Distributed Memory Multiprocessors*". In EDMCC2, Proc. of the 2nd European Distributed Memory Computing Conference, Munich, April 1991, LNCS 487, Springer-Verlag.

[2] Jon L. Bentley and Brian W. Kernighan. "*A System for Algorithm Animation*". Technical report, AT&T Bell Laboratories, Murray Hill, NJ, USA, February 1987.

[3] Cynthia A. Funk-Lea, Tasos D. Kontogiorgos, J.T. Robert, and Larry D. Rubin. "*Interactive Visual Modeling for Performance*". IEEE Software, Vol. 8, No. 5, Sep. 1991, pp. 58–68.

[4] Dieter Haban and Dieter Wybranietz. "*A Hybrid Monitor for behaviour and Performance Analysis of Distributed Systems*", IEEE Transactions on Software Engineering, Vol. 16, No. 2, February 1990, pp. 197-211

[5] Michael T. Heath and Jennifer A. Etheridge. "*Visualizing the Performance of Parallel Programs*". IEEE Software, Vol. 8, No. 5, Sep. 1991, pp. 29–39.

[6] C.A.R. Hoare. "*Communicating Sequential Processes*", Englewood Cliffs etc.: Prentice-Hall 1985

[7] R. Hofmann, R. Klar, N. Luttenberger, and B. Mohr. "*Zählmonitor 4: Ein Monitorsystem für das Hardware- und Hybrid-Monitoring von Multiprozessor- und Multicomputer-Systemen*". In Messung, Modellierung und Bewertung von Rechensystemen. GI/ITG Fachtagung, Sept./Okt. 1987, Proceedings, Springer-Verlag

[8] Inmos Limited. "*ANSI C Toolkit Handbook*", August 1990

[9] Ottmar Krämer-Fuhrmann and Thomas Brandes. "*— GRACIA — A Software Environment for Graphical Specification, Automatic Configuration and Animation of Parallel Programs*". International Conference on Supercomputing, June 1991, pp. 67–74.

[10] L. Lamport. "*Time, Clocks and the Ordering of Events in a Distributed System*". Communications of the ACM 21(7), 1978.

[11] Thomas J. LeBlanc, John M. Mellor-Crummey, and Robert J. Fowler. "*Analysing Parallel Program Executions Using Multiple Views*". Journal of Parallel and Distributed Computing, Vol. 9, No. 2, June 1990, pp. 203–217.

[12] Allen D. Malony, David H. Hamerslag, and David J. Jablonowski. "*Traceview: A Trace Visualization Tool*". IEEE Software, Vol. 8, No. 5, Sep. 1991, pp. 19–28.

[13] Mark A. Linton, John M. Vlissides, and Paul R. Calder. "*Composing User Interfaces with InterViews*". Computer, 22(2):8–22, February 1990.

[14] Erik Maehle, Wolfgang Obelöer. "*Monitoring-Werkzeuge zur Leistungsmessung in Multi-Transputersystemen*". In 2nd Int. Exhibition and Conference on RISC/Transputer-Architectures and Applications, Proceedings, VDE-Verlag 1991.

[15] Jeff Magee, Jeff Kramer, Morris Sloman, and Narakner Dulay. "*An Overview of the REX Software Architecture*". In Second IEEE Computer Society Workshop on Future Trends of Distributed Computing Systems, Cairo, October 1990.

[16] Barton P. Miller et al. "*IPS-2: The Second Generation of a Parallel Program Measurement System*". IEEE Transactions on Parallel and Distributed Systems, Vol. 1, No. 2, April 1990, pp. 206–217.

[17] Heinz Mühlenbein, Ottmar Krämer, Franz Limburger, Monika Mevenkamp, and Siegfried Streitz. "*MUPPET: A Programming Environment for Message Based Multiprocessors*". Parallel Computing, 8(1–3):201–221, October 1988.

[18] Papadopoulos. "*The New Dataflow Architecture Beeing Built at MIT*" Proceedings of MIT-ZTI-Symp. on "Very High Parallel Architectures", Nov. 1987.

[19] Oliver Vornberger and Klaus Zeppenfeld. "*Graphical Visualization of Distributed Algorithms*". NATUG 3, Sunnyvale, Ca, USA, April 1990.

[20] C. Q. Yang, and B. P. Miller. "*Critical path analysis for the execution of parallel and distributed programs*" Proceedings of the 8th International Conference on Distributed Computing Systems, June 1988, pp. 366–375.

[21] Martina Zitterbart. "*Monitoring and Debugging Transputer-Networks with Netmon-II*" In CONPAR–VAPP IV, Proc. of the Joint Int. Conf. on Vector and Parallel Processing, Zurich, Sept. 1990, LNCS 457, Springer Verlag.

PROGRAMMING ENVIRONMENTS FOR PARALLEL COMPUTING
N. Topham, R. Ibbett and T. Bemmerl (Editors)
Elsevier Science Publishers B.V. (North-Holland)

© 1992 IFIP. All rights reserved.

The Enterprise Distributed Programming Model

Duane Szafron, Jonathan Schaeffer, Pok Sze Wong, Enoch Chan, Paul Lu and Carol Smith

Dept. of Computing Science, University of Alberta, Edmonton, Alberta, CANADA T6G 2H1

Abstract

Workstation environments have been in use for more than a decade. Although a network of workstations represents a large amount of aggregate computing power, single users often cannot utilize these resources for their applications. *Enterprise* is a programming environment for designing, coding, debugging, testing, monitoring, profiling and executing programs in a distributed hardware environment. Programs written using *Enterprise* look like familiar sequential C code; the parallelism is expressed graphically. The system automatically inserts the code necessary to handle communication, synchronization and fault tolerance, allowing the rapid construction of correct distributed programs. *Enterprise* programs run on a network of computers, absorbing the idle cycles on machines. The system supports load balancing, limited process migration, and dynamic distribution of work in environments with changing resource utilization. This paper concentrates on the user's view of programming in *Enterprise*.

Keyword Codes: D.2.6; D.1.3; C.2.4
Keywords: Programming Environments; Concurrent Programming; Distributed Systems

1. Introduction

Enterprise is a programming environment for designing, coding, debugging, testing, monitoring, profiling and executing programs in a distributed hardware environment. It represents the evolution of our successful *Frameworks* system [14][15]. Programs written in the *Enterprise* environment look like familiar sequential C code since the parallelism is expressed graphically. The system automatically inserts all code necessary to handle communication, synchronization and fault tolerance, allowing the rapid construction of correct distributed programs. This bridges the complexity gap between distributed and sequential software. *Enterprise* programs run on networks, absorbing the idle machine cycles. The system supports load balancing, limited process migration, and dynamic distribution of work in environments with changing resource utilization. *Enterprise* offers a cost-effective method for increasing the productivity of programmers and the throughput of existing resources.

This paper concentrates on the model that the programmer uses for writing distributed applications. A discussion of the implementation and run-time issues (such as process-processor assignment, process migration, load balancing, debugging, etc.) can be found in [7]. From the user's point of view, *Enterprise* has a number of features that distinguish it from other parallel and distributed program development tools (see Section 4):

- Programs are written in a sequential programming language (C) that is augmented by new semantics for procedure/function calls that allows them to be executed in parallel. The semantic changes are simple and have the important property that parallel code is indistinguishable from sequential code. Users do not deal with implementation details such as communication and synchronization. Instead, *Enterprise* automatically inserts all of the necessary communication protocols into the user's code.

- *Enterprise* can automatically generate these protocols because most large-grained parallel programs make use of a small number of regular techniques, such as pipelines, master/slave processes, divide-and-conquer, etc. In *Enterprise*, the user specifies the desired technique at a high level by manipulating icons using the graphical user interface. The user-written code that implements the parallel procedure is independent of the parallelization technique selected (although the code generated by *Enterprise* certainly is not). The decoupling of the procedure that is to be parallelized and the parallelization technique allows applications to be easily adapted to a varying number and type of processors, usually without changing user-written code. It also provides a simple mechanism for experimentation and evaluation of how the various parallelization techniques fare on the user's particular application.
- For simplicity in expressing parallelism, *Enterprise* uses an analogy between the structure of a parallel program and the structure of an organization. The analogy eliminates inconsistent analogies used in the past (pipelines, masters, slaves, etc.) and replaces it with a uniform set of *assets* (contracts, departments, individuals, etc.). An organizational analogy was chosen because organizations are common and inherently parallel. This allows the programmer a different (but familiar) model for designing parallel programs.
- Several of the parallelization techniques supported by *Enterprise* can distribute work dynamically in environments with changing resource utilization. For example, a *contract* can be used to distribute work to a variable number of identical subordinates. A contract uses as many idle machines as possible to help complete the task. During peak hours, a program may only be able to use a handful of processors, while in the evening many more may be available to help fulfill the contract.
- In most parallel/distributed computing tools, the user is required to draw communication graphs. The user usually draws a diagram connecting nodes (processes) by arcs (communication paths). In *Enterprise*, a similar diagram is created, but the user is spared the tedium of drawing the details. Instead, the user need only edit the diagram by coercing and expanding nodes that represent assets. Coercion provides the user with a high-level technique to alter the method that a process (asset) uses to communicate with its neighbors and corresponds to the choice of a common parallelization technique. Expanding a node allows the user to explore the hierarchical structuring of the application.

Using the graphical user interface, the user manipulates a diagram of the parallel computation and writes sequential code that is devoid of any parallel constructs. Based on the user's diagram, *Enterprise* determines where to insert the parallel code. It then compiles the routines, dynamically assigns processes to processors and establishes the necessary connections. Processes run in the background, taking advantage of idle machines and recognizing when machines become heavily loaded. In this way we can keep the user community happy, while having applications profitably using machines that would otherwise be idle.

Section 2 contains a typical *Enterprise* session, illustrating the model and the graphical user interface. Section 3 describes the two key components of the *Enterprise* model: the semantics of the sequential code that the user writes, and the kinds of parallelism (assets) supported. Section 4 discusses other parallel programming environments and contrasts them with *Enterprise*. The current status of *Enterprise* is discussed in Section 5.

2. Program Design in Enterprise

This section presents a simple example of how *Enterprise* can be used to construct a distributed program. Consider an animation program that displays a group of fish swimming across a display screen. There are three fundamental operations in the program: *Model*, *PolyConv* and *Split* with the following functionality:

- *Model*: Computes the location and motion of each object in a frame, stores the results in a file, calls *PolyConv* to process the frame and proceeds to the next frame.
- *PolyConv*: Reads a frame from the disk file, performs some data format transformations, viewing transformations, projections, sorts and calls *Split*, passing it a transformed frame and a sequence number.
- *Split*: Performs hidden surface removal, anti-aliasing and stores the image in a file.

This problem comes from a Departmental research group and is more complex than portrayed by our brief description. However, examining the structure of the program shows that *Model* consists of a loop that, for each frame in the animation, performs some work on the frame and calls *PolyConv* with the results. *PolyConv* manipulates the image received from *Model* and calls *Split*. *Split* does the final polishing of the frame and writes the final image to disk.

An *Enterprise* user manipulates icons that represent high-level program components called *assets* (defined in the next section of this paper). For this example, assume that an asset represents a single C procedure/function, called an *entry procedure*, together with a collection of support procedures used by the entry procedure, all contained in a single file. A program consists of several assets. In this example, there are three assets: *Model*, *PolyConv* and *Split*.

After starting *Enterprise* and choosing *New Program* from the main menu, a dialog box appears asking for the name of the program. After entering the name of the program, *Animation* in this case, a single asset appears that represents the entire program. Each asset is represented by a box, with the arrow indicating the flow of data. In *Enterprise* diagrams, the length of the critical data path is represented by the height of the diagram, while the degree of replicated (non-line) parallelism is represented by the width of the diagram.

The *Enterprise* window consists of an asset palette containing one icon for each asset kind and a canvas containing the program. A new program contains one *individual* asset that represents a sequential program component. The code for the procedures *Model*, *PolyConv* and *Split* could be associated with this single individual asset and run as a sequential program. However, there is no reason why *Model* should wait until *PolyConv* completes execution of the first animation frame to start processing the second frame. Similarly, *PolyConv* does not need to wait for *Split*. Therefore, the *individual* asset can be *coerced* to (replaced by) a *line* asset (pipeline in more traditional terminology) by selecting the individual asset and then selecting the *line* icon from the asset palette. After entering three as the length of the line, the *individual* is coerced to a three component line as shown in Figure 1.

The line shown in the figure is *collapsed*; that is, its components cannot be seen. By selecting the line and choosing *Expand Asset* from a pop-up menu, the *line* is expanded so that the three *individual* assets that it contains are visible.

To name an asset, the user selects it, chooses *Name Asset* from a pop-up menu and enters the name of the asset in the dialog box that appears. When the dialog box is closed, the name appears on the icon. To associate code with an asset, select it, choose *Edit Code* from a pop-up menu and enter the C code using your favorite text editor. Note that *Enterprise* automatically names the output file for the code you enter as the name of the asset with a ".c" suffix. In the example, the *Model* code would be saved in the file Model.c, illustrating the close relationship between *Enterprise* code and sequential C code.

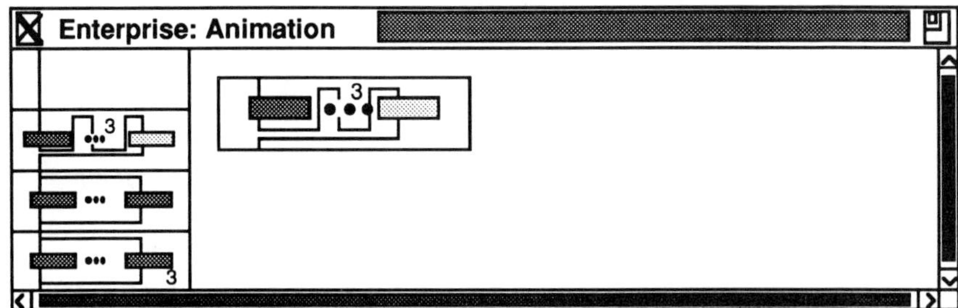

Figure 1. A Collapsed Line Asset Composed of Three Assets

To compile the application, the user selects *Compile* from a menu and the *Enterprise* system automatically inserts the code to handle the distributed computation, compiles the program and reports any errors back to the user. Once the program is compiled, the user selects the *Execute* menu item and *Enterprise* finds as many processors as are necessary to start the program, initiates processes on the processors, monitors the load on the machines and (if a contract is used) dynamically adds additional processors to the application as they become needed. For this animation example, a speed-up of 1.7 was obtained by using a line running on three processors instead of a single individual asset (a sequential program). Note that any timings are subject to large variations, depending on the number of available processors and the amount of traffic on the network.

The strength of the *Enterprise* model can be seen by the ease with which it is possible to take a program and experiment with alternate parallelization techniques *usually without changing the C source code.* For example, by selecting the *Split* asset and selecting a *contract* asset from the asset palette, the *Split* asset is coerced from an *individual* to a *contract* as shown in Figure 2.

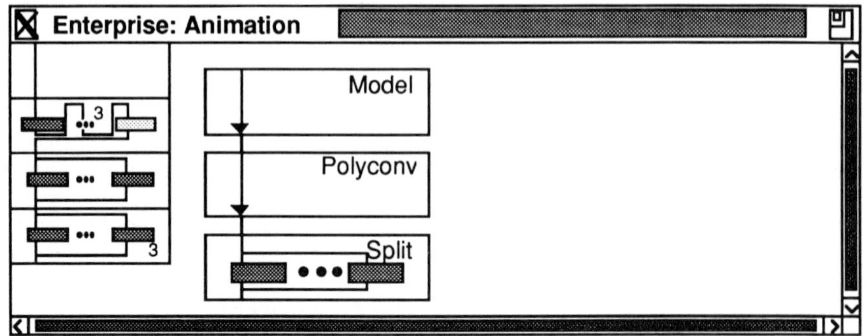

Figure 2. A Collapsed Contract Asset in a Line

In *Enterprise*, each asset represents at least one process. If a call is made to the *individual Split*, it is executed as a process and if a subsequent call is made to *Split* before the first call is complete, the second call must wait for the first call to finish. However, when a *contract* is executed, multiple processes can be used to execute multiple calls concurrently. That is, when *PolyConv* calls *Split*, a process is initiated and if a subsequent call is made to *Split* before the first call is done then a second process is initiated (if there is an available machine). *Enterprise* contracts are dynamic so as many processors as are available are used.

Coercing the *Split* asset to a contract results in as much as a 5.7-fold speed-up (using a dynamically varying number of processors) compared to the sequential animation program, depending on when the program is run. Of course, there is no reason why the user cannot coerce the *PolyConv* asset from an individual to a contract as well. However, in this case, a speedup of only 6.0 was obtained. This implies that the *Split* procedure is the real bottleneck in the animation program. That is, an individual *PolyConv* can almost keep up with its calls by *Model* but an individual *Split* cannot keep up with its calls by *PolyConv*.

If the C code for the individual *Split* contained a sequence of procedure calls (or even a single procedure call at the end of it), then *Split* could be expanded to reveal its individual asset components that could then be coerced to a line. Each of the assets in the line would represent one of the procedure calls. Several other asset kinds are supported by *Enterprise* and they can be combined in arbitrary hierarchies. The next section details the asset kinds that are available.

3. The Enterprise Model

The organization of a parallel or distributed program in *Enterprise* is similar to the organization of a sequential program. The structure of a program is independent of whether it is intended for sequential or distributed execution. The user views an *Enterprise* program as a collection of modules. Each *module* consists of a single *entry procedure* that can be called by other modules and a (possibly empty) collection of *internal procedures* that are known only within that module. No common variables among modules are allowed. In many ways, this is analogous to programming with abstract data types, which provide well-defined means for manipulating data structures while hiding all of the implementation details from the user.

Within any module, the code is executed sequentially. For example, a sequential program simply consists of a single module whose entry procedure is the main program. *Enterprise* introduces parallelism by allowing the user to specify the way in which the modules interact. Module interaction is specified by two factors: the *role* of a module and the *call* to a module. The role of a module defines which one of a fixed set of parallelization techniques (*asset* kinds) the module will use when it is invoked. The call to a module defines the identity of the called module, the information passed and the information returned. The role of a module is specified graphically while the call is specified in the code.

3.1 Module Calls

In a sequential program, procedures communicate using procedure calls. Procedure A contains a call to procedure B, that includes a list of arguments. When the call is made, procedure A is suspended and procedure B is activated. Procedure B can make use of the information passed as arguments. When procedure B has finished execution, it can communicate results to procedure A via side-effects to the arguments and/or by returning a value if the procedure is in fact a function.

Enterprise module calls are similar to sequential procedure calls. As with procedure and function calls, it is useful to differentiate between module calls that return a result and those that do not. Module calls that return a result are called *f-calls* (function calls) and module calls that do not return a result are called *p-calls* (procedure calls).

Enterprise module calls differ from sequential calls in the following ways:

- Arguments cannot be pointers, nor can they contain any pointers.

- When module A, calls another module, B, module A continues to execute. However, if the call to module B was an f-call, then module A would suspend itself when it tried to use the function result, if module B had not yet finished execution.

There is no syntactic difference between procedure calls and module calls. This makes it easier to transform sequential programs to parallel ones and makes it trivial to change parallelization techniques using the graphical user interface, usually without making changes to the user's code.

In *Enterprise*, an f-call is not necessarily blocking. Instead, the caller blocks only if the result is needed and the called module has not yet returned. Consider the following example:

```
result = B(data);
/* some other code */
value = result + 1;
```

When this code is executed, the calling module, say A, only blocks when the statement "*value = result + 1;*" is executed and only if module B has not yet returned the value of *result*. This concept is similar to the work on futures in object-oriented programming [6]. The p-call in the statement:

```
B(data);
/* some other code */
```

is non-blocking, so that A continues to execute concurrently with B. Of course in this case, B does not return a result to A.

3.2 Module Roles and Assets

The role of a module is based solely on a parallelization technique and is independent of its call. There are a fixed number of pre-defined roles corresponding to *asset* kinds. For example, in the previous section, the role of the *Split* module was changed from an *individual* to a *contract* without changing the call.

We have created an analogy between *Enterprise* programs and the structure of an organization to help describe module roles. In general, an organization has various assets available to perform its tasks. For example, a large task could be divided into sub-tasks where various sub-tasks are given to different parts of the organization (divisions, departments, pools, lines and/or individuals) to perform in parallel. Some tasks could even be completed by contract where the organization is not directly concerned about the nature or number of individuals that perform it. In addition, an organization usually provides many standard *services* (like time keeping, information storage and retrieval, etc.) that are available on demand to improve its functionality.

Currently, *Enterprise* supports the roles corresponding to seven different asset kinds: individual, line, pool, contract, department, division and service, with more being developed.

3.2.1 Individual

An *individual* contains no other assets. It is analogous to an individual person in an organization. When called, an individual executes its sequential code to completion. Therefore, any subsequent call to the same individual must wait until the previous call is finished. An individual may be called by any external asset using its name.

3.2.2 Line

A *line* contains a fixed number of heterogeneous assets in a fixed order. Each asset contains a call to the next asset in the line. A line is analogous to a construction, manufacturing or assembly line in an organization where at each point in the line, the work of the previous asset is refined. For example, a line might consist of an individual who takes an order, someone else to fill it and a third person to address the package and mail it. A subsequent call to the line waits only until the first asset is finished its sub-task of the previous call, not until the entire line is finished. The first asset in a line serves as the *receptionist* for the line and is the only asset that is externally visible. That is, the first asset of a line is the only asset that may be called from an external asset and it shares its name with the line asset for this purpose. Lines are often referred to as pipelines in the literature.

3.2.3 Pool

A *pool* contains a fixed number of identical assets. It is analogous to a pool in an organization where each member performs an identical task. For example, consider a pool of telephone operators. When a call is received, an idle operator services the call. However, if all the operators are busy, then the call waits for one of them to finish. Since pool members are externally indistinguishable, an external call cannot select a particular pool asset. Therefore, they are called by external assets using a single name that is shared with the pool asset for this purpose. Since all assets in a pool are identical, they also share the same code. A pool is analogous to a master-slave construct with a fixed number of slaves.

3.2.4 Contract

A *contract* contains a collection of identical assets, so it is similar to a pool. However, the number of assets in a contract is dynamic and depends on the number of processors that are free at any time. A contract is analogous to a contract that an organization lets for the performance of a collection of identical tasks. For example, an organization might sign a contract to a courier company for the delivery of its packages. When a package must be delivered, the courier company is informed. The organization doesn't care how many resources the courier company uses or the route it takes to deliver the packages. The delivery time can be affected by the number of resources used by the courier company and the amount of competing traffic. Similarly when an *Enterprise* call is made to a contract, an idle asset executes the call. However, if all assets are busy and no more are available for hire, then the call waits for an asset to become available. As is the case with a pool asset, a contract asset shares a common name with the identical assets it contains and these component assets also have common code. A contract is equivalent to a dynamic master-slave construct, where the number of slaves varies in response to program needs (demand) and resource utilization (environment).

3.2.5 Department

A *department* contains a fixed number of heterogeneous assets. Every department has a single receptionist asset that shares its name with the department so that it can be called by external assets. However, unlike a line, the other assets in a department do not call each other in a fixed sequential order. Instead, all other assets in the department are called directly by the receptionist. A department is analogous to a department in an organization where a receptionist is responsible for directing all incoming communications to the appropriate place. Note that in our analogy, a department consists of a collection of assets of any kind: individuals, departments, lines, etc. The department has no analogous term in the literature.

3.2.6 Division

A *division* contains a hierarchical collection of identical assets with a fixed breadth and depth where work is divided and distributed at each level. Every division has a single receptionist asset that shares its name with the division so that the division can be called by external assets. Divisions can be used to parallelize divide-and-conquer computations.

3.2.7 Service

A *service* contains no other assets. However, unlike an individual that can only answer a single call at any one time, a service may be used by more than one asset at the same time. A service is analogous to any asset in an organization that is not consumed by use and whose order of use is not significant. A service may be called by any asset using its name.

3.3 Enterprise Diagrams

An *Enterprise* diagram can be built from any combination of assets. For example, one can construct a contract, where each asset is itself a line of individuals. The model allows the user to coerce an asset from one kind to another *usually without any changes to the user's source code* (there are some problems users can encounter, particularly if pointers are used to alias data). However, some gathering or separation of functions from one file to another may be needed. For example, if a line is used for the animation example, there would be three individuals (*Model*, *PolyConv* and *Split*) each having their code in a separate file. If the line is coerced into an individual, the code needs to be gathered together (either in the same file or by using libraries). There are ways that *Enterprise* could do this management automatically, but there are some issues we have yet to resolve.

4. Related Work

In recent years, graphical parallel programming environments have been an area of active research. In these environment, a parallel program is specified as a graph with nodes containing a textual description of a sequential program. Most of the environments specify parallelism based on the large grain dataflow model developed by Babb [2] (for example: CODE [4], DGL [11], LGDF [8], Paralex [1], PPSE [12], TDFL [19]). In these models, an application is usually defined as a dataflow graph whose nodes contain sequential modules and the edges represents data dependencies between the modules.

TDFL introduces the idea of mutable computation graphs to support the mutable execution of recursive functions. If the data input to a function is above a threshold size, then additional processes are created to help process the data. The creation of nodes continues until the data size is within the threshold. However, data size may not be the best criteria to determine the degree of mutability, since processor usage is usually not necessarily proportional to data size. *Enterprise* also supports the mutable execution of recursive functions, but the criterion for creating additional processes is the depth of recursion instead of data size.

The dataflow approach has a number of drawbacks. Usually it requires the programmer to supply low-level information which is often not intuitive to the programmer. Parallelism by replication of processes is hard to specify. In many of the systems, the programmer has to draw the data dependencies connecting every node. The graph can become a dense structure, even with a small number of modules, and it is often time consuming and error prone to draw.

Another research area is in graphical environments to support dependency analysis of programs which are usually written in Fortran and run on machines with a small granularity (for example: PAT [16], E/SP [17], CAPER [18]). Yet another class of approaches provide a set of predefined parallel objects which define the communication and execution behavior of the enclosed module. Among the earlier efforts, PIE [13] made available to the programmer pre-coded templates of parallel structures such as master-slave, pipeline and systolic multidimensional pipeline. A template provided an implementation of the communication and synchronization structures and the programmer needed only to provide the sequential code. However, the parallelism supported is at a much smaller grain size than that offered by *Enterprise*. In contrast, *Enterprise* focuses on problem solving at a higher level, using the analogy to the structure of organizations. This allows new parallel templates to be defined whenever necessary. In our earlier system, *FrameWorks*, dynamic initiation of replicated process according to available idle processors was introduced [14][15]. The programmer also needed to specify parallelism, in a less intuitive way, through templates defining the input and output communication pattern of the process.

Linda, although not a graphical environment, is an important parallel programming model [5]. Linda uses the concept of a virtual shared memory, called the *tuple space*, for communication between concurrent processes. Processes use atomic operations to read, add, or delete a tuple to/from the tuple space. In contrast, *Enterprise* (and Paralex) is implemented using the object-based, message passing ISIS system [3]. Processes communicate by broadcasting messages to a message handler of a specified process.

Another relevant parallel programming model is the Chare-Kernel [9]. A *chare* is a module to be executed in parallel. It can have multiple entries in which enclosed program segments and new chares can be created (even recursively) to execute the entries. The portability of applications is a tremendous asset, however the onus is still on the programmer to use the supplied programming language enhancements and explicitly code all the parallelism.

5. Project Status

Enterprise is built on a number of available tools. The user interface was implemented using X Windows [10] (Motif), and is written in C++. It is currently 50% completed, but a textual interface is available now. Enterprise programs are executed using the communications and fault tolerance facilities of ISIS [3] and lines, pools, services, contracts and individuals have been implemented. A code librarian uses the UNIX *make* facility to automatically recompile source code when needed. The GNU C compiler has been modified to insert *Enterprise* code into the user's source program. The Monitor and debugging tools are in the design phase.

In recent years, there has been an enormous increase in the number and quality of parallel programming tools described in the literature. The authors of these tools have diverse opinions as to where and how in the software development cycle they can be used to increase a programmer's productivity. The *Enterprise* project aims for a complete, integrated programming environment that is suitable for the complete software development life cycle. By capturing an application's parallelism through the use of diagrams that are simple to edit, it is not difficult for the user to make the leap from sequential to parallel programming. Although the complexity of parallel systems, as portrayed in the literature, has been a powerful deterrent to growth in this area, we believe that with a simple model, all of the complexity of parallel programming can be hidden from the user. The analogical model used in *Enterprise* represents a different way of viewing an old problem.

Acknowledgement

This research was supported in part by research grants from the University of Alberta's Central Research Fund and the Natural Sciences and Engineering Research Council of Canada, grants OGP-8173 and infrastructure grant 107880. Also, Rasit Eskicioglu provided us with a number of useful references.

1 O. Babaoglu, L. Alvisi, A. Amoroso and R. Davoli. *Paralex: An Environment for Parallel Programming in Distributed Systems*, 1991, Technical Report UB-LCS-91-01, Department of Mathematics, University of Bologna, Bologna, Italy.

2 R. Babb. *Parallel Processing with Large Grain Data Flow Techniques*, IEEE Computer, 1984, Vol 17, No 7, pp 55-61.

3 K. Birman, R. Cooper, T. Joseph, K. Marzullo, M. Makpangou, K. Kane, F. Schmuck and M. Wood. *The ISIS System Manual, Version 2.1*, 1991, ISIS Project, Computer Science Dept., Cornell University.

4 J. Browne, M. Azam and S. Sobek. *CODE: A Unified Approach to Parallel Programming*, IEEE Software, 1989, Vol 6, No 6, pp 10-18.

5 N. Carriero and D. Gelernter. *Linda in Context*, CACM, 1988, Vol 32, No 4, pp 444-458.

6 A. Chatterjee. *Futures: A Mechanism for Concurrency Among Objects*, Supercomputing '89, 1989, pp 562-567.

7 E. Chan, P. Lu, J. Mohsin, J. Schaeffer, C. Smith, D. Szafron, P. Wong. *Enterprise: An Interactive Graphical Programming Environment for Distributed Software Development*, 1991, TR 91-17, Dept. of Computing Science, University of Alberta.

8 D. DiNucci and R. Babb II. *Architecture of the Parallel Programming Support Environment*, IEEE COMPCON, 1989, pp 102-107.

9 W. Fenton, B. Ramkumar, V. Saletore, A. Sinha and L. Kale. *Supporting Machine Independent Programming on Diverse Parallel Architectures*, ICPP, 1991, pp 193-201.

10 J. Gettys, P. Karlton and S. McGregor. *The X Window System, Version II*, Software - Practice and Experience, 1990, Vol 20, No s2, pp s35-s67.

11 R. Jagannathan, A. Downing, W.T. Zaumen and R.K.S. Lee. *Dataflow-based Methodology for Coarse-Grain Multiprocessing on a Network of Workstations*, ICPP, 1989, pp 54-58.

12 T. Lewis and W. Rudd. *Architecture of the Parallel Programming Support Environment*, IEEE COMPCON, 1990, pp 589-594.

13 Z. Segall and L. Rudolph. *Pie (A Programming and Instrumentation Environment for Parallel Processing)*, IEEE Software, 1985, Vol 2, No 6, pp 22-37.

14 A. Singh. *A Template-Based Approach to Structuring Distributed Algorithms Using a Network of Workstations*, 1991, Ph.D. Thesis, Dept. of Computing Science, University of Alberta.

15 A. Singh, J. Schaeffer and M. Green. *A Template-Based Approach to the Generation of Distributed Applications Using a Network of Workstations*, IEEE Transactions on Parallel and Distributed Systems, 1991, Vol 2, No 1, pp 52-67.

16 K. Smith, B. Appelbe and K. Stirewalt. *Incremental Dependence Analysis for Interactive Parallelization*, Supercomputing '90 , 1990, pp 330-341.

17 K. Sridharan, M. McShea, C. Denton, B. Eventoff, J. Browne, P. Newton, M. Ellis, D. Grossbard, T. Wise and D. Clemmer. *An Environment for Parallel Structuring of Fortran Programs*, ICPP, 1989, pp 98-106.

18 B. Sugla, J. Edmark and B. Robinson. *An Introduction to the CAPER Application Programming Environment*, ICPP, 1989, pp 107-111.

19 P. Suhler, J. Biswas, K. Korner and J. Browne. *TDFL: A Task-Level Dataflow Language*, Journal of Parallel and Distributed Computing, 1990, Vol 9, No 2, pp 103-115.

PROGRAMMING ENVIRONMENTS FOR PARALLEL COMPUTING
N. Topham, R. Ibbett and T. Bemmerl (Editors)
Elsevier Science Publishers B.V. (North-Holland)

© 1992 IFIP. All rights reserved.

ADE — An Application Development Environment for Transparent Use of Scalable Parallel Architectures

Karsten M. Decker
René M. Rehmann
IAM, University of Berne, Länggassstrasse 51, CH-3012 Berne, SWITZERLAND

Abstract

The acceptance of parallel architectures with distributed memory in the scientific community will crucially depend on the existence of appropriate software. In this paper, we argue that the provision of libraries providing efficient parallel algorithms is not sufficient, because they do not address the problem, how to build full-scale applications for parallel distributed architectures. We introduce the application development environment ADE which is part of the SPADE system, an integrated environment for program and application development for the scientific market segment. ADE provides transparent parallel computing for applications modeled by either the master-slave or the farmer-worker computational model, where the latter is realized as a limiting case of a generalization of the former. ADE features automatic generation of complementary master- and slave-drivers from a sequential application description, transparent filesystem I/O from any process, data coherence for shared variables, support for unique return code handling, and automatic data structure partitioning and scope adjustment.

Keyword Codes: D.1.3; D.2.2; D.2.6
Keywords: Programming Techniques, Concurrent Programming
Software Engineering, Tools and Techniques; Programming Environments

1. Introduction

MIMD Distributed memory parallel processor (DMPP) architectures can deliver scalable performance over several orders of magnitude based on a single architectural principle, from the workstation with a few processors to massively parallel systems comprising thousands of processing nodes with a peak performance in the TFLOPS range. Scientific applications characterized by their large uniform data structures with data parallelism which scales with the size of the problem under investigation, are ideally suited to exploit this performance potential. The major problem with these machines is their difficult programming, and efficient parallel algorithms which are tailored to exploit their performance are rare. The scientist, who uses high performance computing devices as a *tool* to solve his problems, often characterized by literally unlimited demands for computing cycles, is confronted with a almost bare machine, rendering the programming and thus the use of these machines too time-consuming to be of practical value.

There exist several tool sets [1, 2] which address the problem of parallelizing existing applications. Whereas this approach has certainly its importance, when *existing software packages* need to be ported which represent a major investment in terms of development time, it is not sufficient, when highest possible performance is the primary objective.

Libraries comprising efficient parallel algorithms are frequently quoted as a recipe which can 'solve' the software problem [3] of parallel computing from the scientist point of view. While libraries certainly play an important role, they are in general not so simple to use as on sequential architectures. More importantly, libraries don't address at all the problem of building full-blown applications from these libraries. Because of the distributed nature of the parallel processor system, several new problems are introduced which do not exist in the sequential case. Thus the scientist in general is not even aware of them. Examples include the partitioning of data structures, data coherence for shared variables, and transparent access to the filesystem. What scientists really need, whose requirements and technical skills are indeed representative for a much wider class of application users, is an environment hiding the distributed nature of the architecture, supporting as closely as possible the programming model of shared memory (sequential) computers without sacrificing the performance issue.

The *Application Development Environment* ADE is tailored to the needs of the scientific community. It is developed as part of the SPADE project[1] [4] which aims at creating an integrated environment for program and application development for the scientific market segment, featuring the design goals *performance, simplicity, expandability* and *portability*. SPADE consists of a core of libraries which are application specific and hierarchically organized. On the upper hierarchy level, we have the *Application Task Libraries* (TLs). Task library functions provide complete components of applications and are designed to run concurrently on any number of processor nodes. They provide the parallel building blocks of applications. Task library functions are built on top of *Application Kernel Libraries* (KL) and *Communication Libraries* (CL). Whereas the former provide basic algorithmic building blocks, designed to run on a single processor, which are compute-intensive and/or often used, the latter provide a message-passing interface to the distributed architecture. These two libraries guarantee the primary design goal of the SPADE system, performance, while keeping architectural features transparent. The lower library hierarchy levels also ensure portability over a variety of parallel architectures. The SPADE core is completed by three tools, the Application Development Environment ADE which we shall discuss in detail in this paper, the *Program Development Environment* (PDE), which supports the development of new parallel distributed algorithms and their efficient implementations, and a *Run-Time Environment* (RTE). The entire system presents itself in a homogeneous through the common *User Interface* (UI).

2. Requirements for Application Development on Distributed Architectures

To illustrate the assertion made in the previous section, we here assume that appropriate parallel libraries (e.g., TLs) do exist, and explain what else is required for convenient and transparent application building for scalable architectures. The more general case, where such libraries are not available, will be discussed at the end of the paper.

The most important requirement from the scientist point of view is that a sequential application description can be retained. This description which we call *driver* represents

[1]SPADE — Scientific Program and Application Development Environment.

the coarse-grained structure of the application, i.e., sequence of calls to the parallel library, repetitions of calls, and whether certain library functions should be executed conditionally. Since scientific applications are characterized by data parallelism, it is sufficient to support the master-slave and the farmer-worker computational model. As in the sequential case, reading and writing from and to files should be possible everywhere in the program, shared variables should be available, and error condition handling should be possible in a simple and efficient way. In addition, depending on the problem size and the number of requested processors, the problem should be decomposed and distributed across the parallel architecture in a fully automatic fashion.

3. Functionality

The application development environment ADE is designed to meet all the requirements described in the previous section. Its functionality is summarized as follows:

1. Automatic generation of complementary master- and slave-drivers from a sequential application description.

2. Data coherence for shared variables.

3. Transparent filesystem I/O from any process, organized via shared variables.

4. Support for return code handling to provide unique continuation of all processes in case of irregular or faulty operation of any single process.

5. Automatic data structure partitioning and scope adjustment.

As usual, the attribute *shared* is used for a variable which is known to all processes. Data coherence for shared variables is organized by automatic addition of communication operations. Transparent filesystem access requires different actions for the master- and the slave-processes, respectively. The master-process is in general mapped to the host, and thus has immediate access to the filesystem. this is not true for the slave-processes. I/O operations from slave-processes consequently require the execution of the corresponding operation in the master-process, and in addition a communication operation. This is exactly how ADE provides transparent filesystem access. In order to realize that this action is required, the variable to be read or written must carry the attribute *shared*. Consistent handling of return code created by functions on termination in a distributed environment is a tough problem. The functionality provided in this respect by the ADE relies again on shared variables, and provides the basis for consistent error condition handling, avoiding tedious communications operations to be programmed explicitly by the scientist.

We finally comment on the computational model which is supported by ADE. As has been argued above, most scientific applications can be modeled with either the master-slave or the farmer-worker type of computational model. Therefore the model which we have chosen is one which consists of one or several instances of the *Master-Slave Model* (MSM), where the distinct instances may communicate among each other via either any pair of master-processes or via the common host-process. This is illustrated in Fig. 1.

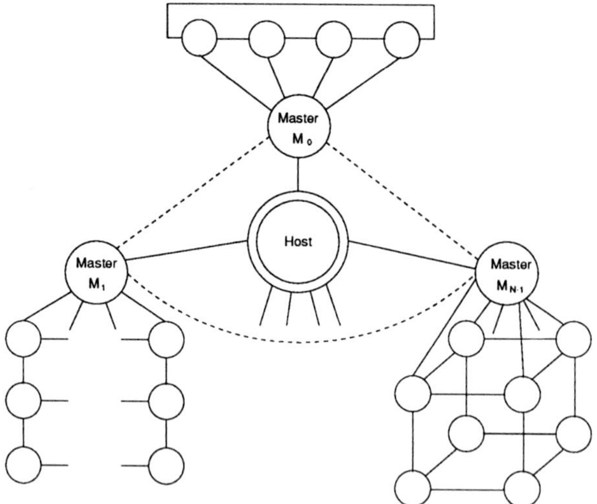

The SPADE computational model

Figure 1. The computational model supported by the ADE.

Within each master-slave model, arbitrary interconnections are possible. In the limit of vanishing interconnections among the slave-processes, we obtain a model which reflects the topological properties of a collection of communicating instances of the farmer-worker model. Due to our application model, the computational concept of farming is realized on the application task level. This, however, does not imply any restrictions, since an application may very well be described by a single application task only.

4. Operational Principle

ADE expects two files for input, the *Application Specification File* ASF and the *Hardware Topology Specification File* HTSF.

The general organization of the ASF is sketched in Fig. 2. It is structured into one section for each instance of the master-slave model. Each section of the ASF consists of four parts. The first part contains the definition of shared variables, and the definition of data structures which should be partitioned and distributed across all processes. The latter data definitions are always *static*, i.e., their size is known at compile time. The main reason why we have chosen a static storage class for these variables, is that we want to avoid the need for a run-time kernel, which would be necessary otherwise in order to partition the data structures at run-time. In addition, static data structures allow more optimization of the communication pattern between slave-processes, which we believe is

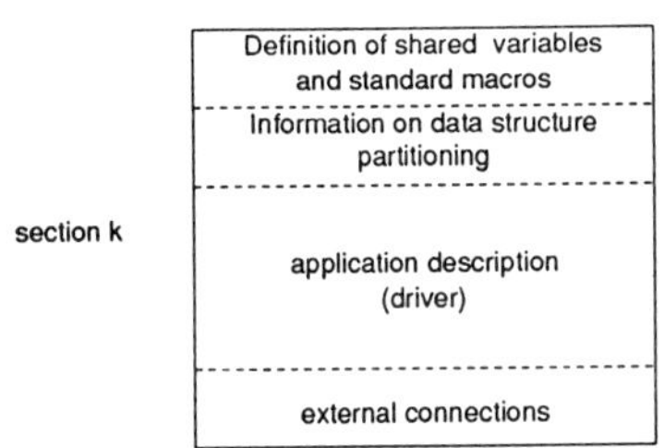

Figure 2. The organization of the Application Specification File ASF.

a very important issue. The first part of each ASF section also contains standard macro definitions. All definitions use standard ANSI-*C* notation [5].

The second part of each ASF section contains information for ADE which data should be partitioned across the slave-processes, how many slave-processes should be used for this application, and which process topology (ring, torus, cube, etc.) should be used. If none of the regular, predefined topologies is found to be appropriate for an application, the scientist can provide a user-defined topology by specifying the complete partitioning scheme. Such a user-defined topology can be quite irregular and turns out to be useful, if it is known that optimal load balancing of the system cannot be achieved by a regular topology. This second part of an ASF section is implemented as an extension to the *C*-language by adding new keywords to the ANSI-*C* keyword list.

The third part of each ASF section specifies the driver for the corresponding instance of the MSM. It consists of variable definitions and calls to library functions which perform the desired action. These function calls are supplemented by control structures for repetition and conditional execution of sequences of statements which in turn complete the description of the application. The driver is defined as a *C*-function, and all features of the language can be used in this part. This function plays the role of a main function in a well-structured program which does not contain any or only a few application specific parts, but basically calls functions which are defined in other modules or libraries. It is neither possible to define more than one function in the `driver`-part of a section, nor is it possible to defined a function in any other part of a section. All function definitions other than the driver function should be done with the help of the program development environment PDE.

The fourth part of a section lists the connections of the master-process of the actual MSM to master-processes of other MSMs. These connections are established always as uni-directional, outgoing links, using the entry name of the function defined in the `driver`-part of a section. With the ability of interconnecting the various instances of master-slave models, it is possible to portion an application using an optimal decomposition scheme for each part and communicating the results of one part to the other parts.

The second file, the Hardware Topology Specification File HTSF, describes number and type of the desired physical processing nodes and the topology of the processor network on which the application is intended to run.

The ASF input file now runs through a two-stage cross compiler which turns the specification contained in each section of the ASF into two complementary drivers, one for the master-process and the other one for each instance of the slave-process of the corresponding master-slave model. These drivers can be compiled with a usual ANSI-*C* Compiler. In the link phase, they only require a minimal set of system and communication libraries which are supplied with most DMPP architectures.

The steps of operation are illustrated in some more detail in Fig. 3. The first stage of the cross compiler, called Split, produces an intermediate file which is similar to the ASF. The first part of each section of the ASF has now been supplemented by the definitions of those shared variables, which were not explicitly defined before. To qualify for a shared variable, these additional variables must fulfill the following two conditions:

- They are used as arguments to both the master- *and* the slave-version of at least one application task library function.
- They are not defined as being partitioned among slave-processes.

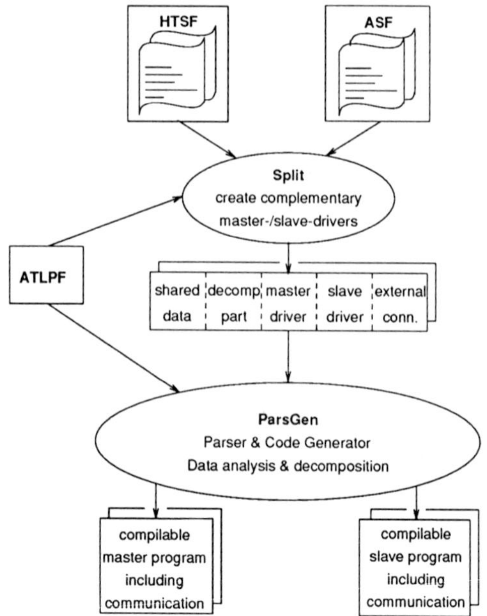

Figure 3. The major steps of operation of the two-stage cross compiler.

The second part of each section of the ASF remains completely unchanged. The major change occurs in the third part, where the driver is now split into two complementary master- and slave-drivers. These two functions define the third and the fourth part, respectively, in each section of the intermediate file. The main difference between the original definition and the two generated drivers is that the application task library function calls are changed to either call the master- or the slave-version of the corresponding application task library function. The fourth part of each section of the ASF again maps without any changes to the fifth part of the intermediate file.

The second stage of the cross compiler, called ParsGen, produces the actual compilable code. It initializes the communication network and the logical node names for the master-process and each instance of the slave-process, if necessary. It generates all inter-processor communication calls which are required to update the shared variables. In addition, ParsGen computes the size of the data structures which should be partitioned among the slave-processes, and inserts the necessary definitions in the definition block of the output files.

As side effect of compiling the ASF, the cross compiler produces a hardware load file which contains information about how many physical processors are used by the application, which processes must be loaded on a single physical, processor and which hardware communication paths should be established. This information is gathered from the ASF and the HTSF and is normally used by the operating system of the distributed memory parallel computer.

5. Example: ADE at Work

In this section we present an example, characterized by its application specification file ASF and the hardware topology specification file HTSF, and show the output produced by ADE. In the example presented, the ASF has one section only. To further reduce the size of the example, some parts which are not needed for understanding are removed.

```
          macro definitions, typedefs and structure definitions
RunParms          run_Parms;
Su2Gfc            su2_gfc[16][16][16][16][4][4];
```

This is the first part containing the macro and type definitions for the application and the data definitions for the shared variables and the variables to be decomposed. `runParms` in the above case is a shared variable and `su2_gfc` is the variable to be decomposed (see second part below).

```
data_split su2_gfc in_one_dimension;
number_of_slaves = 4;
```

This second part provides the information that the variable `su2_gfc` should be decomposed in one dimension; multi-dimensional arrays are always decomposed from 'left to right'. The application will use four slave processes.

```
int example(int argc, char **argv) {
  GridParms       grid_parms;
  Tables          tables;
  UdParms         ud_parms;
```

```
        other data definitions
  ReadRunParms(file_name,&run_Parms);
        other application task library calls
  for (i = 0; i < n_sweeps; i++) {
    rc = Su2Update(su2_link_var_hb_ud,&ud_parms,su2_gfc,&grid_parms,
                   &tables,num_slaves);
    if (rc != 0) {
      printf("SU2UPDATE: error in sweep %d\n", i);
      exit(1);
    }
  }
        other application task library calls
  exit(0);
}
```

This third section now specifies the driver in terms of the two functions `ReadRunParms`, and `Su2Update`. The latter is identified as an application task library function, because a corresponding prototype is found in the Application Task Library Prototype File ATLPF which is maintained automatically by SPADE. Since there exists no corresponding entry for the function `ReadRunParms`, it is identified as user provided.

The second file the user has to define is the HTSF which describes the number of the physical processors, the topology of the network and the processor types. For the example above, we used the following HTSF:

```
master example_master
proc_type host
memsize 16m
slave example_slave for 4
proc_type i860
memsize 8M
topology ring
```

We next show the result produced by the ADE. Because the drivers for the master and the slaves look very similar we only show the slave-driver and will point out the differences between the drivers in the accompanying comment.

```
#define DIMENSIONS 1
#define IS_SLAVE
#define NUM_OF_SLAVES 4
#include "spade.h"
        macro definitions, typedefs and structure definitions
declare_transports_and_names;
RunParms          run_Parms;
Su2Gfc            su2_gfc[4][16][16][16][4][4];
```

As expected, ADE has changed the size of the first dimension of the variable `su2_gfc`. Additionally, some macros and function prototypes needed for the communication calls are added at the beginning of the driver. The definition of `su2_gfc` is only present in the slave version of the driver to avoid allocation of a possibly (huge) data structure on the master process which would be never used.

```
int main(int argc, char **argv) {
  const int     num_of_slaves = NUM_OF_SLAVES;
```

```
  GridParms       grid_parms;
  Tables          tables;
  UdParms         ud_parms;
         other data definitions
  open_and_register_transports_and_names;
```

Here the ADE has defined all variables necessary for communication, has declared the data structures used by the communication system and has opened and registered the communication paths between the master- and all slave-processes. Additionally, the constant `num_of_slaves` is defined which holds the number of slaves of this application.

```
  (ReadRunParms(file_name,&run_Parms),
   send_fnctn(run_Parms,sizeof(RunParms),MasterSlaveLink,
             MasterSlaveNetid,NUM_OF_SLAVES));
         other application task library calls
  for (i = 0; i < n_sweeps; i++) {
    rc = Su2Update_slave(su2_link_var_hb_ud,&ud_parms,su2_gfc,&grid_parms,
                         &tables);
    exchange_return_codes(&(rc));
    if (rc != 0) {
      printf("SU2UPDATE: error in sweep %d\n", i);
      exit(1);
    }
  }
         other application task library calls
  exit(0);
}
```

In this code section, we can clearly see that the ADE has changed the function name of the application task library module such that the appropriate version of the task is called. Additionally, the number of arguments has been changed to reflect the needs of the corresponding version of a task. The second observation is that the call to the function `ReadRunParms` is immediately followed by a communication call which transmits the current value of the variable `run_Parms` to every slave-process. This ensures that all processes use the same value of the shared variable `run_Parms`. At the end of each task, the return codes of all slave-processes are communicated to the master-process, combined to a single value, and returned to the slave-processes. This ensures that all processes behave exactly in the same way, if an error happened during a task call.

6. Summary

Starting from a sequential description of the application building on existing parallel library functions, and a specification of the desired hardware, the ADE fully automates the tedious steps of partitioning the data structures, setting up the required communications, performing the data analysis, and creating the two complementary application drivers for applications modeled with the master-slave computational model. From the application user point of view, the ADE thus allows to realize full-scale applications by simply expressing his application in terms of parallel library modules in a high-level language which is exactly what he would be required to do on a shared memory sequential computer. He then only has to specify the desired hardware size on which he wants to run his application. The rest is done by the ADE. In other words, the ADE provides transparent programming of parallel distributed computers. Since the ADE puts no constraints on either the size of the problem nor on the hardware, full software and hardware scalability is ensured.

An interesting question is what happens, when no appropriate application task library functions are available in any of the libraries in the core of the SPADE system. This is where the Program Development Environment PDE comes into play. The major task of the PDE is to give tool support to the development of new (application task) library modules. At the time of writing, the PDE is not as far advanced as the ADE. So far, we have described a methodology for the design and implementation of efficient algorithms for scalable parallel architectures [6], which will provide the conceptual basis of the program development environment. There exist a number of further activities, including the development of a tool for automatic generation of communication frames starting from a specification of the elementary computational operation [7], the investigation of the usefulness of a knowledge-based system based on hierarchical parallel algorithm frame libraries for parallel algorithm development and implementation, and the analysis of automatic program synthesis techniques. A progress report on these activities will be given in due time.

Acknowledgement.

The SPADE project is supported by Grant 20-31057.91 from the Swiss National Science Foundation.

1 ParaSoft Corporation, Pasadena, CA 91107, USA. *Express User's Guide*, 3.0 edition, 1990.

2 T. Bemmerl. TOPSYS: Eine integrierte Werkzeugumgebung für Multimikroprozessoren. (Artikelsammlung) TOPSYS Tools for Parallel Systems, 1990.

3 J. E. Boillat, H. Burkhart, K. M. Decker, and P. G. Kropf. Parallel Computing in the 1990's: Attacking the Software Problem. In K. M. Decker, editor, *Proceedings of the 3rd Graduate Summer Course on Computational Physics: Parallel Architectures and Applications. Crêt-Bérard (Puidoux), Switzerland, September 3 - 7, 1990.* North-Holland, 1991.

4 K. M. Decker and R. Rehmann. An Environment for Parallel Scientific Computing: The SPADE System and its Functional Units. In R. Glowinski, editor, *Proceedings of the 10th International Conference on Computing Methods in Applied Sciences and Engineering, Paris, France, February 11–14, 1992*, pages 547—557, New York, 1991. Nova Science Publishers, Inc.

5 B. W. Kernighan and D. M. Ritchie. *The C Programming Language.* Prentice-Hall, second edition, 1988.

6 K. M. Decker. A Methodology for the Design and Implementation of Efficient Algorithms for Scalable Parallel Architectures. Technical Report IAM-91-018, IAM, University of Berne, 1991.

7 M. Roth. Thesis. in preparation.

PROGRAMMING ENVIRONMENTS FOR PARALLEL COMPUTING
N. Topham, R. Ibbett and T. Bemmerl (Editors)
Elsevier Science Publishers B.V. (North-Holland)

© 1992 IFIP. All rights reserved.

HyperDEBU : a Multiwindow Debugger for Parallel Logic Programs

Junichi TATEMURA, Hanpei KOIKE, Hidehiko TANAKA
{tatemura,koike,tanaka}@mtl.t.u-tokyo.ac.jp
Tanaka Laboratory, Department of Electrical Engineering,
Faculty of Engineering, The University of Tokyo
7-3-1 Hongo, Bunkyo-ku, Tokyo, 113 JAPAN

Abstract

Debugging parallel programs is more difficult than debugging sequential programs. Since a Committed-Choice Language (CCL), which is a kind of parallel logic programming language, enables fine-grained highly parallel execution, it is very hard to examine and to manipulate its numerous complicated control/data flows. A debugger, whose role is to show users a model abstracted from execution of a program, needs a model applicable to represent execution of fine-grained highly parallel programs. To represent execution of a CCL program, we propose a communicating process model which has flexible levels and aspects of abstraction. Then we introduce a debugger which represents this model. A parallel program has multiple complicated control/data flows which are considered to be high-dimensional information. Therefore, a high-dimensional interface is necessary to debug it. Since a user compares a model represented by a debugger with the expected behavior of the program and finds a bug in the program, the debugger must provide a view of the kind he/she wants. Accordingly, the debugger must provide views which have flexible levels and aspects of abstraction. We developed a multiwindow debugger HyperDEBU which provides a high-dimensional interface. HyperDEBU provides windows flexible enough for programmers to examine and manipulate complicated structures composed of multiple control/data flows.

Keyword Codes: D.2.6;D.2.5;D.1.3
Keywords: Programming Environments; Testing and Debugging; Concurrent Programming

1. Introduction

Debugging parallel programs is much more difficult than debugging sequential programs because many processes run simultaneously and interact with each other. While most traditional debuggers only trace each process, they can hardly handle inter-process communication. To comprehend inter-process communication, some prototype systems have been developed : a time-process diagram and an animation of program execution

[1]. The time-process diagram represents execution of a program in a two-dimensional display with time on one axis and individual process on the other axis. The animation displays snapshots of processes one after another.

A Committed-Choice Language (CCL), which is a kind of parallel logic programming language, enables fine-grained highly parallel execution. It is very hard to trace many small processes in a CCL program. The time-process diagram cannot easily display numerous flows of data and control. It is hard to understand an animation displaying many processes created dynamically. To understand execution of a fine-grained highly parallel program such as a CCL program, the relation among control/data-flows is more important than time-stamps of events.

A debugger which shows a model of program execution needs a model able to represent execution of a fine-grained highly parallel program. In this paper, we introduce a communicating process model to represent execution of a CCL program, and describe a multiwindow debugger HyperDEBU which represents this model on a high-dimensional interface. This debugger provides flexible views which enable a user to examine and manipulate complicated structures composed of multiple control/data flows of a fine-grained highly parallel program.

2. Committed-Choice Language Fleng

Committed-Choice Languages (CCLs) such as Guarded Horn Clauses (GHC) and Concurrent Prolog are parallel logic programming languages which introduce a control primitive "guard" for synchronization [4]. Fleng [2] is a CCL designed in our laboratory. We are developing the Parallel Inference Engine PIE64 [3] which executes Fleng programs. Fleng is a simpler language than other CCLs ; Fleng has no guard goal, and only a head realizes guard mechanism.

A Fleng program is a set of horn clauses like:

$$H{:-}B_1, \cdots, B_n. \quad n \geq 0$$

The side to the left of :- is called the *head part*, and the right side is called the *body part* whose item B_i is called a *body goal.*

Execution of Fleng program is repetition of rewriting a set of goals in parallel. For each goal, one of the clauses whose head can match with the goal, is selected, and then the goal is rewritten into the body goals. The new goals are added to the set of goals. The execution begins when initial goal is given and is completed when no goal remains. The rewriting operation is called *reduction*, and the matching operation is called *unification.*

Unification is an algorithm which attempts to substitute values for variables such that two logical terms are made equal. To realize communication and synchronization in concurrent logic programs, unification in CCL is divided into two classes : *guarded unification* and *active unification.* Guarded unification is applied in a head part of a clause and variables in a goal are prevented from being substituted. Such unification is *suspended* until these variables have values. Active unification is applied in a body part of a clause and is able to substitute values for variables of goals.

The synchronization mechanism of guarded unification prevents reading a variable before it is bound to value and eliminates many nondeterministic bugs due to synchronization.

For example, assume that the following program is given :

```
init :- send(X),receive(X).                     (1)
receive([D|S]) :- do(D), receive(S).            (2)
send(S) :- S = [0|S1], send(S1).                (3)
```

If an initial goal `init` is given, this is unified with the head of the clause (1) and two goals `send(X)` and `receive(X)` , which have a shared variable `X` , are generated by reduction. The goal `receive` is tried to unify with the head of clause (2), however, the argument of `receive` is required to be structured data `[D|S]` (it is called *list cell*) in order to complete guarded unification. Then this reduction of `receive` is suspended if its argument is a variable at this time. On the other hand, the goal `send` is unified with the head of the clause (3), and reduced into two goals `S = [0|S1]` and `send(S1)`. The goal `S = [0|S1]` is a system predicate for active unification which unifies two terms `S` and `[0|S1]`. After this unification, the guarded unification of the goal `receive` and the head of (1) can be completed, and then the reduction of `receive` is resumed and two goal `do` and `receive` are generated.

When a Fleng program is executed, many goals are reduced in parallel, synchronizing each other in the way described above.

Fleng is a fine-grained highly parallel programming language in which goals are executed in parallel. Since many goals are created and terminated dynamically, it is more difficult to examine and manipulate execution of a goal than when there are a few processes statically.

3. Modeling Execution of Fleng Program

3.1. Requirements for Model of Program Execution

The role of a debugger is to show users a model abstracted from the execution of a program. A programmer examines and manipulates the execution of the program through this model, compares the model with an intended model, and finds bugs from the difference between them.

In this section, some requirements of a model which represents execution of a CCL program are described from the following two aspects.

Parallel Logic Program

Since a synchronization primitive "guard" makes a difference of semantics between CCL and a pure logic program language, some operational meaning must be added to the declarative semantics for CCL. The problem with the semantics has been discussed in several works [5] [6]. We must consider the causality relation between input and output of a program. Accordingly, a model which represents execution of CCL program must take account of the input-output causality.

Fine-Grained Highly Parallel Program

A model which represents execution of a fine-grained highly parallel program is required to abstract essential data from numerous information on execution of a highly parallel program, and to assist a user, who can deal with only a limited amount of information, to find a bug from it. Such a model is expected to have the following features :

- flexible levels of abstraction
- flexible aspects of abstraction

3.2. Process Model

We model execution of a Fleng program using processes which communicate each other. In this section we describe the process model for execution of a Fleng program.

Notion of Process for CCL

The conventional notion of process for CCL is associated with one goal or one sequence of goals. The process model proposed in this paper is equivalent not to one goal but to all of its subgoals generated by reduction. From outside, the execution of the process is looked upon as the input-output behavior of the process. The substance of the process is a set of goals derived from a goal. Since a goal is reduced to sub-goals, a process can be divided into sub-processes. It corresponds to execution tree which represents a computation of a logic program. The tree has subtrees whose roots are the nodes of the tree. The tree corresponding to the process can be divided into subtrees, and each subtree corresponds to the sub-process of the process.

In the process model described above, the definition clause is considered to be defining a relation between a process and its sub-processes.

Definition of Process Model

The process model described above is formalized as follows. Our debugger provides this model to programmers.

Let G be a goal which is computed in a Fleng program and Q be a set of goals which are derived from G. We call the process P whose substance is Q "*the process with respect to G*", and call G "*the topgoal of P*".

The process P with respect to G is represented as follows from outside.

$$\langle G_{skel},\ I/O,\ S,\ G_{ins} \rangle$$

G_{skel} is the skeletal predicate of G whose arguments are replaced by distinct variables like this :

$$p(v_1, \ldots, v_i).$$

$v_1, \ldots, v_i$ are distinct variables which are ports for communication with outer processes.

I/O is I/O data flow which represents the communication of the process P. They show how the variables of G_{skel} are substituted by unifications outside and inside of the process. Details of I/O data flow will be described later.

S is the state of P, which is one of the following states:

- *terminated*
  indicates that all of the goals in P have terminated.

- *suspended*
  indicates that there are no active goals in P and that there are some suspended goals. When one of the suspended goals is activated by input data which is substituted by unifications outside of P, the state turns into *active*.

- *active*
  indicates that some active goals exist in P and that P can be executed.

The above definition makes the model suitable for running program or a program which runs perpetually.

G_{ins} is the *instance* of G. It is regarded as the result of the substitution for G_{skel} by I/O.

Input/Output of a Process

I/O data flow of a process is represented as a tree structure which we call an *I/O tree*. This is a tree of causality among active unifications and guarded unifications.

Consider the I/O tree of a process with respect to a goal G. Since the arguments of G_{skel} can be regarded as ports for communication, there are I/O trees corresponding to each port.

The construction of I/O tree O can be represented as follows :

$$\begin{array}{rcl} O & ::= & C \text{ '|' } O \\ & | & U \text{ '}\times\text{' } O \\ & | & O \text{ '+' } O \\ & | & \text{'}Nil\text{'} \end{array}$$

Each factor has the following meaning respectively :

1. $C|O$
   This indicates input-output causality; O exists if input satisfying the condition C exists. C consists of guarded unifications. It is also graphically represented as:

```
cond(Condition)
 |- O
```

2. $U \times O$
   This indicates that the active unification U exists and is followed by O. It is also graphically represented as:

```
T1 = T2
  |- O
```

where `T1 = T2` is an active unification and `O` is the I/O tree which substitutes variables in the term `T2`.

3. $O + O$
   This indicates that the path of I/O is divided. It is also graphically represented as:

```
|- O1
|- O2
```

A horn clause describes not only the relation between a process and its sub-processes, but also describes the relation between I/O tree of the process and I/O tree of the sub-processes. I/O tree is defined recursively by the clauses committed (selected) in the execution of the program. Detail of the definition is described in [7]. In this paper, we will not explain the details but show a simple example of I/O tree.

Assume that the following program and an initial goal `append([1,2],[3],R)` are given.

```
append([H|X],Y,Z) :- Z = [H|Z1], append(X,Y,Z1).
append([],Y,Z) :- Z = Y.
```

This program connects a list given in the first argument and a list given in the second argument, and returns it through the third argument. The result will be `R = [1,2,3]`.

Then we will show I/O tree of the process with respect to the initial goal. G_{skel} of the process is represented as $append(A, B, C)$. The output of C is represented as the following I/O tree :

```
cond(A = [D|E]) <= (A = [1,2])
  |- C = [D|F]
      |- cond(E = [G|H]) <= (E = [2])
          |- F = [G|I]
              |-cond(H = []) <= (H = [])
                  |- I = B
```

This meaning is as follows : The active unification `C = [D|F]` exists on condition that the guarded unification `A = [D|E]` succeeds. There is the subsequent I/O tree to substitute variable `F` in the term `[D|F]`. `F` is unified with `[G|I]` on condition that the guarded unification `E = [G|H]` succeeds.

We can also abstract the I/O tree by replacing its subtree with its sub-processes as follows :

```
cond(A = [D|E]) <= (A = [1,2])
  |- C = [D|F]
      |- F / append(E,B,F)
```

`append(E,B,F)` is the subprocess of `append(A,B,C)` and unifies `F` by the inner unification of it.

3.3. Features of Process Model

The process model proposed in the previous section has the following features :

- hierarchy of processes
  A process consists of some subprocesses.

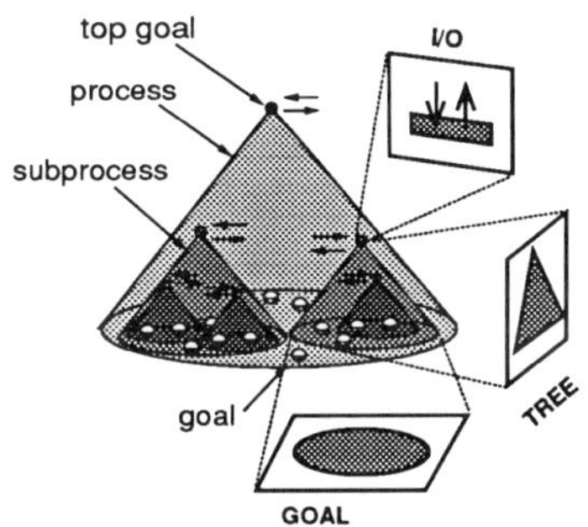

Figure 1. The Process Model

- multiple views of a process
  A process has three views; a set of goals, an execution tree, and communicating process.

Figure 1 shows the process model. This model satisfies the requirements for a model of a fine-grained highly parallel program. The other notions of process such as one goal and one sequence of goals do not seem applicable to debugging a highly parallel program.

Representing input-output causality, the process model also satisfies the requirements for the semantics of CCL. We have applied this model to *algorithmic debugging* of Fleng programs [7].

4. Multiwindow Debugger HyperDEBU

4.1. Design of Debugger for Fine-grained Highly Parallel Programs

A sequential program has only one thread of execution, which can be debugged with a sequential interface. On the other hand, a parallel program has multiple complicated control/data flows which are considered to be high-dimensional information. If a sequential interface is used to debug a parallel program, the bottleneck between a programmer and the program makes it difficult to examine and to manipulate the execution of the program. Therefore, a high-dimensional interface is necessary to debug a parallel program.

Since a user compares a model represented by a debugger with the expected behavior of the program when he/she debugs a program, the debugger must provide a view of the kind he/she wants. Accordingly, the debugger must provide views which have flexible levels and aspects of abstraction.

Most of conventional multiwindow debuggers use a window as a sequential debugger assigned to one of the processes. However, high-dimensional information cannot be handled well in this way. HyperDEBU provides windows flexible enough for programmers to

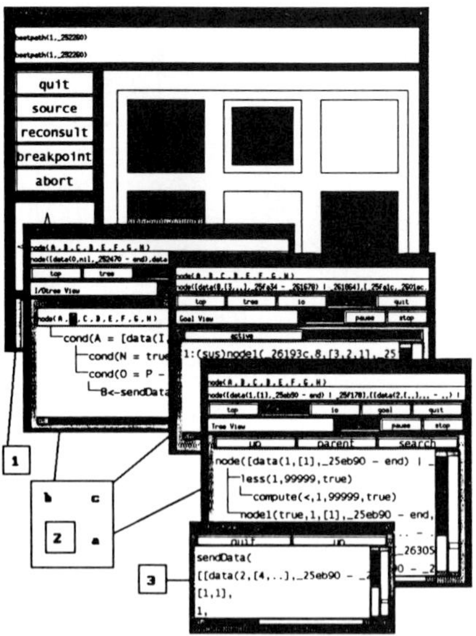

Figure 2. Overview of HyperDEBU

examine and manipulate complicated structure composed of multiple control/data flows. Tracing links on a window which displays information of a program execution, a user can get an expected window.

HyperDEBU consists of the following windows.

1. toplevel-window

2. process-windows
   (a) TREE view (b) I/O tree view (c) GOAL view

3. structure-windows

Figure 2 shows an overview of HyperDEBU.

4.2. Requirements of The Debugger

In this section, we will mention some requirements of the debugger design in accordance with the concept described in the above section.

Comprehending the Global Situation of the Execution

When a program shows unexpected behavior, the first task for a programmer to debug it is comprehending the situation of the execution of this erroneous program. A programmer can debug a sequential program by tracing one thread of execution through some event filters. On the other hand, it is very difficult to trace a complicated structure composed of a large number of control and data flows of a highly parallel program. Even if he tries to trace some threads of these flows through an event filter, it is a hard problem to determine what should be extracted from such an enormous amount of data, and, furthermore, he can not comprehend their relationship with each other. That is to say, it is very much more difficult to comprehend a global situation of the execution of a highly parallel program than of a sequential program.

To solve this problem, a debugger is required to provide a macroscopic view abstracted from the information of the execution in order to help a programmer to comprehend the situation of the erroneous program. So our main approach to realize such a view is our method of showing the information to a user clearly and easily.

Zooming on the Location of the Bug

After the user judges the area where bugs are seemed to exist by comprehending the global situation, he must examine this area more minutely and, at last, reach the erroneous points. Since the information of the execution is enormous and complicated, it is necessary to zoom gradually in on the location of the bug as the breadth of a view (that is, a level of abstraction) is kept properly.

To zoom in on the location of the bug efficiently, it is important to extract as much useful information from a user as possible, with the amount of data to treat limited to as little as possible. For this reason, a debugger's view is required to have the flexibility of the plane on which the high-dimensional information of the parallel program is projected. Moreover, it is a essential problem that this abstracted information is displayed so as to be easy to understand and that the directions the user can give to the display are elastic. A high-dimensional interface plays a important role in solving this problem.

Grasping the Static Information of the Program

Since a programmer has to grasp the static information of the program to debug it, he refers to the source code as required throughout debugging. To debug a concurrent program, he must trace multiple flows in the source code simultaneously. Although most of conventional multiwindow debuggers provide a window as a source level debugger for each process, this method is not applicable to a highly parallel program.

Control of the Execution

To debug a program, a programmer examines and manipulates its execution. Therefore, a mechanism to control the execution is needed. For a sequential program, the programmer sets up breakpoints in desirable places to make the execution stop there and to examine the state of the program. However, a new control method is required to debug a highly parallel program which has many threads of execution.

The nondeterminism of a parallel program is also important. To debug such a program, a debugger has to control this nondeterministic behavior. Note that the synchronization mechanism of guarded unification of CCL eliminates many nondeterministic bugs.

4.3. Features of HyperDEBU

In this section, we will describe the debugger's functions which satisfy the requirements described in the above section.

4.3.1. Various Views for Bug Locating

Toplevel-window and Process-windows

For the needed flexibility of levels of views from global to local, HyperDEBU provides a toplevel-window and process-windows.

A toplevel-window, which provides a global view, is opened initially, and a user provides initial goals into it. The user can examine and manipulate execution of a program in the global scope with this window. Moreover, the user can get a process-window to examine detail of any process displayed on the toplevel-window. The toplevel-window manages all of process-windows.

A process-window, which can be opened for any process, enables examination and manipulation of the process. To locate bugs, a user can get a subprocess as another window from this process.

Moreover, HyperDEBU has a structure-window which provides a data-level view. A user can get it from any data displayed on windows of HyperDEBU. Since all of the data on HyperDEBU are updated as the program runs, a user can examine state of the program dynamically.

Three Views of Process-window

A process-window enables bugs to be located efficiently using the flexible levels and aspects of abstraction of the process model. The process-window has three windows as views of the process model.

- TREE view : This shows an execution tree (control flow relationship of the computation).
- I/O tree view : This shows a tree of input-output causality (data flow relationship of the computation).
- GOAL view : This shows a set of goals (snapshot of the computation).

They enable flexible examination from multiple aspects. A user can get a subprocess as a window from their windows.

4.3.2. Program Visualization

The global view of the toplevel-window visualizes execution of a Fleng program. Execution of a CCL program is represented by visualizing the following two flows :

- control flow: goal reduction
- data flow: guard and unification

Their histories correspond to an execution tree on TREE view, and a tree of input-output causality, respectively. However, visualizing all goals and data is hard to comprehend.

The toplevel-window visualizes only processes with respect to some particular goals and only some particular data-flows. A user needs to specify what is "*particular*" , depending on the user's intention. HyperDEBU provides "*breakpoints*" to specify it.

Note that one of problems on the visualization of Fleng program execution is the need for dynamic location of display objects since goals and data themselves are created dynamically.

Control-flow

The toplevel-window visualizes processes with respect to some particular goals to provide a global view. Figure 3 shows an overview of the toplevel-window. It is regarded as the top view of Figure 1. Each process is displayed as a rectangle.

- A color of the rectangle indicates the state of the process (white, light gray and dark gray indicate active, suspend,and terminated respectively)
- A nest of rectangles indicates the relation between a process and its subprocess.
- A topgoal of a process is displayed when the mouse cursor enters the corresponding rectangle.
- Clicking a rectangle generates a new process-window for this process.

Contents of all the windows are updated reflecting the state of the execution dynamically. By observing creations and state transition of processes, and by observing modification of data in the arguments of topgoals, a user can comprehend the execution of Fleng program correctly and easily.

Data-flow

Though data flow is represented as a tree of input-output causality in the I/O tree view, the display of the I/O tree view is too complicated to understand global data flow of a large scaled program. To solve this problem, the toplevel-window should visualize some particular data flows. Although the visualization of data flow has not been implemented yet completely, we consider that visualizing streams between processes which are displayed as rectangles is helpful to solve the problem. An experimental version of this facility is under development.

4.3.3. Breakpoints for Parallel Execution

The conventional approach to debugging a sequential program is to stop the program at a breakpoint and to examine the state of execution. However, this approach is not applicable to a parallel program which has multiple control flow.

We extend "breakpoints" as a debugger's knowledge given by a user before the execution of the program. The debugger uses this information to control the execution, visualization and static debugging.

Breakpoints are specified as pairs of "point" and "direction". The following place in a program can be specified as a point :

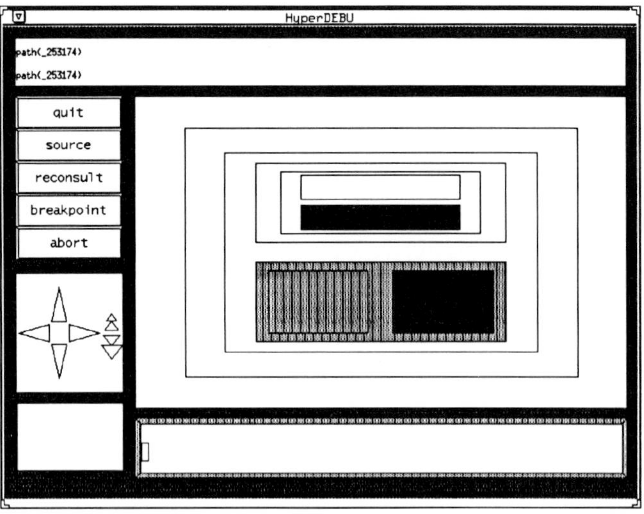

Figure 3. A Toplevel-window

- predicate (a set of clauses which have the same name)
- clause
- body goal
- argument of goal

There are directions as follows :

- pause : This directs to stop a goal there.
- process : This directs to visualize a process with respect to a goal.
- notree : This directs not to keep execution history.
- stream : This directs to visualize a data as a stream.

Since the need to set breakpoints before execution may be a burden to a user, a debugger is expected to aid a user to comprehend static information with which a user decides breakpoints. The program code browser of HyperDEBU is provided for this purpose.

4.3.4. Browsing Program Code

To comprehend static information of Fleng programs, HyperDEBU has a prototype of the program code browser which supports following functions :

- tracing a graph of predicates (procedures) created from cross references
- navigating from execution of a program to source program
- searching history and program code etc. with name of predicate

These functions are applicable to the following aids to a user :

- setting breakpoints
- static debugging
- correcting a source code

5. Examples

In this section, we will demonstrate the effectiveness of HyperDEBU by showing two examples of debugging using HyperDEBU.

Example 1

The following example is a program to solve "good-path problem".

```
path(A) :- token(start,[],A,[]).

token(Node,History,H,T) :-
        (Node == goal ->
           H = [[goal|History]|T]
        ;
           next(Node,Next),
           checknext(Next,[Node|History],H,T)).

checknext([],History,H,T) :- H = T.
checknext([N|Ns],History,H,T):-
        member(N,History,Result),
        gonext(Result,N,History,H,T1),
        checknext(Ns,History,T1,T).

gonext(true,_,_,H,T) :- H = T.
gonext(false,Node,History,H,T):-
        token(Node,History,H,T).

next(start,Next) :- Next = [a,d].
next(a,Next):- Next = [start,b].
next(b,Next):- Next = [a,c,goal].
next(c,[b,d,goal]).                 %erroneous
```

```
%next(c,Next):- Next = [b,d,goal]. %correct
next(d,Next):- Next = [start,c,e].
next(e,Next):- Next = [d,goal].

member(_,[],R) :- R = false.
member(X,[Y|Z],R) :-
        (X == Y -> R = true ; member(X,Z,R)).
```

This program searches the paths on the directed graph and finds all paths from **start** to **goal**. The **next** clauses specify the directed graph; for example, the first clause tells the node **start** has two arrows directed to **a** and **d** respectively. To get the solution, an initial goal **path(X)** is given at first. Then it matches with the first clause of this program and a new goal **token** is generated and spawned. The **token** goals spawn themselves and search the paths from **start** for **goal**. A **token**, which has a node as the first argument **Node**, spawns a goal **checknext** if **Node** is not **goal**. The **checknext** spawns goals **gonext** for the nodes next to the **Node**. Each **gonext** generates a **token** goal if the path from **start** to the node has no loop. If a **token** reaches the node **goal**, it links the solution with the variables H and T to make the list of the solutions. However, the erroneous definition of **next** makes this program suspend illegally without returning the solutions.

At first, breakpoints for visualization are placed in order to observe the creation of **token** goals which make the main control flows of this program. Figure 4 shows the visualization of control flow on the toplevel-window. The light-gray rectangles indicate the processes concerned with them are suspended. Then, one of these processes, which fails to output results, is opened as a process-window (Figure 5). The third argument of its topgoal is still an undefined variable which must have been fixed. Figure 5 shows the display of an I/O tree view to examine the output of the third argument. It shows that **checknext** is suspended without outputting intended result. The structure-window which displays the instance of **checknext** shows the first argument of **checknext** is an undefined variable. The I/O tree view tells that the input of the first argument E must have come from next(A,E) which is suspended illegally. From this part on I/O tree view, we can open a window to display the clauses which defines **next** and get the definition clause which includes a bug.

Example 2

Next example program has a bug involving input-output causality. Although two program have same input and output, their results are different.

```
ex1(A,Z) :-
        multi1([A|X],Y,Z),
        filter(Y,Yout),filter(Z,Zout),
        merge(Yout,Zout,X).
ex2(A,Z) :-
        multi2([A|X],Y,Z),
        filter(Y,Yout),filter(Z,Zout),
        merge(Yout,Zout,X).

multi1([A,B|X],Y,Z) :-
```

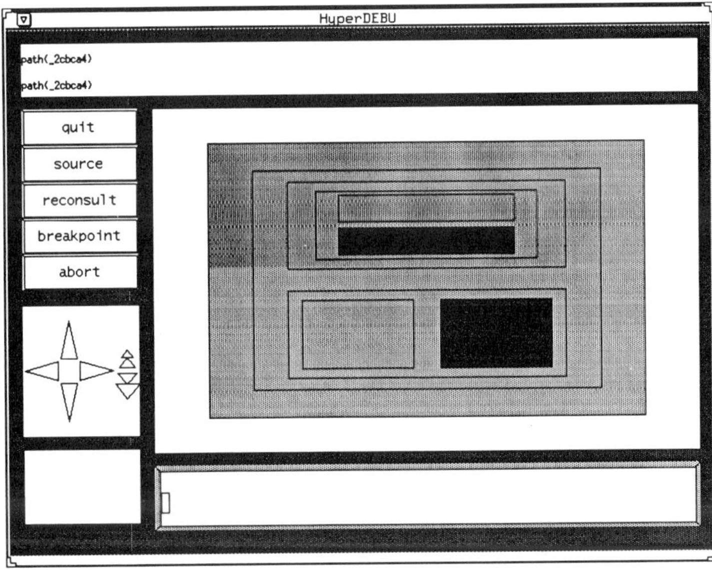

Figure 4. example 1-1: the visualization of the toplevel window

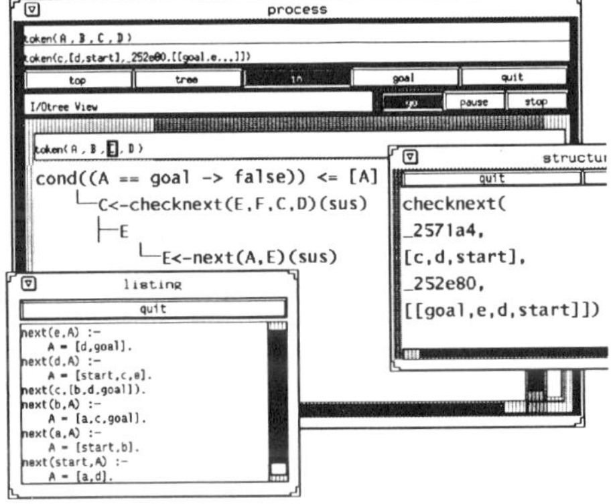

Figure 5. example 1-2: the process window and its I/O tree view

```
            Y = [A|Y1],Z = [B|Z1],multi1(X,Y1,Z1).
    multi1([],Y,Z) :-
            Y = [], Z = [].

    multi2([A|X],Y,Z) :-
            Y = [A|Y1],multi21(X,Y1,Z).
    multi2([],Y,Z) :-
            Y = [], Z = [].
    multi21([A|X],Y,Z) :-
            Z = [A|Z1],multi2(X,Y,Z1).
    multi21([],Y,Z) :-
            Y = [], Z = [].

    filter([A|In],Out) :-
            (A > 0 ->
                sub1(A,A1),
                Out = [A1|Out1],
                filter(In,Out1)
            ;
                Out = [A]).
    filter([],Out) :- Out = [].

    merge([A|X],Y,Z) :- Z = [A|Z1],merge(X,Y,Z1).
    merge(X,[A|Y],Z) :- Z = [A|Z1],merge(X,Y,Z1).
    merge([],Y,Z) :- Z = Y.
    merge(X,[],Z) :- Z = X.
```

Although both of `multi1` and `multi2` split the input of the first argument into the second argument and the third argument, they are different with respect to input-output causality. While `ex2(5,X)` returns a result `X = [4,2,0,0]`, `ex1(5,X)` falls into deadlock and outputs nothing. Figure 6 and Figure 7 show I/O tree views displaying the results of `ex1(5,X)` and `ex2(5,X)` respectively.

According to the output of `ex1`, `multi1` is suspended without output to `B`. It has got input `C = [A|F]` and waiting for next input from `merge` which is waiting for inputs of `G` and `E`. However, two `filter` which must output to `G` and `E` are both waiting for output of `multi1`. This loop of input-output causality brings this program into deadlock.

On the other hand, according to the output of `ex2`, the output of `B` exists on condition that `C = [D|E]` and `E = [F|G]`. This condition is satisfied by the existence of the output of `merge` to `O` which requires the input `P`. A goal `filter` can output to `P` because the input `Q = [D|I]` exists on condition to `C = [D|E]`.

6. Discussions

6.1. Related Works

PIMOS [8], the operating system on the parallel inference machine PIM, has a tracer for KL1 which is a realistic version of GHC on PIM. It traces a particular thread of execution. However, when we have to deal with many threads of a highly parallel program, it is

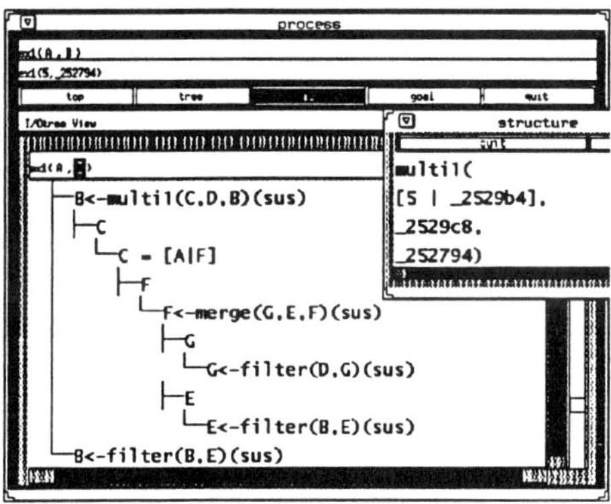

Figure 6. example 2-1: the I/O tree view for ex1

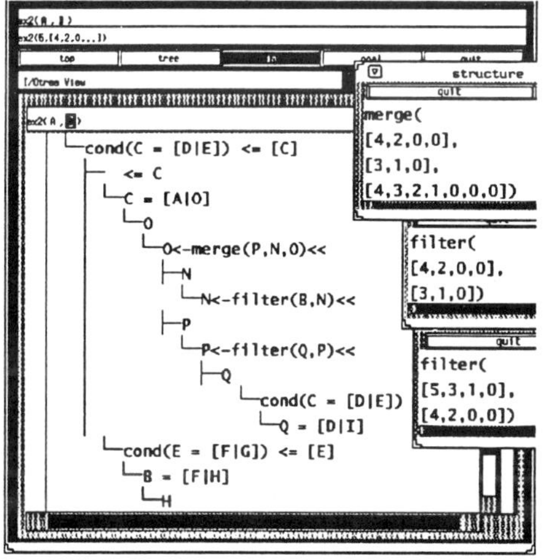

Figure 7. example 2-2: the I/O tree view for ex2

almost impossible to understand them. Moreover, some facilities to trace data flows are required. Although PIMOS can also report some goals fall into deadlock, these relation and histories must be presented for users to find bugs. On the other hand, HyperDEBU enables to solve this problem since it provides flexible views from global to local view point and enables for users to examine expected control/data flows and to locate bugs efficiently.

There are some debuggers which visualizes execution of a CCL program as processes and their communication. For example, [9] is one of their debuggers. However, they regard one sequence of goals as a process. For this reason, they can hardly visualize execution of a highly parallel program concisely. The flexibility of abstraction, which HyperDEBU has, is required to debug such a highly parallel program.

6.2. Nondeterminism

Nondeterminism of a CCL program is caused by the following factors.

1. racing active unifications

2. nondeterministic commitment of clauses

In case 1, a programmer can find a failure of one of these unifications which does not happen in a correct program. Then, using an I/O tree view, the programmer can find the race of outputs to one variable in a tree of active unifications and guarded unifications.

In case 2, introducing some extension such as an OR-tree of input-output causality, an I/O tree view will be able to represent nondeterministic commitment. To analyze how this nondeterminism effects the results of the program execution, some tools need to be developed. However an OR-tree of input-output causality is too complex to compute in practical time. Unlike verification, we think that a debugger needs only to report the existence of nondeterminism without computing all possible execution of the program. We are planning to introduce some breakpoints for nondeterministic commitment to enable user's control of nondeterminism.

6.3. Costs of Time and Space

When a program is executed with a debugger, there is some overhead such as time to execute codes for debugging and memories for event histories. Although the performance of HyperDEBU is enough for practical use now, more improvement is desired.

HyperDEBU takes much time since it uses meta-interpreter to manage execution of goals. We will design an improved version of the goal management mechanism which is realized by adding some primitives to the interpreter or the compiler.

Although event histories are useful to debug parallel programs, it is almost impossible to record whole events. Therefore, HyperDEBU provides a breakpoint to determine if the history of goal (execution tree) is recorded. The visualization of program execution also helps to decrease data of history to store.

7. Future Work

We have realized a realistic debugger for parallel logic programs. For more improvement, we have some subjects as follows:

- visualization of data flow
- support of compiler, operating system, and architecture to debugger
- control of nondeterministic behavior
- static analysis to help debugging
- performance debugging
- total environment for parallel programming

8. Conclusion

In this paper, we introduce a communicating process model to represent execution of a Fleng program, and present a multiwindow debugger HyperDEBU which represents this model on a high-dimensional interface.

HyperDEBU is written in Fleng itself and runs on a Fleng interpreter on UNIX workstations and Mach parallel workstations. Being used in development of application programs, it is being evaluated and improved .

1 Mcdowell,C.E. and Helmbold,D.P.: *Debugging Concurrent Programs*, ACM Computing Surveys, Vol.21 No.4, pp.593-622 (1989).

2 Nilsson, M. and Tanaka, H.: *Massively Parallel Implementation of Flat GHC on the Connection Machine, Proc. of the Int. Conf. on Fifth Generation Computer Systems*, p1031-1040 (1988).

3 Koike, H. and Tanaka, H. : *Parallel Inference Engine PIE64*, in *Parallel Computer Architecture*, bit, Vol.21,No.4,1989, pp.488-497 (in Japanese).

4 (Ed.) Shapiro, E. : *Concurrent Prolog : Collected Papers* , (Vols. 1 and 2), The MIT Press (1987).

5 Murakami, M. : *An Axiomatic Verification Method for Synchronization of Guarded Horn Clauses Programs*, ICOT Technical Report TR-339, ICOT (1988).

6 Murakami, M. : *A Declarative Semantics of Parallel Logic Programs with Perpetual Processes*, ICOT Technical Report TR-406, ICOT (1988).

7 Tatemura, J. and Tanaka, H. : *Debugger for a Parallel Logic Programming Language Fleng*, Proc. of Logic Programming Conference '89 (1989).

8 Chikayama,T. and Suzaki, K. : *PIMOS 1.5 Introductory Manual*, ICOT Technical Memorandum TM-884, ICOT (1989).

9 Maeda, M., Uoi, H. and Tokura, N. : *Process and Stream Oriented Debugger for GHC Programs*, Proc. of Logic Programming Conference '90 (1990).

PROGRAMMING ENVIRONMENTS FOR PARALLEL COMPUTING
N. Topham, R. Ibbett and T. Bemmerl (Editors)
Elsevier Science Publishers B.V. (North-Holland)

© 1992 IFIP. All rights reserved.

Model–driven Validation of Parallel Programs Based on Event Traces

P. Dauphin, M. Kienow, A. Quick
Universität Erlangen–Nürnberg, IMMD VII, Martensstraße 3, D–8520 Erlangen, Germany
email: pdauphin@immd7.informatik.uni-erlangen.de

Abstract

In order to program parallel and distributed systems efficiently, a systematic way of defining and understanding the complex behavior of process interactions in concurrent programs is needed. A proved method for understanding existing programs is model–driven monitoring which abstracts the program behavior to a sequence of events. These event traces are analyzed for debugging and tuning the program. However, model and program are not always consistent. The goal of this paper is using measured event traces to validate the consistency between model and program.

We have investigated a solution to validate model–program consistency automatically: by building a functional model of the parallel program describing all properties for debugging and performance evaluation the definition of monitoring events is automated and carried out systematically. This integration of modeling and monitoring guarantees the same set of events in monitoring and modeling. It enables us to validate the program behavior in an automatic and systematic way by checking the event trace against the behavior represented in the model.

In order to implement validation for different modeling methods only once we analyzed three different methods for a model–type–independent representation of parallel programs. The analysis showed that a model of a real–world application is too complicated to be described in a model–type–independent way. Therefore validation was implemented for two modeling tools: PEPP used for modeling with graph models and GreatSPN used for modeling with Petri nets. Both tools were extended to enable automatic program validation.

Keyword Codes: C.4, D.2.2, D.2.5, D.2.6, I.6.4
Keywords: Performance of Systems, Tools and Techniques, Testing and Debugging, Programming Environments, Model Validation and Analysis

1. Introduction

Efficient programming of parallel and distributed systems is still a hard job! Parallel and distributed data processing is intended to increase performance by distributing a workload on many processors, but this way of getting high performance produces new problems like race conditions, mutual waiting of processes, or access conflicts on interconnection networks. Although parallel and distributed computer systems are getting more and more common, there is a big lack of tools for programming and debugging these systems. Because of signal run times it is hard to define global breakpoints for debugging. Therefore sequential debuggers cannot easily be adapted to parallel and distributed systems [MH89]. For efficiently parallelizing big jobs and successfully designing distributed applications the program must not be regarded as a black box, as it is done in calculating performance indices [Fer78], but insight into the dynamic behavior of at least two processors (computers) at a time is needed. One of the most promising ways of gaining the necessary insight is event–driven monitoring, a technique in which the real–time sequence of interesting events is monitored and stored as an event trace. This technique can be used for event–based debugging, supporting efficient programming, tuning, program analysis, and performance evaluation.

Monitoring is a great help for analyzing these systems but due to the complexity of the system to be measured monitoring itself is a complex task. For monitoring distributed systems a distributed monitor is needed [DHK+92, BM86]. In order to get the desired results with monitoring it should be carried out in a systematic way.

By building a functional model of the parallel program describing all properties for debugging and performance evaluation the definition of monitoring events can be automated and carried out systematically. The integration of modeling and monitoring guarantees the same set of events in monitoring and modeling. But even with a systematic and model–based instrumentation of the program it cannot be guaranteed that the behavior of the program represented by the event trace corresponds to the expected behavior given in the model, making the results of a subsequent evaluation of the event trace senseless. To avoid such a useless evaluation the program behavior should be validated by checking the event trace against the behavior represented in the model before evaluating the event trace. Since the set of events is the same in monitoring and modeling the validation process can be carried out automatically.

In the next section a systematic approach for event–driven monitoring which integrates modeling and monitoring is described. Based on this method and using model–driven instrumentation the set of events used in the model and with monitoring is by construction the same. In section 3 three approaches for a model–type–independent representation of parallel programs are described. This representation was intended to allow a model–type–independent validation of event traces. The result of this analysis is that all three approaches need too much memory and computation time. Therefore we decided to implement the automatic validation for two common modeling methods, graph models and Petri nets. The extension of the tools PEPP [DKM+92] and GreatSPN [Chi91] by a "validation unit" is described in section 4. In section 5 we summarize our results and give a short prospect.

2. Model–driven Monitoring

Event–driven monitoring represents the dynamic behavior of a program by a sequence of events. Only this monitoring method, in contrast to time–driven monitoring (sampling), is suited for efficient program analysis[1]. The events are defined by inserting monitoring instructions into the program under investigation (program instrumentation). The monitoring instructions write event tokens to a hardware interface which is accessible for a hardware monitor (hybrid monitoring) or into a reserved memory area (software monitoring). Defining

1 In the following text "monitoring" always is used in sense of "event–driven monitoring".

events with program instrumentation each monitored event token can be clearly assigned to a point in a program; this provides a problem–oriented reference. Thus, the evaluation of the event trace can be done on the program level which is familiar to the program designer. To minimize the influence of instrumented monitoring instructions on the programs execution (probe effect) we prefer hybrid monitoring.

As the CPU time overhead increases with the number of events monitored, instrumentation must be limited to those events whose tracing is considered essential for an understanding of the problems to be solved. Monitoring complex systems, like parallel or distributed systems, is too complex a task to do it intuitively. Therefore monitoring and especially program instrumentation should be carried out in a systematic way.

Model–driven Instrumentation

In order to define events systematically one needs knowledge about the aim of measurement and about the functional behavior of the system to be analyzed. We agree with Nutt who already postulated in 1975 [Nut75]: "The most important questions to be answered before attempting to monitor a machine are *what* to measure and *why* the measurement should be taken.", and Kobayashi [Kob81]: "The system tuning requires a clear understanding of the complex interactions among the individual system components. A systematic procedure of performing this task is yet to be developed."

Our idea of performance evaluation, tuning, and debugging is to integrate modeling and monitoring to a comprehensive methodology. In using event–oriented models (like graph models, Petri nets, queueing models, or formal specifications) and event–driven monitoring there is a common abstraction, the event, which enables us to integrate both methods. Both rely on the same abstraction of the dynamic program behavior: strategic points are represented as events of interest and the overall dynamic behavior as an event trace. Therefore, the monitoring model can be used to specify the events for monitoring (model–driven instrumentation).

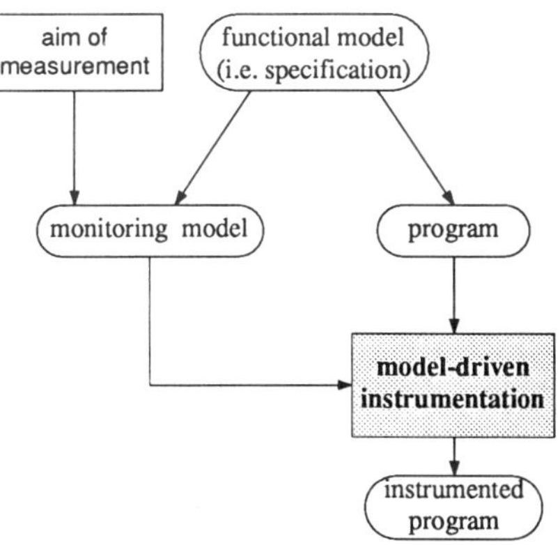

Figure 1: Model–driven Instrumentation

Due to this very close connection between the flow description in modeling and monitoring it is desirable to use the same set of events for modeling and monitoring. Since not every detail of the functional model (i.e. a formal specification) which is used for programming is of interest in terms of performance evaluation and program analysis, the analysis of the program is carried out on another level of abstraction. For monitoring purposes, the so–called monitoring model is created. This model is derived from the functional model considering the aim of measurement. The monitoring model forms the basis for the instrumentation (see fig. 1). All activities represented in the model will be instrumented in the corresponding program.

The difficult questions “Which events should be defined?” and “Where should the program be instrumented?” are implicitly answered by building the monitoring model. Model–driven program instrumentation versus intuitive instrumentation offers the following advantages:

- Instrumentation is no longer an intuitive action, but may be executed systematically.
- Instrumentation can be carried out automatically with the support of tools.
- The interpretations of the instrumented event tokens are known. This knowledge of the event semantic can be used for automatically creating an event trace description in TDL [Moh91], for program animation, and for automatic event trace evaluation.
- There is a one–to–one mapping between the set of events used in modeling and monitoring.
- The measurement can be validated in a systematically way. This leads to an automatic, model–driven validation.

Model–driven Monitoring

Model–driven instrumentation (fig. 1) is the foundation for model–driven monitoring (fig. 2). After model–driven instrumentation the instrumented program can be executed and measured which produces an event trace as result.

The results of trace analysis can be used for creating a performance model with realistic parameters. These parameters can be used for model evaluation and for the prediction of the mean runtime of other implementations, process mappings, or other computer configurations.

Model–driven monitoring is independent of the method used for modeling. In [KQS92] there is an example given for stochastic graph models and programs written in C.

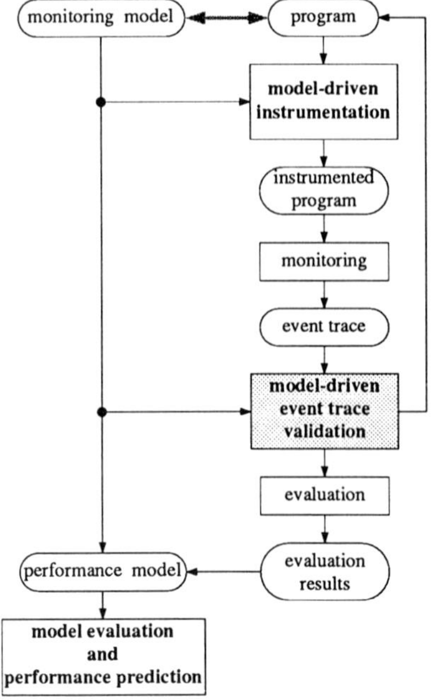

Figure 2: Model–driven Monitoring

Model–driven Event Trace Validation

In the following part of this paper we are going to describe the automatic, model–driven validation of measured event traces. Validating the event trace is necessary in order to evaluate correct results from the event trace. A simple form of validation is to check for increasing time stamps or for the set of monitored event tokens.

Furthermore the monitored behavior can be checked against the behavior represented in the monitoring model.

In the context of this paper only this aspect of validation is considered (in fig. 2 there is only an arc from *validation* to *program* and no arc from *validation* to *monitoring*). The results of the validation are hints for finding program errors or the knowledge about a correct event trace which can be evaluated.

There are some debugging tools for checking the specification against an event trace. The debugger ESCP [BDV86] can only check specified communication behavior and hierarchical fork–join parallelism. In the TSL system [HL85] specifications are automatically checked against events generated by an Ada tasking program. As with model–driven validation, TSL also requires a linearly ordered event trace.

As there are many methods for modeling parallel and distributed programs and various tools supporting these methods we first want to find a model–type–independent way for validation.

3. Model–type–independent Validation

With the model–type–independent way for validation we have to transform the functional behavior represented in the monitoring model into a uniform representation. Concerning the validation, such a model–type–independent solution minimizes the amount of implementation work: The validation algorithm needs only be implemented once for all modeling methods and tools.

As different types of models contain different information of the program to be modeled it is generally impossible to transform them in one another or to choose one model type as a reference for validation purposes. Common, however, to all model types used for modeling parallel and distributed programs is the representation of event ordering and modeling of parallelism and causal dependencies.

As these features are important to our intention it suggests itself to extract the according informations from the model and form a reduced, but standardized and model–type–independent monitoring model out of them which is further used for the event trace validation exclusively.

As described in fig. 3 this approach indeed demands a model–type–dependent model conversion for each modeling tool extracting all possible orderings of the events and forming the model–type–independent monitoring model. But the advantage of this approach is that the validation algorithm itself including the error localization and the error classification need to be implemented only once for all modeling methods and tools.

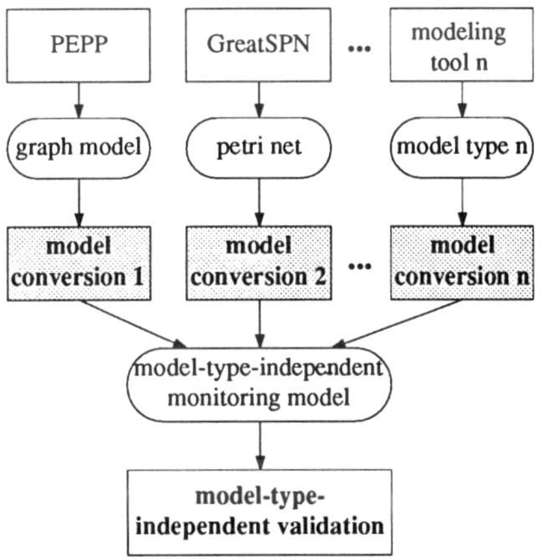

Figure 3: Model–type–independent validation

In this section we examine three formalisms — regular expressions, shuffle expressions, and free partially commutative monoids — whether they are suited to represent the causal ordering of the events in a suitable way and whether models created by different modeling tools can be easily transformed into one of these formalisms. These questions will be answered in respect of graph models, i.e. task dependency graphs [ST87]. Nodes of the graph model represent the tasks and arcs represent the causal ordering. The name of a task (name of a node) in the graph is identical with the event in the trace generated by that task. This bijective function is a prerequisite for validating the event trace against a reference model.

3.1. Regular Expressions

Regular expressions (and the equivalent finite state automata) [HU69, Sal73] are often used to describe patterns or even parallel and distributed systems, e.g. to test protocols in communication systems. A regular expression consists of atoms (single events). The operators sequence (→) and alternative (|) combine single atoms or expressions to form new expressions. Parentheses around expressions are used to override operator precedence. The ordering of events in an event trace can be described by such a regular expression; the event trace validation becomes a pattern matching problem. In fig. 4 a simple graph model with tasks $a, \ldots, e$ and the corresponding regular expression is given.

When converting the graph model in fig. 4 into a regular expression, every possible order of the events b, c, and d must be explicitly given in the regular expression. There is no other way to express parallelism in one regular expression than to enumerate every possible sequential order of the events in different alternatives of the expression.

Figure 4: Graph model and regular expression

For checking an event trace against a regular expression, first a deterministic finite state automaton must be derived from the expression. Then the event trace is given as input to the automaton. If the trace matches the regular expression, the automaton reaches its final state, otherwise an error will be detected.

With increasing size and parallelism of the model the time needed to convert the model into the corresponding regular expression and the memory necessary for storing the regular expression explode so that this formalism is unsuitable as an efficient model–type–independent description. Even simple graph models with about 20 nodes may lead to a regular expression with millions of atoms, depending on the complexity of the causal dependencies between the specified events.

3.2. Shuffle Expressions

As seen above, the regular expressions are not well suited for a model–type–independent description of parallel systems. By extending the concept of regular expressions by the so–called shuffle operator (&) we get shuffle expressions. The shuffle operator represents the parallel composition of two expressions. Thus, the ordering of events in a parallel system can be described much more compactly than with a regular expression.

To convert a graph model into a shuffle expression, the graph is processed recursively as follows: let N be the set of nodes and $E \subseteq N\text{x}N$ be the set of edges in the graph model. We define the set of predecessors of a node n by $pred(n) = \{n' \in N | (n', n) \in E\}$, the set of successors of a node n by $succ(n) = \{n' \in N | (n, n') \in E\}$. For a set M of nodes we define $succ[M] = \bigcup_{m \in M} succ(m)$. $P \subseteq N$ is the set of nodes already processed during the model conversion. The nodes which may be processed next is given by $ready(P) = \{n \in N |\ pred(n) \subseteq P\}$. When starting the algorithm P is the empty set ($\emptyset$) and $ready(P)$ is the set of start nodes, i.e. nodes without a predecessor.

For a finite set $R = \{r_1, ..., r_j\}$ with $j \leq |N|$ and $r_i \in N$ the notation $\&(R)$ represents the shuffle product $(r_1 \& r_2 \& \ldots \& r_j)$. If we finally define $R_n = (pred(n) \cap ready(P))$ with $n \in succ[ready(P)]$ as an abbreviation the shuffle expression $SE(P)$ can be computed recursively by the following equation:

$$SE(P) = \begin{cases} \&(ready(P)) & \text{if } succ(ready(P)) = \emptyset \\ \mathop{\Big|}\limits_{\substack{n \in succ[ready(P)] \\ R_n \subset ready(P)}} (\&(R_n) \rightarrow n \rightarrow SE(P \cup R_n \cup \{n\})) \quad | \\ \qquad (\&(ready(P)) \rightarrow SE(P \cup ready(P)) & \text{else} \end{cases}$$

Then, by $SE(\emptyset)$ the shuffle expression for the whole graph is given. A shuffle expression generated by this algorithm contains only shuffle products of single events. To produce shuffle products of composed expressions, i.e. shuffle products of shuffle products, which are much more compact than a shuffle product of single events, appropriate alternatives in the shuffle expression must be combined. This is easy in the case of series parallel graphs, but it is difficult to solve for general graph models.

To check an event trace against a shuffle expression, a shuffle automaton is built from the shuffle expression [Bat86]. The shuffle automata are similar to the finite state automata. The difference is, that instead of a single symbol sets of symbols are used in the transitions of the automata. A shuffle automaton collects input symbols in an input register until a transition is possible. Therefore, concurrency can be handled since the ordering of events in the input register is unimportant.

In fig. 5 a graph model and the corresponding shuffle expression together with the shuffle automaton is given. The letters $a, \ldots, f$ represent instantaneous events.

Both, the transformation and the validation algorithm as described above were implemented and tested with two representative models: a model with N–structure and a model with X–structure (see table 1).

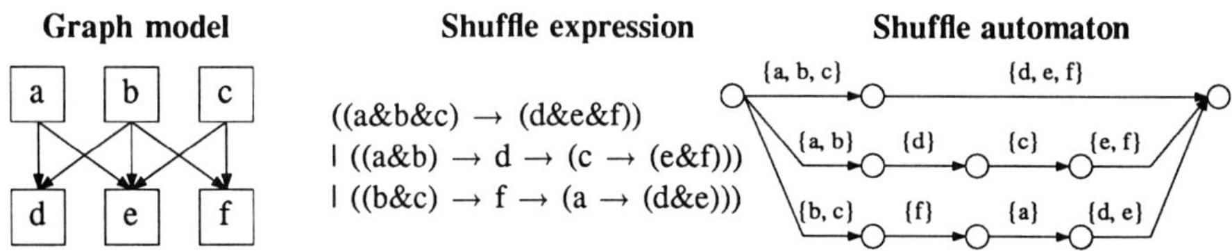

Figure 5: Graph model, corresponding shuffle expression and shuffle automaton

Both models are examined with varying width (w), i.e. number of parallel jobs, and height (h), i.e. number of tasks per job. The results are summed up in table 1. *Nodes* represent the number of nodes in the underlying graph model which is equal to the number of events in the event trace. The columns titled with *create shuffle expression* refer to the transformation of the graph model into a shuffle expression: for both model structures it can be seen that with increasing number of parallel jobs as well as with increasing number of tasks per job the *memory* necessary for the transformation, the number of *atoms* in the final shuffle expression, and the amount of *time* to perform the transformation augment dramatically. For the (4,7)–N graph model the availability of 115 MB of memory (swap space) is not enough to succeed in transforming the graph model into a shuffle expression.

	Model	Nodes	create shuffle expression			trace validation	
			Memory	Atoms	Time	States	Time
N-structure (w, h)-N	(3,5)-N	15	155k	3943	3s	869	22s
	(4,4)-N	16	485k	14259	10s	1694	140s
	(4,5)-N	20	5.5M	172711	100s	?	?
	(4,7)-N	28	>115MB	>6487020	>2340s	?	?
X-structure (w, h)-X	(3,5)-X	15	16k	313	0.3s	142	1.1s
	(4,4)-X	16	164k	5088	4s	1142	33s
	(4,5)-X	20	1.4M	44174	30s	6991	420s
	(4,7)-X	28	75MB	3329626	1440s	?	?

Table 1: Validation using shuffle expressions (computation time for SUN–4/110)

The last two columns deal with the *trace validation* itself: *states* describes the number of states of the deterministic shuffle automaton; the values in the column *time* include the building of the deterministic automaton and the subsequent validation step. The question marks (?) indicate that 115 MB of memory is not sufficient for executing the validation algorithm based on shuffle automata. In both columns the tremendous decrease of the performance of the validation algorithm with increasing model size becomes obvious.

3.3. Free Partially Commutative Monoids

The free partially commutative monoids (FPCM) are used in theoretic computer science as a model of concurrency in parallel systems [Maz86, Kön91]. A FPCM M is defined by the free monoid A^* over the set A and a commutation relation $\theta \subseteq \binom{A}{2}$ where $\binom{A}{2}$ is the set of all two–element subsets of A: $M(A, \theta) = A^*/\{ab = ba \mid (a, b) \in \theta\}$, i.e. every subset θ defines a FPCM by allowing two elements a and b to commute iff $(a, b) \in \theta$. A monoid $M(A, \theta)$ can be represented by a graph $G(M)$ with nodes A and arcs θ. If two elements of A can commute there is an undirected edge between the two elements in the graph. If an element of A cannot commute with any other element it is represented as an isolated node in the graph. Thus $G(M)$ need not be a connected graph (see fig. 6). The set $C \subseteq A$ is called a *clique* of $G = (A, \theta)$ iff the inclusion $\binom{C}{2} \subseteq \theta$ is valid. On the contrary, the set $L \subseteq A$ is called an *anticlique* iff L is a clique of the graph $\overline{G} = (A, \binom{A}{2} \setminus \theta)$. Cliques are sets of nodes which may commute; anticliques are sets of nodes which must not commute. In our context the elements of A represent the events defined in the graph model. Cliques are sets of events which may occur in any order of time during the execution of the program. Anticliques are sets of events where a causal connection exists between each other.

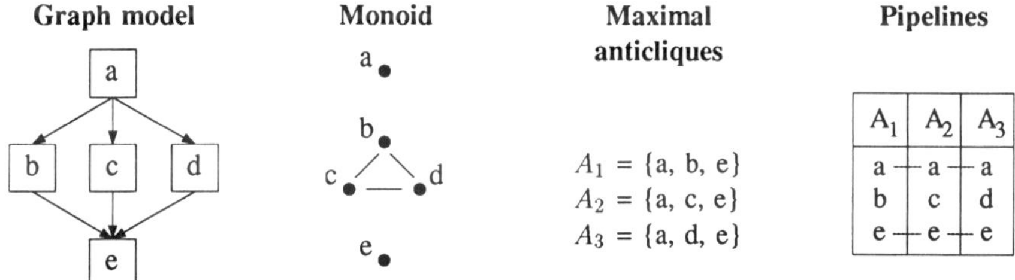

Figure 6: Graph model and corresponding monoid, anticliques and pipelines

As we only want to check the causal ordering of the events by trace validation, the computation of the maximal anticliques[1] of the monoid is sufficient. They may be found by tracing every possible path from a start node to an end node in the graph model. When transforming a graph model into a FPCM the directness of the graph is lost. This loss can be compensated by storing a synthetically created reference trace additionally to the set of anticliques. Thus the synthetically created reference trace together with the set of anticliques are a possible model–type–independent description of the program behavior.

During validation a pipeline will be attached to every anticlique of the monoid. These pipelines will be filled by events of the event trace: the events are inserted into the pipelines in the order they appear in the trace. Each event is only inserted into those pipelines, for which the corresponding anticlique contains the event. Every correct trace fills the pipelines in the way the reference trace will do it. This enables us to distinguish between correct and wrong traces. The synthetically created reference trace acts as a template to enable the recognition of

[1] If a maximal anticlique is extended by an additional element, the anticlique loses its property.

erroneous events in the trace to be validated. Fig. 6 shows a graph model, the corresponding monoid, and anticliques together with the pipelines, filled with a reference trace.

The validation concept described above is implemented and tested for the same models we used to check the efficiency of shuffle expressions applied to trace validation. The results are collected in table 2. Obviously, the formalism comes off well compared with the formalism of shuffle expressions. Nevertheless the examined concept of the FPCMs is inappropriate for our validation purposes when modeling realistic programs (see last line in table 2). When using FPCMs the amount of memory and time needed for validation increases with the number and length of paths leading from a start node to an end node in the graph model.

Model	Anti-cliques	Memory	Time
(3,5)-N	17	8k	0.1s
(4,4)-N	20	9k	0.2s
(4,7)-N	72	28k	0.5s
(4,10)-N	187	73k	1.8s
(3,5)-X	99	25k	0.5s
(4,4)-X	68	18k	0.5s
(4,7)-X	1220	270k	10s
(4,10)-X	21892	4.6M	5400s

Table 2: Validation using FPCMs (computation time for SUN–4/110)

3.4. Results

There was an improvement between the examined formalisms. But the results in table 1 and 2 show, that all examined formalisms are inappropriate to efficiently describe the ordering of events in a model–type–independent way. This is due to the explosion of both, the time needed for validating an arbitrary event trace and the memory used for model–type–independent representation with increasing model size.

Besides, we examined the formalisms concerning graph models only. When using other types of models more problems will probably come up, e.g. FPCMs are not appropriate to represent models containing loops and branches as used in Petri nets.

Last but not least, there has to be a feedback from the validation results to the original monitoring model to give hints for program correction. For this purpose a reference to the representation in the original monitoring model for each task must additionally be stored together with the model–type–independent description used for validation. Sometimes, however, the reference to the original monitoring model cannot be preserved when building a model–type–independent description or when executing the validation algorithm.

These disadvantages absolutely outweigh the advantage of having one single validation algorithm for all types of models. Therefore, we developed validation tools strictly tied to the type of model used for modeling the program behavior.

4. Validation with Graph Models and Petri Nets

Working directly on a model, a specialized validation algorithm is used and there is no need to convert model information into another form. Error localization and error classification can be carried out directly in the model, using all the information contained in the model. When using the model–type–independent approach, a model–related graphical display of the validation is difficult to realize. But for models with a graphical representation, the visualization of validation progress and error situations in the model is a great help in understanding and debugging the program under investigation. This is another great advantage for developing a validation algorithm strictly tied to a modeling tool.

Common modeling tools used in our environment for two different model types are extended for trace validation, namely PEPP (*P*erformance *E*valuation of *P*arallel *P*rograms) [DKM+92] used for modeling with graph models and GreatSPN (*Gr*aphical *e*ditor and *a*nalyzer for *t*imed and *S*tochastic *P*etri *N*ets) [Chi91] used for modeling with Petri nets. The extension of the tools and their use for program analysis and debugging are described in the following sections.

The validation should be able to handle any event trace produced by monitoring arbitrary parallel and distributed systems. Therefore we use the interface POET (*P*roblem *O*riented *E*vent *T*race interface) between the event trace and the tools for consistency validation. POET takes the event traces as a generic data structure and provides uniform trace access. Using this interface trace access is independent of the object system and the monitoring system. The necessary syntactic and semantic information for trace access and trace decoding is taken from a so–called *keyfile*. The keyfile can be obtained from the trace description in TDL (event *T*race *D*escription *L*anguage). Integrating TDL/POET [Moh91, Moh92] into the modeling tools any event trace can be validated by only creating a TDL–description for this event trace.

4.1. Extension of the Tool PEPP

The tool PEPP (*P*erformance *E*valuation of *P*arallel *P*rograms) [DKM+92] is a modeling tool for acyclic stochastic graph models developed at the University of Erlangen–Nürnberg. Its user interface is based on the X–window systems (see fig. 9). With PEPP, graph models can be created interactively and evaluated for performance analysis. Program activities are modeled by an *elementary node*. A *hierarchical node* which contains a subgraph can be used to create hierarchical graph models. Although the graph have to be acyclic loops in a program can be modeled using a *loop node*. This node is similar to the hierarchical node, the body of the loop is modeled by the subgraph of this node. Besides edges which represent the activities' execution order and parallelism, graph models created with PEPP may contain alternative branch edges, e.g. to model if–then–else structures.

The connection between program sources and the model is realized by node identifiers, e.g. procedure names. Up to two events may be specified at a node, the call–event and the return–event of the program activity modeled by that node. These events indicate entry and exit of the activity. The specified events are graphically displayed by little filled rectangles inside the node at the top (for the call–event) and at the bottom (for the return–event) (see fig. 9). Nodes which are not provided with any event are skipped over automatically in the correct way during validation. For trace validation each node must have a unique identifier. If an activity A is processed in parallel on different processors or in different processes, there may be several nodes in the graph model which represent the activity A. When an event 'call A' occurs it is impossible to decide which of these nodes was really processed using only the activities' name. Therefore the mapping of activities on different processors or processes have to be specified in the model. For this the processor or process name is used as an additional node parameter.

The validation algorithm starts to examine for every event of the event trace whether the event can occur in the graph model at the current processing state. The current state of a graph is defined by the set of already processed nodes and the set of ready nodes, i.e. nodes which have no unprocessed predecessor and which related event may occur next. Storing the processed nodes, it can always be decided which nodes are ready to be processed next. Whenever an event of the trace is accepted, the corresponding node in the model — which has to be found in the set of ready nodes — is marked as processed and the new set of ready nodes is computed. Thereby the trace is processed, moving from state to state in the model until end of trace is reached or an error is detected.

This validation algorithm cannot handle situations where an event of the event trace can be mapped to more than one node in the graph model. This situation arises, when two or more nodes with the same event exist in the set of ready nodes. Therefore, the models have to meet some restrictions: different branches may not begin with the same event and loops may not begin with the same event as the first possible event after the loop. Otherwise it cannot be decided if the loop is entered or left. In practice, these restrictions can always be fulfilled.

The validation functions can be selected from a menu (fig. 7). To start validation, the monitoring model must be loaded by PEPP and the event trace must be initialized by pressing the *Init Trace*–button. A window comes up demanding for the name of the trace file and of the key file necessary for event trace access. To get the initial state of the graph model the *Clear Marking*–button is to use.

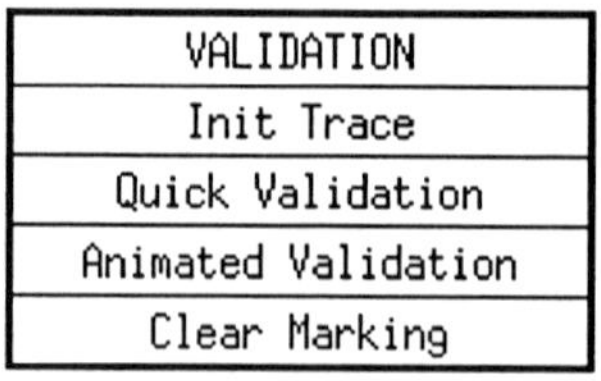

VALIDATION
Init Trace
Quick Validation
Animated Validation
Clear Marking

Figure 7: Validation functions

The validation itself can be executed in two different modes:

Quick Validation: Here the event trace will be checked against the model until an error is detected or end of trace is reached. An error message or the successful closing of the validation is graphically displayed in the model. This mode is useful for a quick error check.

Animated Validation: In this mode the progress of the validation in the model is shown event by event. The nodes of the events are marked so that the status of each node can be recognized graphically at each time during the validation in progress. The monitored behavior will be animated.

Using the animated mode a delay between the processing of the events is selectable by the user, the validation can be interactively stopped and continued as desired to inspect the model's state. In order to stop validation at a specific event, a breakpoint can be defined. One way of using a breakpoint could be as follows: when an error in the trace has been detected by a quick validation, then a breakpoint can be defined some events before the error. Now a new (animated) validation can be started which stops at this point. Then the user can continue to step through the event trace using animated display of the validation. Thereby it can be observed which events precede the error and how the error is reached in the model.

An error in the event trace is detected when there is no ready node named with the current event in the model. Error handling is done completely in the model using the information stored in the model and in the event trace. If an error has been detected, we first *localize* the error in the model by finding a node with the erroneous event assigned. If there is more than one possible node, the node in the model nearest to the actual processing state of the program is selected as error node. To localize an error not only in the model but also in the program sources, every event should have additional parameters 'line number' and 'file name', which helps finding the point where the event occurs in the program sources. Together with the event name it is possible to view the program's state at the moment when the error was detected.

Using the dependency structure of the program represented in the model combined with the information of the event trace concerning the processor's or process's name on which the events occur an error may be *classified* either as a synchronization error or a program flow error. When involving additional knowledge about the syntax and semantics of the programming language used the error classification may be improved. Modeling C–programs with PEPP branches, loops, and hierarchical nodes model corresponding program structures. As there is a mapping between the nodes and certain program structures it is possible to detect some common program faults like missing break–statements between case–statements, wrong continue–statements in loops, or skipped procedure calls.

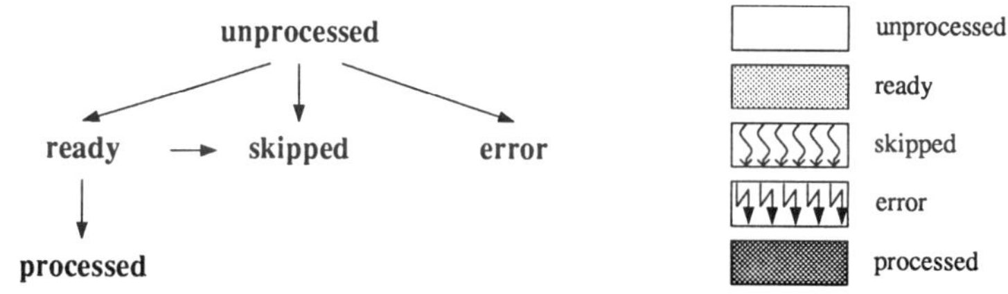

Figure 8: Possible state changes of a node in the PEPP model and their graphical representation

If an error can be classified, the result of the classification will be given together with a description of the event which caused the error and the position in the program sources. In addition, the processing state of every node in the model is displayed graphically. We distinguish five different states of a node (see fig. 8):

unprocessed — An event belonging to the node has neither been occurred in the event trace nor is expected to occur next. Unprocessed nodes are not marked.

ready — The event belonging to the node may occur next in the event trace. Ready nodes are marked with a light hatching.

processed — An event belonging to the node has already been found in the event trace. Processed nodes are marked with a dark hatching.

error — The node is related to the unexpected and erroneous event. The node is marked with flash signs.

skipped — Skipped nodes are nodes with events that should have been occurred in the trace before the erroneous event. Skipped nodes are marked with arrows.

The last two states can be found only if an error was recognized in the event trace under investigation. The possible state changes of a node are given in fig. 8. As there may be a call–event and a return–event assigned to each node a node can be marked with two different states, one concerning to the call–event, the other concerning the return–event.

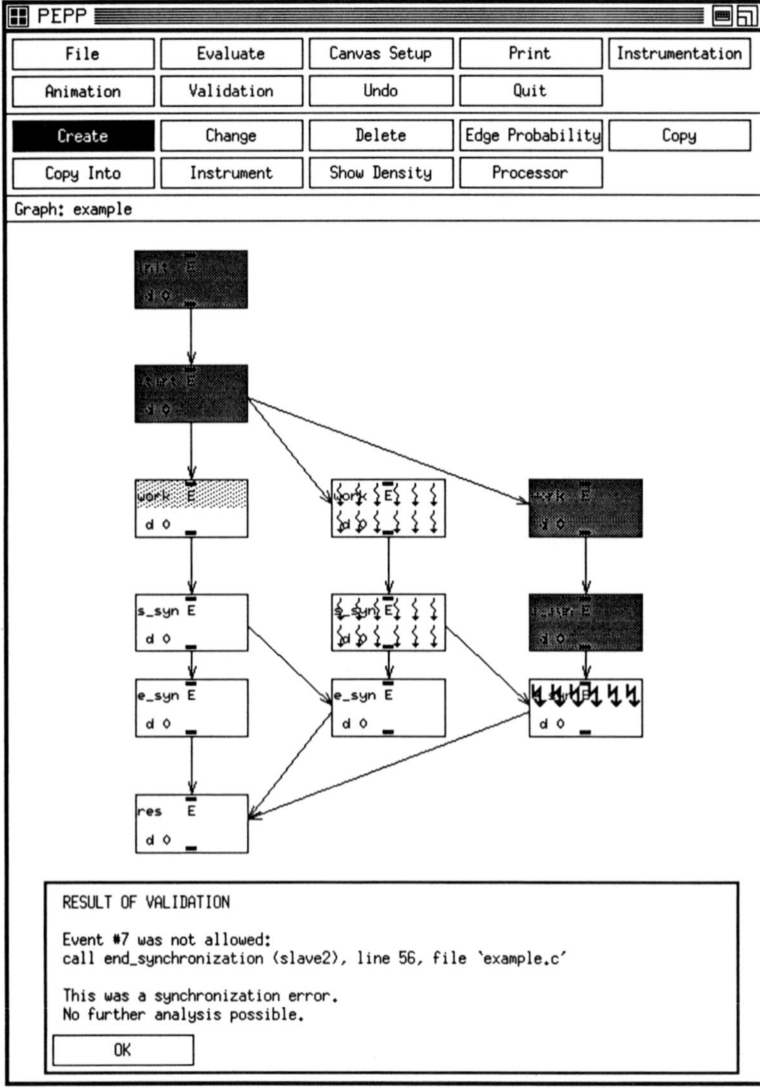

Figure 9: Visualization of an error in the PEPP model after error localization

In fig. 9 the graph model for a simple program is given. An abbreviation of the name of the activity is displayed inside every node. The program starts with the process *master* (left column of nodes). First an initialization takes place (procedure 'init'), then two other processes (*slave1*, *slave2*) are forked (middle and right column of nodes) in procedure 'start'. Now every process does its work followed by a synchronization to its right neighbor (procedures 'work', 's_syn', and 'e_syn'). After synchronization, all processes but the process *master* terminate and the results are collected by the *master* process in procedure 'res'. Fig. 9 shows the graph model after a synchronization error has been detected by trace validation: process *slave2* did not wait for its left neighbor at the synchronization point. The event 'call e_syn' may not occur before the nodes marked with arrows in the middle process have been processed. A subwindow arises displaying

- the number and the name of the erroneous event
- the line number and file name of the program under investigation
- the result of error classification

Obviously, it can be seen in fig. 9 that the graphical display of errors' localization together with the validation results are a great help for debugging.

4.2. Extension of the Tool GreatSPN

The tool GreatSPN (*Gr*aphical *e*ditor and *a*nalyzer for *t*imed and *S*tochastic *P*etri *N*ets) [Chi91] developed at the University of Torino is a modeling tool for generalized stochastic Petri nets (GSPN). With GreatSPN, Petri nets can interactively be created and analyzed for structural properties or performance parameters. Interactive simulation with graphical display is also possible.

The stochastic Petri nets used with GreatSPN are bipartite graphs consisting of places and transitions which are connected by weighted edges. The places represent states of the program under investigation, the transitions correspond to the instrumented events. For validation purposes the name of the activity (called tag in GreatSPN) and a processor/process name is assigned to each transition (see attributes assigned to the nodes in the PEPP model). As two events may be assigned to one program activity, (call–event and return–event) and transitions of Petri nets are able to represent exactly one event it has to be specified whether the event assigned to a transition is the call–event or the return–event of a modeled activity.

Validation with Petri nets works similar to validation with graph models. The events of the event trace control the firing of transitions. For every event in the trace it is checked, if a transition with the corresponding event assigned exists in the model and therefor may fire. When a transition did fire the set of transitions being able to fire next are computed. Priority classes among the transitions and inhibitive edges must be noticed when computing the transitions being able to fire next. The validation algorithm described requires the same model restrictions as mentioned for graph models to work correctly, i.e. different branches may not begin with the same event and loops may not begin with the same event as the first possible event after the loop. In addition, the algorithm implies that every transition in the Petri net model is really assigned to an event, transitions representing no event are prohibited.

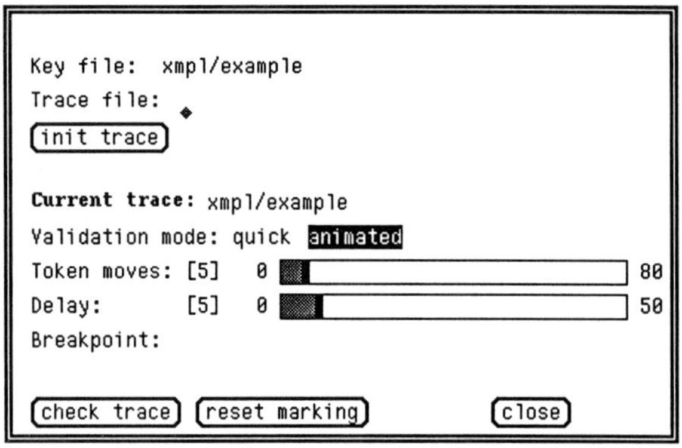

Key file: xmpl/example
Trace file:
init trace

Current trace: xmpl/example
Validation mode: quick animated
Token moves: [5] 0 80
Delay: [5] 0 50
Breakpoint:

check trace reset marking close

Figure 10: Control of validation

In fig. 10 the validation control interface can be seen. By pressing the *init trace*–button the names of the trace file and of the key file are prompted. After trace initialization the event trace chosen for validation is indicated in the control interface. The validation is started by pressing the *check trace*–button. To put the Petri net into a well–defined state, i.e. to guarantee the correct number of tokens on each place of the Petri net, the *reset marking*–button is needed. As already described for graph models the validation can be carried out in two modes, *quick* or *animated.* The quick validation runs without any display during validation is in progress until end of trace is reached or an error is found.

Using the animated validation, the processing of the trace is displayed graphically in the model. When a transition is fired, the tokens moving along the edges are displayed and the transition flashes. Using the slider *Token moves* it can be adjusted how much time it should take to move tokens in the net from one point (place or transition) to another. The speed of the validation can additionally be controlled by the slider *Delay* which gives the time in milliseconds in which the tokens arriving in a place or transition remain unmoved. Both sliders can be changed during the validation progress. These features are used to skip portions of the event trace by quickly passing over them and to concentrate just on the parts of interest. For both validation modes, the display of the validation result is identical. Furthermore the validation can be stopped manually with the *break/continue*–button which appears in the validation control window (see fig. 10) when validation is started or when reaching a user–defined *breakpoint.*

The analysis of errors in Petri nets is more complicated compared to graph models because of the possibly unlimited loops in Petri nets. With graph models, the processing state of a node could be classified as unprocessed or processed. This is not possible for transitions in a Petri net, and so error localization is hard if there is more than one transition as candidate for an erroneous event. Error analysis in graph models is based on the presence of some well–defined structures like branches and loops in the model, these structures cannot be localized in general in Petri nets. This is the reason why a further error classification is not carried out for Petri nets. An analysis of errors is possible using the graphical display of the net's state after the error occurred. The reached net marking is displayed, transitions which are able to fire at the moment the error occurred are displayed inverted, and the error transition is displayed flashing. Using this display, it is recognizable how far the program was executed on every processor or in every process, how a correct execution would have continued, and where the error occurred. Besides the graphical display, the erroneous event and the position in the program, i.e. line number and source file name, are displayed in a text window. For each transition which already fired during validation, the event parameters 'line number' and 'file name' can be viewed, allowing to trace the program's flow in the source code. In addition, the number of fires for every transition is given during and after trace validation. This allows to examine in the model how often a loop was run through or which branch was executed. These features together with the graphical display of the validation process are a great help in debugging parallel and distributed programs.

5. Conclusion and Prospect

The starting points of our investigations are a monitoring model representing the internal behavior of the program under investigation and a monitored event trace. In order to be sure that the real behavior of a parallel program as monitored by the event trace corresponds to the ideal behavior represented by the monitoring model validation is necessary. The integration of monitoring and modeling enables us to perform the validation in a model–driven and automatic way: the monitored event trace is mapped onto the monitoring model for checking the temporal order of the events in the event trace against the modeled behavior in the monitoring model which serves thereby as a reference. The main prerequisite of this validation method is a necessary bijective function between the set of events used to describe the programs behavior and the set of events instrumented. This is guaranteed by the automatic model–driven instrumentation.

As the model–type–independent approach of validation is inefficient we exemplarily choose graph models and Petri nets to prove the realization and the profit of the automatic model–driven validation concept for the development of parallel and distributed programs. The tools PEPP and GreatSPN are extended with a validation algorithm tied to the modeling tool. In model–driven monitoring, they may be applied to debug parallel and distributed programs and to guarantee the correctness of an event trace relative to the underlying monitoring model. Thus, we are able to trust the results of the subsequent evaluation of the event trace. Especially when using for debugging purposes the interactive and graphical display of the validation progress offered by the extended tools are a great help to the user for recognizing errors which may remain unnoticed.

Furthermore, in order to improve error analysis we will try to combine the knowledge about the dynamic program behavior with methods of static program analysis. It is desirable to continue the validation progress after a single error was found and to define error recovery points as known from compiler techniques to find several errors in a single validation run. Last but not least the implemented syntactic–oriented validation concept should be extended to consider semantic aspects, too. One can imagine to specify a runtime distribution of an activity and check during the validation whether the activity fulfills the time specifications or not.

References

[Bat86] P. Bates. *Debugging Programs in a Distributed System Environment.* PhD thesis, University of Massachusetts, February 1986.

[BDV86] F. Baiardi, N. DeFranco, and G. Vaglini. Development of a Debugger for a Concurrent Language. *IEEE Transactions on Software Engineering*, SE-12(4):547–553, April 1986.

[BM86] H. Burkhart and R. Millen. Performance Measurement Tools in a Multiprocessor Environment. Technical Report 86/10, ETH Zürich, Institut für Elektronik, November 1986.

[Chi91] G. Chiola. GreatSPN 1.5 Software Architecture. In G. Balbo, editor, *Proceedings of the 5th International Conference on Modelling Techniques and Tools for Computer Performance Evaluation*, pages 117–132. Elsevier Science Publisher B.V., 1991.

[DHK+92] P. Dauphin, R. Hofmann, R. Klar, B. Mohr, A. Quick, M. Siegle, and F. Sötz. ZM4/SIMPLE: a General Approach to Performance–Measurement and –Evaluation of Distributed Systems. In T.L. Casavant and M. Singhal, editors, *Advances in Distributed Computing: Concepts and Design.* IEEE Computer Society Press, 1992.

[DKM+92] P. Dauphin, M. Kienow, V. Mertsiotakis, A. Quick, and F. Sötz. PEPP: Performance Evaluation of Parallel Programs — User's Guide – Version 3.0. Technical Report 5/92, Universität Erlangen–Nürnberg, IMMD VII, April 1992.

[Fer78] D. Ferrari. *Computer systems performance evaluation.* Prentice Hall, Englewood Cliffs, 1978.

[HL85] D. Helmbold and D. Luckham. Debugging Ada Tasking Programs. *IEEE Software*, 2(2):47–57, 1985.

[HU69] J.E. Hopcroft and J.D. Ullman. *Formal Languages and Their Relation to Automata.* Addison–Wesley, 1969.

[Kob81] H. Kobayashi. *Modeling and Analysis – An Introduction to System Performance Evaluation Methodology.* Addison–Wesley, reprinted and corrected edition, October 1981.

[Kön91] R. König. *Graphs and free partially commutative monoids*, pages 319–346. Theoretical Computer Science. Elsevier Science Publishers B.V., North–Holland, 1991.

[KQS92] R. Klar, A. Quick, and F. Sötz. Tools for a Model–driven Instrumentation for Monitoring. In G. Balbo, editor, *Proceedings of the 5th International Conference on Modelling Techniques and Tools for Computer Performance Evaluation*, pages 165–180. Elsevier Science Publisher B.V., 1992.

[Maz86] A. Mazurkiewicz. Trace Theory. In G. Goos and J. Hartmanis, editors, *Petri Nets: Applications and Relationships to Other Models of Concurrency. Advances in Petri Nets 1986: Part II. Proc. of an Advanced Course*, pages 279–324. Springer, LNCS 255, 1986.

[MH89] C.E. McDowell and D.P. Helmbold. Debugging Concurrent Programs. *ACM Computing Surveys*, 21(4):593–622, December 1989.

[Moh91] B. Mohr. SIMPLE: a Performance Evaluation Tool Environment for Parallel and Distributed Systems. In A. Bode, editor, *Distributed Memory Computing, 2nd European Conference, EDMCC2*, pages 80–89, Munich, Germany, April 1991. Springer, Berlin, LNCS 487.

[Moh92] B. Mohr. SIMPLE — User's Guide Version 5.3. Part A: TDL reference guide, part B: POET reference manual, part C: tools reference manual, part D: FDL / VARUS reference guide. Technical Report 3/92, Universität Erlangen–Nürnberg, IMMD VII, 1992.

[Nut75] G.J. Nutt. Tutorial: Computer System Monitors. *IEEE Computer*, pages 51–61, 1975.

[Sal73] A. Salomaa. *Formal Languages*. ACM Academic Press, New York, 1973.

[ST87] R. Sahner and K. Trivedi. Performance Analysis and Reliability Analysis Using Directed Acyclic Graphs. *IEEE Transactions on Software Engineering*, SE-13(10), October 1987.

PROGRAMMING ENVIRONMENTS FOR PARALLEL COMPUTING
N. Topham, R. Ibbett and T. Bemmerl (Editors)
Elsevier Science Publishers B.V. (North-Holland)

© 1992 IFIP. All rights reserved.

The Design of the General Parallel Monitoring System

M. van Riek [1] [2] and B. Tourancheau [3] [4]
Laboratoire de l'Informatique du Paralléllisme-IMAG-CNRS,
ENS-Lyon, 69364 Lyon cedex 07, France

Abstract
The GPMS project aims to define the specification of an open, scalable, extensible monitoring system. The specifications are presented and an implementation of them is described.

Keywords Codes: D.2.6; D.1.3; D.2.2
Keywords: Software, Programming Environments; Concurrent Programming; Tools and Techniques

Introduction

Programs for parallel MIMD distributed memory multicomputers are difficult to write, understand, evaluate and debug and the parallel algorithm design is much more complex than the sequential one. The motivation behind the monitoring of parallel programs is to improve parallel program development, understanding and performances after a few runs. As these improvements depends on the interaction of the architecture and the algorithm such monitoring tools are essential for today's programmer environment.

One of the aims of the GPMS project is to provide the specifications for a General purpose Parallel Monitoring System. This monitoring system should fulfill the needs of even the most demanding user and at the same time be useful on a wide variety of different machines.

To ensure the generality of GPMS, its specification will be solely define on the needs of the user and some models of parallel computing. Particularities of specific parallel systems will only be taken into account in the implementation phase. The GPMS specifications were used to implement a monitoring systems on an ARCHIPEL Volvox IS860 machine, running the Trollius OS.

In this paper, we will present the design of GPMS and discuss the decisions and considerations that lead to it. We will start by introducing some necessary models. After that we will present the specifications and architecture of GPMS. All along in our discussion we will try to show the generality of our approach. At the end we will describe the implementation that has been done at the LIP.

---

[1]On leave from Delft University of Technology, The Netherlands
[2]This work was partially funded by ARCHIPEL S.A.
[3]This work was partially funded by ARCHIPEL S.A.
[4]This work was supported by the research program C3 of CNRS

1. Defining the required models and concepts

To discuss any of the issues involved in the specification of GPMS, we will need to define a parallel system, a parallel program and parallel monitor model [22].

1.1. Machine model

PMS has been designed for message passing MIMD type parallel machines. Each node in the machine possesses a processor, local resources and a clock. An example of such a local resource is memory.

Every nodes can communicate with one other through a channel of the communication network of the machine. A channel can either be physical or virtual assuming the OS is able to route messages. These communications can either be synchronous or asynchronous. We consider the communications to be fault-free. Synchronizations in the system take places by exchanging messages and no special synchronization mechanism is part of the machine. Multiprocessing is allowed on the nodes, but no assumptions are made about the behavior of the scheduler.

1.2. Defining a programming model

The programming model we have adopted for the design of GPMS, is based upon Communicating Sequential Processes (C.S.P.) [11].

An executing parallel program can thus be seen as a set of sequential processes, that in an alternating way compute locally and interact with each other through communication channels.

The global state of a parallel program P is defined as the state of the communication network and the sum of all individual process states.

1.3. Introducing the main concepts of monitoring

Monitoring is the activity that consists of gathering runtime information about executing programs. This information is used to gain a better insight in the behavior and the performance of the monitored programs.

In the specification of a general purpose monitor such as GPMS, two fundamental questions will have to be answered:

- What types of behavior are fundamental for the understanding of the parallel program?

  The three commonly encountered orientations in monitoring tools are:

  - debugging oriented monitors [3] [4] [15] [16] [19]

  - performance oriented monitors [4] [10] [16] [17]

  - behavioral visualization oriented monitor [1] [12] [19]

- What information should be gathered to describe meaningfully the above types of behavior?

  Moreover, it not sufficient to derive what information describes some type of behavior, at least as important is the availability of the required information or its approximation.

Globally speaking the activity of monitoring programs can be divided into three relatively independent activities following the "3-phased approach to monitoring" [22]:

- Generating the runtime information. This information is stored in trace-records.
- Storing and transporting the information. Usually the information is not used at the same place and time as where and when it is generated.
- Using the information. Analyzing the information to increase its understanding constitutes the last phase of the monitoring activity.

The "event-action paradigm" is one of the most commonly encountered approaches to the generation of runtime information [22].

An event is defined as an action without duration that takes place at a specific point in time and changes the state of a process. The execution of a distributed program is thus viewed as a set of event-sequences.

An execution program is observed to detect occurrences of specific events. When such an event is detected, the action that corresponds is executed. In monitoring system that generate event-records, the "action" consists of the generation of an event-record.

1.4. A classification of the different approaches to monitoring

Following [22] there are 3 different kind of monitoring:

- Software monitors are entirely implemented in software. Therefore they are the most flexible and portable type of monitor, but they also induce the most overhead on the monitored system.
- Hardware monitors consist of completely independent monitoring systems that collect information from the electrical signals of the computing system. They require a considerable amount of additional hardware, but have the advantage to be non-intrusive.
- Hybrid monitors try to combine the best of both worlds by being more flexible than hardware monitors and less intrusive than software monitors.

2. The GPMS specifications

The aim of GPMS is to provide a concise definition of the functionality of a general purpose monitor independently of the underlying computing system. GPMS is an event-driven monitor because the list of events defines what is monitored and what is not, so it is easy to add new events. For portability reasons, GPMS is based on the "3-phased approach to monitoring". Their are a number of implications of choosing this approach: the flow of information is unidirectional and no direct interactions with the executing program are allowed but modifying the behavior of the monitoring system during the execution is possible on the other hand.

The event-record occurrence detection , generation , storage , transportation , processing can be implemented in many different ways in GPMS. Within the same architecture, we can realize and combine different types of monitoring by using different implementations of the basic functions [22]: pseudo 'real-time' monitoring environment [7] where the event-record transportation will have to be immediate, 'post-mortem' environment with 'store-and-unload-afterwards' transportation strategy, distributed processing and centralized analysis can thus be combined into one monitoring system.

The information generated by GPMS is contained in trace-records for simplicity. They will describe the nature of the event that took place but no specific traceformat is specified in GPMS, this is considered an implementation issue to preserve openess and portability.

2.1. The event related information semantics

Some attributes that uniquely identify an event occurrence, are common to all event:

The event-type uniquely define the type of the event that occurred.

The time attribute often referred to as "timestamp", defines the moment of occurrence of an event. The timestamp is used to establish causality relationships between event occurrences [13]. All timestamps should be related to the same clock, if anything valid is to be said about time-relationships between different events. For event occurrences that take place on the same node, this is not a problem since the local clock is used. On the other hand, for event occurrences that take place at different nodes a global clock will have to be simulated [8].

The location attribute defines uniquely where an event took place in a computing system (node, task, process, ...).

2.2. The control-flow related information

The controlflow related information provides the user with the possibility to monitor the execution of any predefined instruction. The user needs to specify to which instructions the monitoring should apply to control the overhead. The power of the monitoring system is not affected by this approach to controlflow monitoring, since the user still has the possibility to monitor any instruction.

2.3. The data-flow related information

The dataflow related information often reveals a powerful aid in the detection of errors (variables that exceed value boundaries, values of communication buffers, ...). GPMS provides dataflow monitoring by offering the possibility to observe the state of predefined data objects. The power of GPMS is not affected by our approach to dataflow monitoring, since the user has the possibility to monitor any dataflow event

2.4. The communications related information

The communication related information are often the cause of errors and performance bottlenecks. Providing the user with information about communications is therefore of crucial importance in monitoring.

Commonly two different types of communication are encountered in message-passing programs: synchronous communications take place according to rendez-vous and block the participating processes and asynchronous communications are always directly executed and cannot block a process.

Obviously, there is some overhead time in communications due to the operating system. In our model of communication, the total time spent in a communication can thus be decomposed in three fundamental periods: the blocked time, i.e. the time the process remains blocked waiting for a rendez-vous to be established the transfer time, i.e. the time used to actually transfer the data the overhead time, that represents the sum of the different overhead that occur during a communication.

The total time defines the duration of a communication and is the sum of all the three preceding durations.

Macro-communications are communications in which more than two processes participate. Examples are one-to-many and many-to-one communications. Macro-communications will be represented by their individual components because GPMS is independent of the type of macro-communications available on a parallel system.

2.5. The process-scheduling related information

Multiprocessing is in our view important to provide scalable solutions for future massively parallel machines [21], but it considerably increases the complexity of communications monitoring. The importance of multiprocessing comes from the fact that it allows the easy mapping of large applications on small machines by virtualizing the notion of a processor. But a communicating process might get suspended in the middle of a data transfer to be resumed later on and a process in communication might be descheduled for the time that it is blocked. Thus, the notion of duration of an activity becomes ambiguous and the notion of causality relationship on a processor is modified.

Few existing parallel monitoring systems offer the possibility to monitor the scheduling of processes. But knowing precisely the state of each process as a function of time can be used for a number of purposes:

- the precise busy/idle time on a node can be computed;
- in process oriented operating systems, the overhead time of the system can be accurately estimated;
- a precise characterization of communications can be obtained.

Monitoring process-scheduling provides some unique possibilities and also generates enormous amounts of runtime information . Grouping processes in different process classes based on their process-id will allow the user to considerably reduce the amount of generate event-records. For example, all the system processes could be grouped into one system process class and only the scheduling or descheduling of this class will be monitored.

2.6. The monitoring related information

Monitoring related information describes the behavior of the monitoring system. It distinguishes itself from the other types of information because it is not directly related to the behavior of the executing program. GPMS generates records that contain global characteristics of the monitoring system such as the number of monitored nodes and process, the total number of processes on the nodes, the total duration of the execution, monitoring off/on, statistics....

3. The design and implementation of GPMS under the Trollius OS on the ARCHIPEL Volvox machine

We develop this monitoring environment for the Trollius parallel operating system [6] to test the GPMS specifications. Trollius is available on wide variety of parallel Transputer based machines, but no monitoring features were provided. Our development effort resulted in two relatively independent parts: One implements the GPMS specifications as a part of Trollius [5] and we have adapted the ParaGraph [10] visualization tool to follow the capabilities of GPMS that are allowed by the Volvox machine [2]. Our principal requirements during the design were:

- A development cycle based on rapid prototyping : Our phased development allowed the rapid construction of a working prototype, that provides the main functionality.
- Openness and extensibility: Openness guarantees the possibility to integrate new concepts, standards and tools from other environments. Extensibility ensures that the tool can be adapted to the requirements of the individual user by allowing the integration of new features and the modification of existing ones.
- Scalable power : Offering scalable power will allow the user to tune the power and thus the induced overhead of the monitoring environment to his needs.

3.1. The TMS architecture

We have adopted a hierarchical layered architecture. The monitor layer ensures event-record generation, storage and transportation and runs on the target-machine. This layer which is operating system-dependent forms the least portable part of our monitoring environment.

The tool layer has a modular structure in which the different processing functions are implemented as separate independent tools. The interface between the monitor and the tool layer is formed by the TMS traceformat, that defines how the information-entities that are exchanged between the two layers are encoded and the protocol on how the information is exchanged. This interface is contain in the TRADE tool.

3.2. Defining the TMS traceformat

This format defines both the syntax and the semantics of the exchanged event-records. The semantics of the traceformat have been based on the GPMS specifications. Two different ways to encode the event-records have been used in TMS. The internal format is used within the monitor layer , whereas the external format is used by the tool layer.

An event-record consists of a sequence of integers. Each integer corresponds to one attribute and the meaning of an attribute is defined "by position", i.e. the position of the attribute in the sequence defines the meaning of the attribute. In the external traceformat, the event-records are encoded in ascii-characters with the advantage that this format is easy to manipulate, provides a good portability accross different systems and is human-readable. In the internal binary format, the event-records are encoded as sequences of integers with the advantage that no ascii conversions are needed to store the runtime information resulting in less overhead.

Most of the events that have been defined in GPMS are implemented in TMS But a few attributes were not available in Trollius and were omitted in our implementation. The overhead of the operating system cannot actually be measured because of the hardware

[5]The authors thanks G. Burns of Trollius Inc. at Ohio Supercomputer Center for its helpful collaboration while visiting LIP.

scheduler utilization in Trollius. The overhead-time of communication is deduced from the sum of the other parameters. This assumption is only valid when the scheduling is not taken into account, but holds for most situations in which monitoring is used.

3.3. Designing the monitor layer

Our aim was to provide a small set of minimum functionalities to built a functional monitoring system. TMS has to be designed in such a way, that new functionalities can be integrated in this minimum set, without the need for a major redesign of the monitoring system. Especially, the integration of different transportation and storage strategies and distributed processing.

For example, many different transportation strategies can be devised and the optimal strategy will depend of the needs of the user. TMS allows for the integration of different transportation strategies in a transparent manner: the information is either considered as a sequence of separate event-records which describe event-occurrences, or as blocks of runtime information of a certain size (in the last case, no assumptions on the contents of these blocks are made).

The key element of our client-server architecture is a trace-server, which provides upon request from clients, most of the basic services required in a monitoring system. Different clients of the server can be distinguished:

- The reception of runtime information from trace-generating clients.
- The storage of runtime information in local buffers.
- The unloading of the runtime information in a file upon request of a trace-using client.
- The signaling of the trace-generating clients.

Controlling clients can request the server to signal a trace-generating client. These signals can be used to modify the behavior of the monitoring system on the fly.

Many other services can be easily added to the trace-server and allowing thus the extension of the functionality of TMS.

In TMS, the trace-generating client is formed by the monitored user-processes. This is due to the use of software monitoring techniques, which imply the detection of event-occurrences within the monitored process.

To unload the generated event-records, the client requests the trace-server the transportation of a block of runtime data. The trace-generating client can be signaled by the server, so that a control process can modify the behavior of a trace-generating client.

The overhead induced by the monitoring is very low (a few percent), but the time spent for the flush of the collected data may be important depending on their size.

3.4. The TRAceDEcoder tool

TRADE interfaces the monitor and the tool layer. Currently the following functions are performed by TRADE:

- Preprocessing of the runtime information.
- Conversion of the runtime information into a verbose human-readable format.
- Conversion of the runtime information into the PICL trace format.
- Converting the internal to the external traceformat.
- Sorting of the runtime information according to their timestamp.
- Adjusting the timestamps of the event-records according to the moment of the beginning of the monitoring is more convenient for the analysis of the runtime information.

- Remapping the node and process id's.

In the current heterogeneous parallel systems however, some remapping of node and process id's can be necessary to analyze the generated traces. To remap the node id's TRADE uses the .MAP file where the user specifies the process-keys of the processes that need to be remapped together with their new node and process id's.

3.5. Designing the Trollius Visualization System

Graphical visualization is a standard technique for facilitating human comprehension of complex phenomena and large volumes of data [14] [20] [10]. The behavior of parallel programs on advanced computer architectures is often extremely complex, and hardware or software performance monitoring of such programs can generate vast quantities of data. It seems thus natural to use visualization techniques to gain insight into the behavior of parallel programs so that their performance can be understood and improved.

ParaGraph [10] is a graphical display system for visualizing the behavior and performance of parallel programs on message-passing multiprocessor hypercube architectures. The visual animation is based on the runtime information generated during the program execution. The resulting information is replayed pictorially to provide a dynamic depiction of the behavior of the parallel program, as well as graphical summaries of its overall performance. The runtime information that is displayed by ParaGraph is generated by the PICL subroutine library [9]. PICL is a Portable Instrumented Communication Library that runs on a variety of message-passing parallel architectures.

ParaGraph currently provides 25 different displays. Some of these displays change dynamically as events occur, with execution time in the original run represented by a simulation time in the replay. All displays of both types are updated simultaneously and synchronized with each other.

Most of the displays fall into one of the following three basic categories:

- Processor utilization related displays are helpful in determining the effectiveness with which the processors are used and how evenly computational work is distributed across the processors.

- Communication related displays are helpful in determining the frequency, volume and overall pattern of communication, and whether there is congestion in the message queues.

- Task related displays provide its users with a mean to observe the control flow in a program.

There are a number of inherent limitations in ParaGraph, that cause its adaptation to our needs:

- The only support for hypercube machines.
- Multiprocessing is not allowed.
- The notion of process id is not supported in PICL nor ParaGraph.
- No support for heterogeneous systems.
- The only support of the PICL traceformat.

ParaGraph was modified in such a way, that a variable number of nodes can be displayed. To solve the incompatability of the monitoring of multiple processes per node, we have chosen the flexible solution of remapping through the intermediary of TRADE The user can:

- Map each process on a given node onto one virtual process

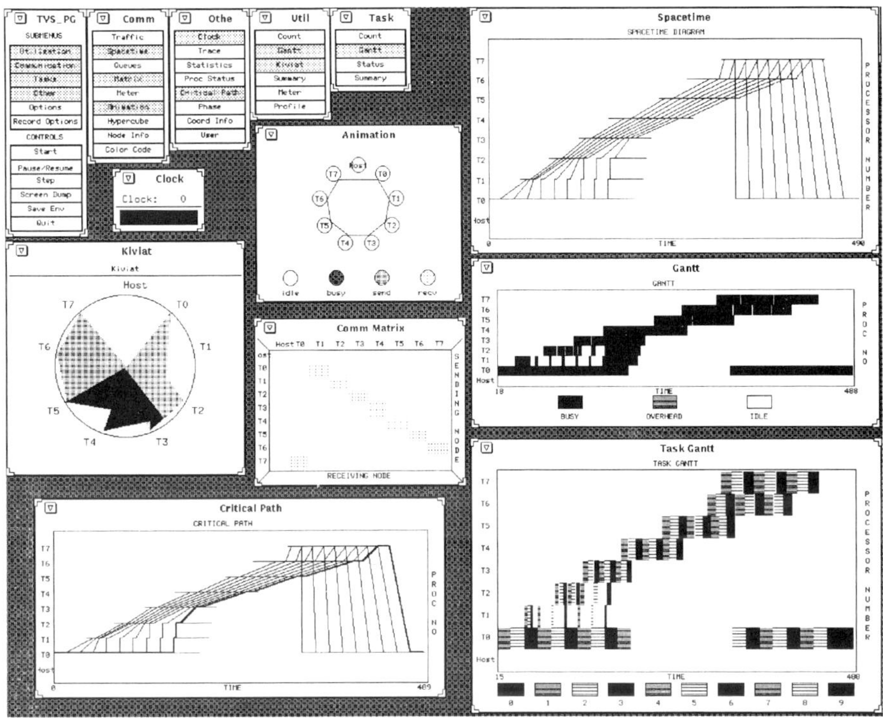

Figure 1. The GPMS modified version of ParaGraph.

- Map each process on a virtual processor
- Deal with the possibility of one of more distinct separate hosts

An example of the use of the GPMS system with a pipeline demonstration program is shown on figure 1.

3.6. Do we meet our requirements?

The portability of the TMS/TVS system is ensured by its layered architecture, the GPMS specifications and the use of software monitoring techniques.

The layered and modular architecture of TMS allowed a phased development cycle. Once the monitor interface has been defined, the monitor and the tool layer can be developed independently. The tool layer itself can also be developed in separated phases, since the different tools form independent modules.

By extending the protocol of the monitor layer, new types of monitoring can be integrated in the monitoring environment.

The monitor interface and the modularity of the tool layer guarantee both the openness and the extensibility of TMS. The integration of an adapted version of ParaGraph in the tool layer clearly demonstrates it.

The modularity of the tool layer and the flexibility of the monitoring features provided, allow the user to entirely scale the impact of TMS.

Conclusion

The parallel monitoring field is still a very young field but the research interests are rapidly growing. The hardware vendors are becoming aware that the users want a comfortable programming environment and the massively parallel architectures open grand challenges for researchers. With the GPMS specification, we hope that we capture most of the functionalities of the today's user demand and we demonstrate that such a system will be able to evolve with the future results. We have prove that our general specifications can lead to a very rapid implementation of a monitoring system on a given machine. The openness of our software is encouraging for the future research and extension of the actual tools. Our futur research is oriented toward the massive parallel challenge which imply distributed processing and new representations of the very important amount of runtime information generated.

References

1 F. Abstreiter Visualizing and Analyzing the Runtime Behavior of Parallel Programs Proceedings CONPAR 1990 - VAPP IV, Sep 1990, Springer-Verlag, pp.828-839

2 ARCHIPEL S.A. Volvox IS860 documentation 1991, ARCHIPEL, PAE du Levray, 74000 Annecy-France

3 P. Bates Distributed Debugging Tools for Heterogeneous Distributed Systems Proceedings of the 8th International Conference on Distributed Computing Systems, 1988, IEEE, pp.308-316

4 T. Bemmerl, R. Lindhof, T. Treml The Distributed Monitor System of TOPSYS Proceedings CONPAR 1990 - VAPP IV, Sep 1990, Springer-Verlag, pp.756-765

5 T. Bemmerl, A. Bode An Integrated Environment for Programming Distributed Memory Multiprocessors Proceedings of the 2nd European Distributed Memory Computing Conference, Apr 1991, pp.131-142

6 G. Burns, R. Daoud Trollius operating system 3th Conference on hypercube concurrent computers and application, ACM, 1988, pp 374-376

7 A. Couch, D. Krumme, Monitoring parallel executions in real time, proceedings of the 5th Distributed Memory Computing Conference, 1990, IEEE, pp 1187-1196.

8 A. Duda, G. Harrus, Y. Haddad, G. Bernard Estimating global time in distributed systems Proceedings 7th Int. Conf. on Distributed Computing Systems, pp 299-306, Berlin, sept-1987.

9 G.A. Geist, M.T. Heath, B.W. Peyton, P.H. Worley PICL, A Portable Instrumented Communication Library ORNL/ TM-11130, Jul 1990, Oak Ridge National Laboratory, TN

10 M. T. Heath, J. A. Etheridge Visualizing the Performance of Parallel Programs Software, Sep 1991, IEEE, pp.29-39

11 C. A. R. Hoare Communicating Sequential Processes Prentice-Hall 1985

12 J. Joyce, G. Lomow, K. Slind, B. Unger Monitoring Distributed Systems Transactions Computing Systems, May 1987, ACM, pp.121-150

13 L. Lamport Time, Clocks and the Ordering of Events in a Distributed System Communications, Jul 1978, ACM, pp.558-565

14 TJ. Leblanc, JM. Mellor-Crummey, RJ. Fowler, Analysing parallel program executions using multiple views Journal of parallel and distributed computing, june 1990, Academic Press, pp 203-217

15 T. Lehr, Z. Segall, D.F. Vrsalovic, E. Caplan, A.L. Chung, C.E. Fineman Visualizing Performance Debugging Computer, Oct 1989, IEEE, pp.38-51

16 J.E. Lumpp, T.L. Casavant, H.J. Siegel, D.C. Marinescu Specification and Identification of Events for Debugging and Performance Monitoring of Distributed Multiprocessor Systems Proceedings of the 10th International Conference on Distributed Computing Systems, 1990, IEEE, pp.476-483

17 A.D. Malony, D.A. Reed, J.W. Arendt, D. Grabas, R.A. Aydt, B.K. Totty An Integrated Performance Data Collection Analysis and Visualization System Proceedings of the 4th Conference on Hypercube Concurrent Computers and Applications, 1989, pp.229-236

18 A.D. Malony, K. Nichols Standards in Performance Instrumentation and Visualization for Parallel Computer Systems: Working Group Summary Available in PostScipt as pub/BOF/LANL.ps via anonymous ftp from eagle.cnsf.cornell.edu

19 D.C. Marinescu, J.E. Lumpp, T.L. Casavant Models for Monitoring and Debugging Tools for Parallel and Distributed Software Journal of Parallel and Distributed Computing, Jun 1990, Academic Press, pp.171-184

20 D. Socha, ML. Bailey, D. Voyeur, Voyeur: Graphical views of parallel programs, proceedings SIGPLAN/SIGOPS Workshop on parallel and distributed debugging, may 1988, ACM, pp 206-215

21 JM Stone, A graphical representation of concurrent processes, Proceedings SIGPLAN/SIGOPS workshop on parallel and distributed debugging, May 1988, ACM, pp 206-215.arldk

22 M.G. van Riek, B. Tourancheau A General Approach to the Monitoring of Distributed Memory Machines Research Report 91-28, Sept 1991, L.I.P. / Ecole Normale Supérieure de Lyon, 69364 Lyon, France.

PROGRAMMING ENVIRONMENTS FOR PARALLEL COMPUTING
N. Topham, R. Ibbett and T. Bemmerl (Editors)
Elsevier Science Publishers B.V. (North-Holland)

© 1992 IFIP. All rights reserved.

Generic Visualisation and Performance Monitoring Tools for Message Passing Parallel Systems

Ian Glendinning, Stephen A. Hellberg, Piers A. Shallow [a]
Martin J. Gorrod[b]

[a]Department of Electronics and Computer Science, The University of Southampton, Southampton S09 5NH UK

[b]Goldman Sachs International Ltd., Peterborough Court, 133 Fleet Street, London UK

Abstract

With the increasing complexity of parallel programs there is a need for performance monitoring for both optimization and debugging. Many tools that perform such tasks are either specific to a machine or alternatively to a communication library or harness. Work carried out at Southampton within the GENESIS project, which forms part of the European ESPRIT initiative, has investigated generic performance monitoring tools for message passing parallel systems. This paper describes a visualisation tool that has been developed from the existing *ParaGraph* tool, and how the use of *trace filters* has enabled it to be used in conjunction with a number of different communication libraries running on a wide range of machines. The overheads incurred by performance monitoring are also briefly discussed.

1. Introduction

Parallel performance monitoring tools are needed in order to understand the behaviour and inner workings of programs, and help to identify possible trouble spots such as communications bottlenecks. They may be used to to evaluate and compare the performance of similar programs and variants of algorithms, and are also an aid to debugging [20].

Since the execution of parallel programs is often highly complex, monitoring a program's execution can produce a large volume of data. It has long been accepted that humans can manipulate complex information more efficiently in the form of pictorial images [16] and graphical techniques for visualisation of serial programs have been considerably studied [4, 20]. The visualisation of parallel programs is a major current area of research [11, 15, 17] and has been an important component in many programming environments.

Within the Esprit-2 GENESIS project we have developed a graphical visualisation tool based on ParaGraph [12], written at Oak Ridge National Laboratory, Tennessee. It is a post-execution tool for visualising the behaviour of parallel programs on message passing multiprocessor machines. Data recorded during program execution may subsequently be repeatedly viewed from many different perspectives in order to gain maximum insight into the execution of the program. The multiplicity of ways offered by ParaGraph to view the information is an advantage it has over many other tools. Multiple views have been emphasized in many reports [3], and a much larger base of perspectives is provided than with most packages [10].

ParaGraph was initially written for use with the PICL *Portable Instrumented Communication Library* [8, 9], which runs on a variety of message passing parallel architecture. PICL can optionally generate a *trace file* containing a record for each event of interest that occurs during the execution of a program. It is this trace file that forms the input to ParaGraph.

The combination of PICL and ParaGraph is already generic over a number of target systems, but we wish to go even further and remove the restriction that ParaGraph be used exclusively with PICL, making it generic over communication libraries as well. A number of other communication libraries for message passing systems are also instrumented to produce trace files, but there are at present no standards in this area and their formats differ. Nevertheless, if there is sufficient similarity in the kind of information recorded in the trace files, it is possible to write *trace filter* programs to convert from one to another, possibly with some restrictions. We have demonstrated this by implementing trace filter programs to convert traces generated by the PARMACS [18] and Express [7] libraries into the format recognised by ParaGraph.

2. ParaGraph

Performance visualisation can be thought of in terms of either a static or dynamic visualisation. A static visualisation summarizes the performance at a given time (snap shot) while a dynamic approach gives a re-enactment of the performance of the system. Both may display either the current or a cumulative view of the system. The dynamic approach captures a sense of motion and evolvement and, provided the simulation speed can be controlled, all the information may be viewed. The static approach allows the user more control over the data which is viewed (time may be altered from one value to another, either backwards or forwards), although the intuitive dynamic behaviour of the program is lost. ParaGraph, although based on a dynamic approach, tries to encompass most of the major advantages of a static visualisation as well.

2.1. Design Objectives

The principal design objectives of the original version of ParaGraph were:

- *Ease of Understanding*

  The aim has been to provide a simple and easy to comprehend visualisation of the information from the trace file. In order to achieve this it is important to make the display as intuitive as possible and aesthetically pleasing. Each display should not be over cluttered and the main aims of the display must be self evident. Often it will be necessary to provide many different perspectives of the same information, since no single view is likely to be able to convey all the information available. A standard colour system is used in all the diagrams to simplify comprehension of information.

- *Ease of Use*

One of the main aims must be to make anything the user may wish to do as easy as possible. The use of a graphical interface, based on X windows and a mouse achieve this.

- *Portability*

  There are two main ways in which our tool is portable. Firstly the graphical output is portable, requiring only the support of standard X windows and a C compiler. This is independent of any particular vendor or workstation. Output to grey scale and monochrome monitors is also supported, although it is most effective in colour, and this is automatically detected and the output modified accordingly. Secondly, the system is portable in the sense that it is capable of displaying the execution behaviour of a number of different parallel message passing machines available from different vendors with different communications harnesses. Portability reduces the user learning curve as the same front end interface can be used to monitor and analyse output from a large number of different hardware platforms and communications tools.

2.2. Modifications

Many modifications have been made to ParaGraph, including the removal of a number of bugs. The graphical interface has been enhanced by improving the resizing of windows and providing backing store, when available, to retain information when a window is obscured and reexposed. Changes in the accessing of X events and trace records, so that priority is given to any user interaction, has led to an improved user response time that permits pausing in the middle of scrolling trace records. Buffering has also been added to record multiple sends from a process before they are received and error detection in time stamping to detect receives before data is sent, due to incorrect clock alignment on processors [11]. Other additional features include a simple X window save and load to user-specified files, display of processor state in the Feynman diagram, display of processes waiting to send and receive in the Animation diagram and output of trace record histories (in a verbose form) by expanding the trace file window.

ParaGraph has also been modified from being biased towards a hypercube connectivity machine towards a more general purpose monitoring tool. This involved replacing the selection of a gray coding option with the ability to have any ordering and any number of processors (rather than just a power of two).

The most significant modification made to ParaGraph was the enhancement of its repertoire of recognised trace records to include blocking sends, which are not part of the PICL model of communication, while retaining the ability to recognise standard PICL format traces. This extension was found necessary in order to properly visualise traces produced by other libraries that include blocking sends in their communication model. The new type of event involved adding a “sending” processor state analagous the the existing “receiving” state, represented visually by different colours on the display.

2.3. The Trace File

In order to achieve hardware and software independence, the interface to generic tools such as ParaGraph must be abstracted away from the operations supported by particular systems (figure 1). It is important to define the semantics and syntax for the trace records, which can be thought of as declaring the operations permitted on an abstract machine (table 1). The trace file then just specifies a CSP trace of the abstract machine with the records of table 1 comprising its alphabet [14].

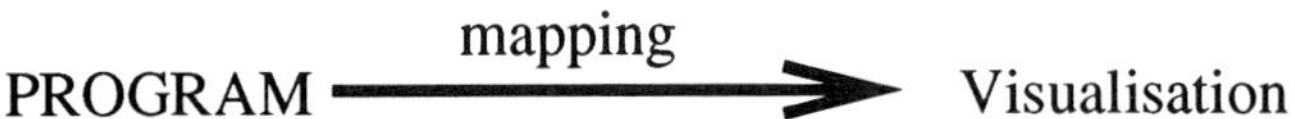

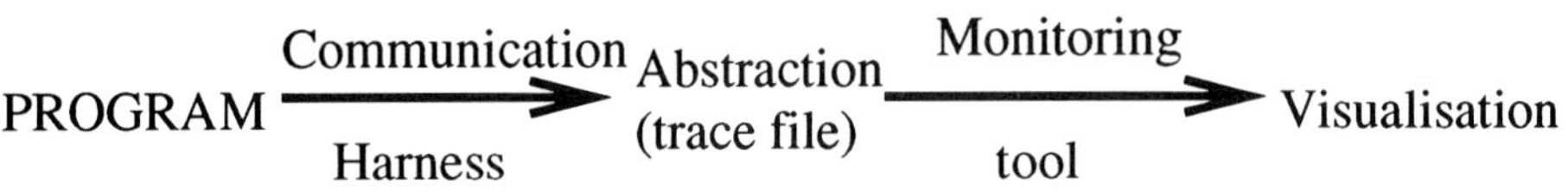

Figure 1. abstract model

All types of ParaGraph events have a time stamp indicating when they were generated. This is represented as two integers (seconds followed by microseconds since tracing was enabled) and an integer identifying the processor which generated it. The *type* indicates the message type and is user defined and *lth* is the message length in bytes. The record types defined form a superset of those recognized by ParaGraph with the addition of synchronous sends. PICL generates other record types but these are ignored by the current version of ParaGraph.

Trace Record						meaning
trace_start	clock 0 0	node #				start of tracing
message	clock # #	node #	"message"			user message.
trace_mark	clock # #	node #	type #			user defined event.
trace_exit	clock # #	node #				end of trace execution.
compstats	clock # #	node #	busy # #	idle # #		cumulative busy and idle times.
send	clock # #	node #	to #	type #	lth #	send a message
send_waking	clock # #	node #				message received after a send_blocking.
send_blocking	clock # #	node #	to #	type #	lth #	blocking send until message received.
receive	clock # #	node #	from #	type #	lth #	receive message in system buffer.
recv_waking	clock # #	node #	from #	type #	lth #	end of receive blocking.
recv_blocking	clock # #	node #	type #			receive executed but message not in buffer

Table 1
Trace file records

2.4. Displays

ParaGraph is menu driven with most user input provided by mouse operation, although some options require minimal keyboard input. The user selects how the trace file is to be visualised and preprocessing of the trace file determines all relevant parameters automatically (eg. timescale, number of processors) before 'playback' of the trace commences. However, these values may be overridden by the user. Many different display views are supported, and any combination of them may be viewed at the same time. Figure 2 illustrates a selection of displays:

- *Feynman*

  This is the most useful of the displays for getting an overall impression of the state of execution of the program. The thread of execution of each processor is represented by a horizontal line, drawn from left to right, which changes colour to indicate whether the processor is active, idle, or waiting for a send or receive to complete. In addition, message transfers are represented by diagonal lines from source to destination. The points where the communication lines meet the processor lines mark the send and receive times. This display shows particularly clearly if particular processors are idle because they are blocked waiting for a message to be sent or received. The sample trace depicted in figure 2 illustrates the point. After about 200 time units, the execution becomes sequentialized, as a single message is passed from one processor to the next, while the other processors wait. (The waiting is indicated by a colour change in the horizontal lines, which is more obvious on a colour display.)

- *Animation*

  Nodes are depicted as circles, with each node representing a communicating sequential process of the multiprocessor system. Communications between nodes are represented by lines and the status of each node is displayed by a colour which may be either busy, idle, sending or receiving. The line is drawn when there is a send and deleted when it is received. At the conclusion of the simulation all the lines of communication are displayed, indicating the logical communication links between the processors.

- *Message Lengths*

  Messages are represented by a coloured square in a grid whose rows and columns correspond to sending and receiving processors. The length in bytes of each message is indicated by the colour of this square which is related to an accompanying legend. Each square displays the current information, which is cleared once the data has been received. At the end of the simulation the display shows the cumulative communication volume for the entire run between pairs of processors. The colour indicating messages of a given size may be modified by the user via keyboard input in the appropriate window of the legend.

- *Kiviat*

  A geometric representation of individual processor utilization and overall load balance. Each processor is depicted as a spoke of a wheel. The fractional utilization of each processor portrays a point on the spoke, with the hub of the wheel representing zero (completely idle) and the edge of the spoke representing one (completely busy). Taken together all these points on the spoke determine the vertices of a polygon whose size and shape indicates the load balancing and utilization of the system. There is also a high water mark indicating the maximum utilization so far achieved.

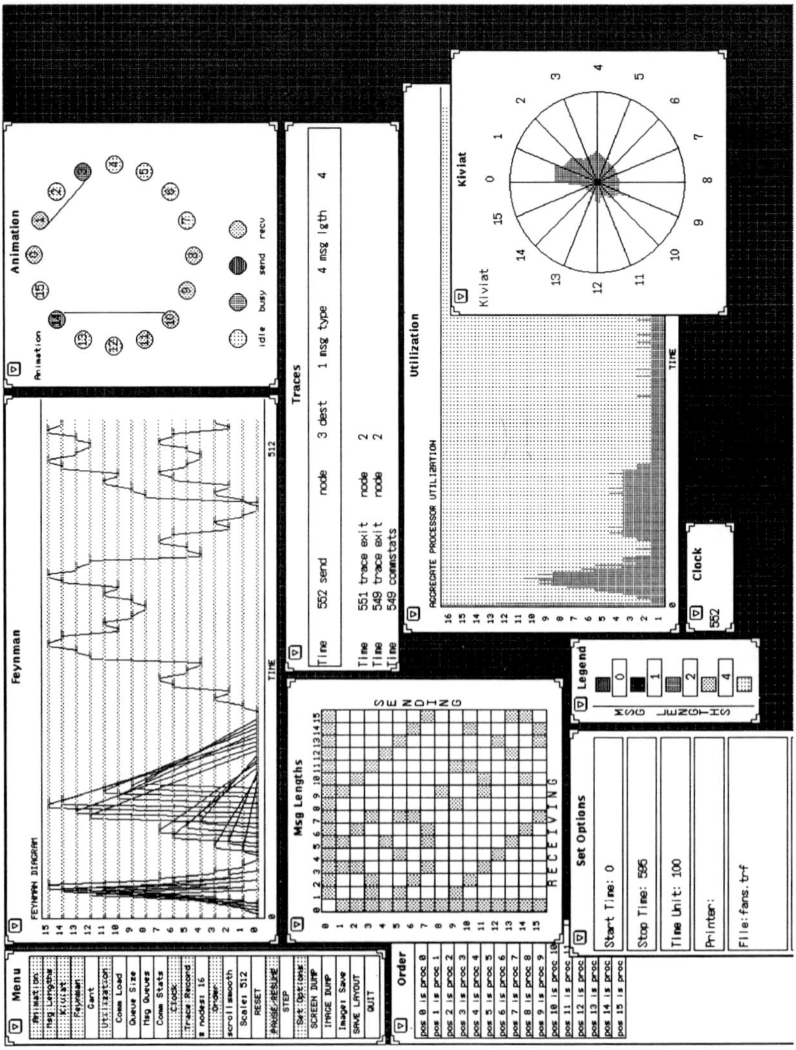

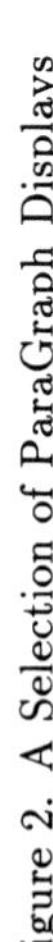

Figure 2. A Selection of ParaGraph Displays

- *Utilization*

  A scrolling display of the total number of processors that are busy as a function of time. The same information can be obtained from the Feynman diagram, by adding up the number of busy processors at any given time, but it is usefully summarised here.

- *Clock*

  Indicates current time in the simulation.

- *Trace Record*

  The current trace record being processed and optionally by expanding the window, past trace records.

- *Order*

  Enables the user to specify the ordering of processes in the displays, or to select a subset of the processes to display using keyboard input in the appropriate box. Automatic reordering ensures that a given process is not multiply displayed.

- *Set Options*

  Enables the user to modify, using keyboard input when the cursor is in the required window, the start, end, time step, printer for screen dump, trace file and image dump file name.

- *Menu*

  This is ParaGraph's main menu. Display windows may be selected or de-selected by toggling their corresponding buttons, and replay of the trace may be started, stopped or single-stepped. A number of display options may be adjusted, and screendumps may be taken.

3. Trace Filters

Many other packages generate trace file like output and it is possible in many cases to devise transformations that will convert it into the syntax described previously. A trivial example is that PICL can generate two formats of trace file that are semantically equivalent; verbose and compact, both ASCII. The verbose format is easier to comprehend, where each trace record is identified by a keyword and all numeric data preceded by a descriptive keyword. The compact format contains just an integer representing the keyword and the numerical values as before, with no descriptive keywords. More complex transformations need in general to combine many records from the input trace to generate each output record.

The PARMACS [18] and Express [7] packages, which are each implemented on a wide range of systems, were selected as test cases to investigate the feasibility of developing trace filters in practice. EXPRESS generates three files: a profile of program functions called, a profile of the communication functions called, and an event profile. The last profile file contains all the information required to allow it to be mapped into ParaGraph format. PARMACS does not generate all the information required, although enough is produced to generate some of the trace records previously described. Typically this provides enough information on the execution of the system to make monitoring useful.

Implementation of both filters proved to be easier than had been expected. In the case of Express it is was found that the implemenation of the filter took significantly less time to complete than that of an implementaition of PICL for the same target hardware (transputers), despite having to reverse-engineer the trace file format.

4. Systems Supported

The use of ParaGraph is currently supported with the following combinations of hardware and software. Except in the case of PICL and CSTools, the use of a trace filter is assumed. PICL does not require one, and the latest i860 version of CSTools has been instrumented to produce trace data in an enhanced PICL format, which can be displayed by Meiko's version of ParaGraph, called CSN_Graph. Although the trace format recognised by CSN_Graph is not identical to that of our version of ParaGraph, it is so similar that filtering would be trivial, and it is included here for completeness.

- PICL
  - Intel iPSC/2
  - Intel iPSC/860
  - nCUBE/3200
  - Cogent
- PARMACS
  - Cray Y-MP
  - Intel iPSC/2
  - Intel iPSC/860
  - nCUBE 2
  - SUPRENUM
  - Meiko (Transputer & i860 versions of CSTools)
- Express
  - Transputers (PC hosted)
- CSTools + CSN_Graph
  - Meiko i860

In addition to the above, an implementation of PICL on a transputer based system, using VCR [5] as the underlying message router, is currently under development at Southampton. Many other groups and companies are also working on either generating trace file output identical to that of PICL or at least similar. The Manchester Graphics Unit is currently working on an implementation of PICL on top of CSTools and investigating trace file generation from other harnesses [6]. Work has been done at Daresbury to generate trace file information from their FORTNET harness [2].

5. Performance Impact

To get an idea of the order of magnitude of the performance degradation caused by the addition of performance monitoring, some measurements were made for the PARMACS library with and without tracing enabled. The measurements were taken using the COMMS1 benchmark from the GENESIS distributed-memory benchmark suite [1] on the iPSC/860 machine at Daresbury. PARMACS itself incurs a 5% overhead in the start-up time compared to the native Intel primitives. The measurements showed a constant increase of 72 μs in the start-up time when the trace generation was switched on, corresponding to 47% and 11% of the total communication time (with tracing enabled), for message lengths of 1 and 1000 bytes respectively.

6. Future Work

One aspect of the user interface to ParaGraph which could be improved is the control of the scale and range of times displayed in the scrolling windows. Some degree of control over the speed of scrolling and the ability to move backwards in time would also be desirable.

There is no reason in principle why ParaGraph could not be used to visualise data in real time, provided the display workstation could keep up with the data rate. It would then no longer be necessary to store an entire trace file, saving disk space.

A limitation of the programming model supported by ParaGraph is that it assumes that there is only one process per processor. This assumption is becoming increasingly untrue of real machines and ought to be removed.

The most serious limitation of the current version however, is in the number of processors that can be effectively visualised. For massively parallel systems containing thousands of processors it will be necessary either to adapt the existing displays, to aggregate or select information, or to devise new ones based on new programming abstractions [19]. Such abstractions would also help reduce the volume of trace data, which is already a problem and would inevitably become worse for larger systems.

7. Conclusion

Tools such as Paragraph help to understand the behaviour of code and to locate possible performance bottlenecks, with only a moderate performance overhead. The use of traces and trace filters allows such tools to be largely independent of hardware platforms and communication libraries, although it would be desirable to standardize the models that trace files are based on as far as possible. For massively parallel systems, it is clear that many of the graphical representations will not scale well and the users ability to understand such volumes of information will soon degrade. Monitoring tools for such large scale parallel systems will require new ways of displaying the information at a higher level of abstraction.

1 C. Addison, V. Getov, A. Hey, R. Hockney, I. Wolton, *The GENESIS Distributed-Memory Benchmarks*, to be presented at the conference *'Parallel Processors - Benchmarking and Assessment'*, Teddington, March 1992

2 Robert Allen, Daresbury Laboratory, Private communication.

3 J. M. LeBlanc, J. M. Mellor-Crummey, R. J. Fowler, *"Analyzing parallel program execution using multiple views"*, Journal of Parallel and Distributed Computing, 9, pp 203-217, 1990

4 M. H. Brown and R. Sedgewick, *"Techniques for algorithm animation"*, IEEE Software, pp 28-39, January 1985

5 M. Debbage, M. Hill, D.A. Nicole, *Virtual Channel Router Version 2.0 User Guide*, Southampton University, October 1991

6 Robert Dickens, University of Manchester Computer Graphics Unit, Private communication.

7 *Express User's Guide, Version 3.0*, Parasoft Corporation, 2500, E.Foothill Blvd., Pasadena, CA 91107, USA

8 G. A. Geist, M. T. Heath, B. W. Peyton, P. H. Worley, *"PICL: A portable instrumented communication library, C reference manual"*, tech. rep., Oak Ridge National Laboratory. ORNL/TM-11130, 1990

9 G. A. Geist, M. T. Heath, B. W. Peyton, P. H. Worley, *"A Users' guide to PICL, A portable instrumented communication library"*, tech. rep., Oak Ridge National Laboratory. ORNL/TM-11616, 1991

10 I. Glendinning, M.J. Gorrod, S.A. Hellberg, P.A. Shallow, *"Tools for Parallel High Performance Systems – Comparative Evaluation"*, Southampton Novel Architecture Research Centre tech. rep. SNARC 92-01, January 1992

11 D. Haban, D. Wybranietz, *"A hybrid monitor for behaviour and performance analysis of distributed systems"*, IEEE Trans. on Software Eng., 16(2), pp 197-211, 1990

12 M.T. Heath, 1990. *"Visual Animation of Parallel Algorithms for Matrix Computations"*, Proc. of the fifth distributed memory computing conference, Charleston, South Carolina, U.S.A. Volume II, pp 1213-1222

13 M. T. Heath, J. A. Etheridge, *"Visualizing Performance of Parallel Programs"*, tech. rep., Oak Ridge National Laboratory. ORNL report TM-11813, 1991

14 C. A. R. Hoare, *"Communicating Sequential Processes"*, Prentice Hall, 1985

15 T. Lehr, Z. Segall, D. F. Vrsalovic, E. Caplan, A. L. Chung, C. E. Fineman, *"Visualizing Performance Debugging, IEEE Computer"*, pp 38-51, October 1989

16 B. Melamed, R. J. T. Morris, *"Visual Simulation: The performance analysis workstation"*, IEEE Computer, pp 87-94, August 1985

17 B. P. Miller, *"DPM: A measurement system for distributed programs"*, IEEE Trans. on Comp., 37 (2), pp 243-248, 1988

18 *PARMACS Performance Analysis Tools Documentation*, PALLAS GmbH, Hohe Str. 73, W-5300 Bonn 1, Germany

19 G. Roman, K. C. Cox, *"A declarative approach to visualizing concurrent computations"*, IEEE Computer, pp 25-36, October 1989

20 J. T. Stasko, *"Tango: A framework and system for algorithm animation"*, IEEE Computer, September, pp 27-39, September 1990

PROGRAMMING ENVIRONMENTS FOR PARALLEL COMPUTING
N. Topham, R. Ibbett and T. Bemmerl (Editors)
Elsevier Science Publishers B.V. (North-Holland)

© 1992 IFIP. All rights reserved.

Adapting the Portable Performance Measurement Tool PATOP to the Multi-Transputer Monitoring System DELTA-T

Thomas Bemmerl, Olav Hansen [a] and Wolfgang Obelöer, Harald Willeke [b]

[a] Institut für Informatik, TU München, Arcisstr. 21, 8000 München 2, Germany
[b] FG Datentechnik, Universität-GH Paderborn, Pohlweg 47-49, 4790 Paderborn, Germany

Abstract

Tools for performance analysis are important parts of programming environments for parallel computers. This article describes how PATOP (a tool of the TOPSYS-project) was used as the basis for the new evaluation program ΔVIEW, which works in a different environment (called DELTA-T). At first, the design and implementation of PATOP are presented. The next part covers the DELTA-T project, considering particularly the differences and similarities to PATOP´s design. Finally, an example measurement evaluated by both tools is shown.

Keyword Codes: C.4 ; D.1.3; D.2.6
Keywords: Performance of Systems; Concurrent Programming; Programming Environments

1. Introduction

In the last ten years computer science research has lead to commercially available, scaleable distributed memory computers. Although it has been shown that performance increases by numbers of magnitudes are feasible with parallel machines, they are not widely used in the production process. This is due to the necessity for explicit parallelization, which makes the programming more complicated than for sequential systems. Another reason is a lack of adequate programming tools for parallel architectures. Thus the Technische Universität München was motivated to develop a methodology within TOPSYS (TOols for Parallel SYStems [Bem90]) project for a more automatic way of using and programming scaleable (distributed memory) parallel architectures. In the project´s first step, interactive tools for specification, mapping, debugging, testing, performance analysis, tuning, and visualization (animation) were developed [FLM89]. A prototype of the TOPSYS environment on an iPSC/2 hypercube with 32 processors has been available since the end of 1989. The performance analysis tool of the TOPSYS environment, PATOP (Performance Analysis TOol for Parallel systems), offers a sophisticated user interface with a set of display windows to visualize performance data. The data is evaluated and visualized *on-line*, parallel to program execution.

The DELTA-T (Debugging and Evaluating of the Load of Transputer Applications and Topologies) project at the Universität-GH Paderborn had a similar motivation. Target systems are multi-transputer machines. As the first step, a software monitor was implemented that records traces of transputer programs. In contrast to PATOP DELTA-T supports detailed interactive *off-line* evalutaion and visualization. While developing the performance evaluation tool for DELTA-T (ΔVIEW), it seemed adequate to base it on existing developments made for the performance analysis tool PATOP, thus avoiding re-development.

2. Objectives in the Development of PATOP

2.1 Motivation

The programming of parallel systems is more complicated than that of sequential ones. On the one hand, writing *correct* programs is more difficult because parallelism in execution is an additional factor to be dealt with. Thus the first tool developed in the TOPSYS project was the debugger DETOP (DEbugging TOol for Parallel systems) with special features to regard parallelism in execution. On the other hand, an efficient use of parallel hardware resources is necessary to gain performance compared to a sequential machine´s version of the program. Therefore, PATOP´s necessity for performance analysing was immanent from the beginning [MiY87, Moh90].

2.2 Target System Independent Requirements

The debugger DETOP is a tool to support the search for functional bugs in a program, whereas PATOP supports the search for performance bugs [BHL90] by enabling the programmer to detect performance bugs and to track them down to their origin. Therefore, PATOP can be considered as a performance debugger. Further objectives in PATOP´s design were defined considering desirable attributes of debuggers:

- The instrumentation has to be transparent to the programmer.
- The tool must support an interface that allows the user to specify which information is required interactively and that retrieves this information as fast as possible.
- The way of presenting data should be adapted to the user´s view of the system.
- The displayed data should be reduced to the relevant information and be visualized in an easily comprehensible manner.

2.3 The Target System and Environment

Target systems in the TOPSYS project are Intel's iPSC/2 and iPSC/860 multicomputers and networks of SUN workstations.

Within the TOPSYS project, the multi-threaded programming library MMK was developed [BeL90]. It offers the programmer a virtual machine model consisting of tasks such as parallel execution units, mailboxes as means of communication, and semaphores to support inter-task synchronization. These components (the so-called objects) exist within a global name space to achieve direct access among one another. Mailboxes are implemented as FIFO buffers. Any task can send messages to and receive messages from them. All objects can be created and deleted dynamically.

The second step entails mapping the virtual machine to the real hardware. This is accomplished by a special description language. Most of the performance bugs are produced in this phase because the complex, critical timing of the parallel execution is often unpredictable.

All tools of the TOPSYS environment use the same graphical interface to the application. The performance data is supplied by a monitor [MCN90] linked to the application on each node. The monitor can influence and observe the application's execution. For these functions, hardware support is also available to reduce the distortion caused by the monitor itself. The funtionality, however, is unchanged.

Since the monitor only collects data, it offers a very low-level interface. Data transformation to a high-level language symbolic format, filtering out and evaluating the relevant information is done on the host. All tools are used interactively and are based on common graphical primitives to interface the user. Data is presented in direct response to the user's request.

3. Design and Implementation of PATOP

3.1 Design of PATOP

PATOP's goal is to aid programmers in the optimizing a parallel program's performance. It offers the user a methodology that allows him to do this in a top-down manner. The symptoms of performance bottlenecks are inefficiently used hardware resources. The performance values measured on the individual granularity levels show either the usage of a hardware component by a program part or the delay of program entities at hardware resources. There are multiple levels of granularity on which a user can see the performance of his parallel program (see figure 3.1):

- The coarsest level is the *system* level, which displays combined performance values for the complete system. For instance, the system idle time and the summed-up length of the ready queue for all nodes can be seen. Using these values, it can be determined whether hardware components are used inefficiently.
- On the next level, similar values are measured for individual *nodes*. This makes it possible to determine the inefficiently used hardware components.
- On the finest levels, the library *objects* and program parts that produce the performance bottlenecks can be detected. This level reflects the programmer's view when he develops his application, but only supported down to the tasks level.

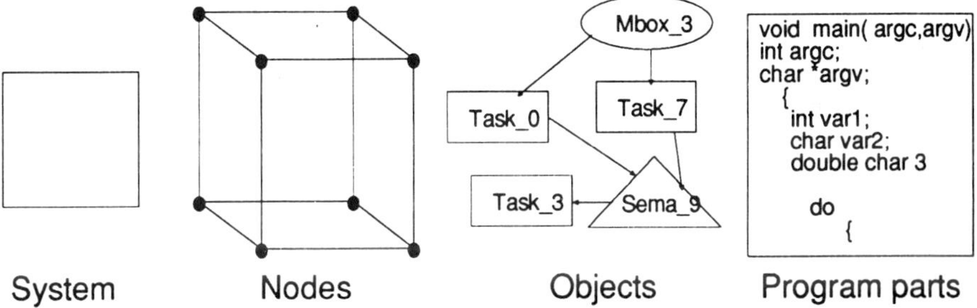

Figure 3.1. Levels of Granularity

On the coarse grained levels, the existence of performance bottlenecks can be detected. The finer levels of granularity must be used to track performance bottlenecks down to the program parts that produce them.

Measurement results are displayed in bargraphs and time histograms. Bargraphs adequately compare average values of various measurements, time histograms show more detailed timing information.

3.2 Implementation of PATOP

Two different instrumentation techniques are used in the monitor to collect performance values. Counters are used for measurements requiring little resolution in respect to time. In this procedure, streams of events are combined to single counter values. Much information is lost, but the amount of data is reduced dramatically. For many measurements, this method is absolutely sufficient. Traces are used for measurements that require detailed timing information. The complete event stream is written into a trace buffer from which outputs of any level of timing detail can be produced. It is sometimes necessary to use traces for measurements that require such a high resolution but the amount of data that this method produces is hard to deal with, if it is to be processed on-line. In PATOP, traces can be used only for very few measurements in parallel because they are evaluated on-line.

PATOP´s software structure was designed modular. Three major components are linked by a central component that controls others´ execution. The monitor collects the performance data in the parallel system and sends it, if requested, to the host. Data is represented either as trace stream or as counter value. The actual time and the time of the last reading of the according measurement unit (trace, counter) is transmitted, together with the values. The data collection is done with the help of hooks that are inserted into the multitasking library or the user application itself. These hooks mark the discrete events. When the execution reaches a hook, functions are called that update the contents of the according measurement unit. Functions for either type of measurement unit may exist on every hook. If hardware support is used, the counters and a trace buffer exist as dedicated hardware. On the host a module evaluates the data delivered by the monitor. In the first step of evaluation, the values from the different monitors must be adjusted to a common time base. These values are then transformed into an output format independent of the measurement unit type. In the common output format, the resolution of trace measurements is reduced to fit the given requirements of the output unit. Finally, different measurements are combined to produce values that give an overview of the complete system.

The output module is a set of independent types of output windows. So far bargraphs and time histograms are given (see figure 6.1 and 6.2). Performance values are given to the output windows in the form that is output by the evaluation module. Output windows may support operations on the data they display. For example the time histogram windows support the calculation of average values for any part of the displayed curve. As such operations are special to each kind of output window, they are performed independent of other program modules in the output window. The central component controls the other components´ execution. It is controlled by the user interface and is the only component where there must be knowledge about the semantic of individual measurements.

4. Using PATOP for DELTA-T

4.1 Motivation and New Requirements

At the University of Paderborn the distributed software monitor DELTA-T was developed. Target systems for this 'performance debugging tool' are transputer based multiprocessors, which are members of the MIMD class - the same class Intel's IPSC/2- and IPSC/860-hypercube belong to. This gave the inspiration to use substantial parts of PATOP for the graphical presentation of measurement data in the DELTA-T project.

The procedure of performance debugging is similar for all kinds of parallel computers: At first, the programmer is interested in general, more or less statistical information such as average system load or utilization of global resources. At this level he probably gets only a first hint where the bottleneck of his application is. Thus a more detailed insight into the program behaviour is required, e.g. the load of the various processors, the communication durations, the execution time of individual processes etc. The hierarchical architecture of multiprocessor systems demands a hierarchical approach to performance debugging tools. PATOP supports this top-down search for performance bottlenecks. Another reason to adapt PATOP instead of developing a new program is that the implementation of a user interface is a time-consuming, difficult task. For the TOPSYS-project an extensive library of graphical functions was implemented. They can be used to build up menus in a very convenient way.

In order to adapt PATOP to the DELTA-T environment, we had to respect some new, important aspects:

- *Transputer based target system with a different programming model (CSP):* To evaluate the performance of transputer programs, the representation of the monitoring data must correspond with the programming model CSP (Communicating Sequential Processes [Hoa78]) - compared to MMK, no semaphors and mailboxes are used for synchronization and communication.

- *Event-driven software monitoring*: The concurrent programs are observed by a distributed software monitor (see chapt. 4.2), which generates an event trace. The event-driven monitor produces an exact history of the states of processes and communications among them. Thus a new visualization form was needed for the scheduling of the processes and the communication.

- *Off-line evaluation:* The main difference between PATOP and ΔVIEW is the source of the input data. In contrast to the runtime tool PATOP, an *off-line* evaluation of an event-trace was desired. Therefore, the calculation and graphical visualization of the performance data demand no 'real time' conditions.

- *Additional requirements:* Performance debugging is usually an iterative, time-consuming task. In ΔVIEW, the user should have the option to compare two or more versions of his computation. Therefore monitoring data of different measurements stored in a file system must be managed.

The various requirements for ΔVIEW result from the different target systems and the implementation of the software monitor. Both aspects are discussed in the following chapter.

4.2 Multi-Transputer Systems and DELTA-T

The software monitor DELTA-T [MaO91], which can be used on every transputer-based system, has been tested on the commercially available Parsytec Supercluster [FLM92] and the DAMP system [BBM91], developed at the University of Paderborn.

The Parsytec Supercluster consists of clusters (of 16 nodes each), connected via crossbar switching units (NCUs). The network allows one to define a topology before the program starts. During runtime, the topology remains unchanged (quasi-static topology). The target system was a 320-Processor Supercluster at $(PC)^2$ (Paderborn Center of Parallel Computing).

The DAMP system consists of 64 transputer nodes connected by a distributed switching-network. On each node a local crossbar switch is implemented. This supports dynamic reconfiguration (change of the communication topology at runtime), which also is important for fault-tolerance [BaM91].

The nodes (PMUs) of these multi-transputer systems are built up by a processor (transputer) and local memory [INM88] (nodes are connected via links). Usually, Workstations or PCs act as front-end-computers for the programming and as servers for such transputer systems.

To observe the behaviour of concurrent applications with DELTA-T, a *monitor process* is started on each node parallel to the target program. During program execution this process collects and manages the monitoring information which consists of primitive events (e.g. 'start process', 'start communication'). To obtain a global system view, the monitor process provides them with a globally valid time-stamp (resolution: 1 μs), which is either supplied by hardware (as e.g. in the DAMP system) or is obtained by software synchronization (additional details in [MaO91]). A part of the local memory organized as a ring buffer is used to store the information. Thus the storage capacity only determines the duration of the event-recording. It does not reduce the measurement time.

DELTA-T offers different ways to extract the required data sent to the monitor process:

- *Observing and manipulating the hardware scheduler:* A monitoring process is attached to the last (node spy) or inserted at the second location (process spy) of the transputer's process queue [BiO91]. While the node spy extracts information at node level, the process spy obtains data on the states of all processes and link-communications. This instrumentation is transparent to the user and allows him to track the scheduler´s behaviour.

- *Instrumentation of the source code or using instrumented libraries:* At interesting locations of the program or library, additional instructions are inserted. This method is also transparent to the user if the source code instrumentation is carried out by a tool or instrumented libraries are used.

The process and communication level is the most detailed level of monitoring for both techniques. After a measurement is completed, the locally buffered information is merged, ordered by time and stored in a file (trace), which is the input for succeeding off-line evaluation tools at the front-end-workstation. For a first impression of the parallel program's behaviour, the animation tool ΔGINA can be used. It visualizes the load of processors, processes and communications by colours or gray scales. For more detailed information ΔVIEW was developed.

Software monitors often have the disadvantage of slightly influencing the computations they observe. However, experience has shown that the DELTA-T monitor raises the execution time of typical programs by only 4 to 5 percent. Reasons are the transputer´s fast process switching and the short runtime of the spy. In addition the off-line concept produces no communication overhaed during runtime.

5. Realization in Respect to the New Requirements

PATOP´s modular structure (C++) and the output module´s independence from the target and host system (Unix, X Windows) were the main reasons to use this program within the DELTA-T project. For using various target systems with a different monitoring concept, the evaluation of the measured data and all lower level parts of PATOP had to be replaced. In contrast, PATOP's visual user interface is suitable for ΔVIEW. The interface between these two parts consists of several functions: defining, starting and terminating the measurement, and reading out the evaluation results. PATOP was split up at this interface. The next section describes the modifications and extensions of the parts taken over from PATOP. The interaction among the different modules of trace evaluation is shown. Figure 5.1 shows ΔVIEW's structure and its integration into DELTA-T.

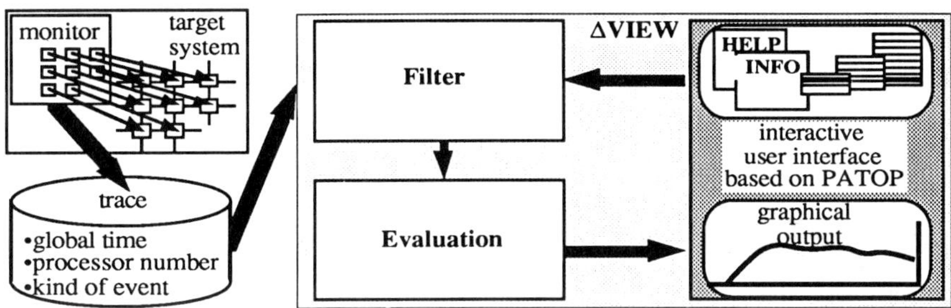

Figure 5.1. The Structure of ΔVIEW

5.1 Alteration of the User Interface and the Output Windows

The appearance of the graphical interface with the output windows and the meaning of the menus had to be adapted for the new requirements. In contrast to PATOP's system and node-level, which resemble the corresponding components in ΔVIEW, the MMK model's objects (tasks, semaphores and mailboxes) had to be replaced by processes and synchronous communication.

A new histogram showing the distribution function of the measured application's parallelism was developed for the evaluation on the system level. This output form visualizes statistical data to give the programmer a quick overview of his parallel program's efficiency (parallelization profile). On the level of processes and communications, a second, new output form was added. A Gantt-diagram reproduces the exact time behaviour of processes and communications for (performance) debugging (see figure 6.4). The states of several processes and communications are represented by different colours or gray scales. All processes running on a selected node can be displayed to track their busy and idle phases and to visualise the CPU's time-sharing. The reasons for bad performance can be discovered as well as the visualization of link-communication among the processes on different nodes.

5.2 Evaluation of the Event Trace

Central points of ΔVIEW's evaluation part are a data structure to store the results, a filter and a set of evaluation functions. The data structure and filter are built up and initialized, according to the desired evaluation. The evaluation reads the data from the trace-file, computes the values and stores them in the data structure. Although the trace consists of all events collected by the monitor, a specified evaluation requires only a certain part of them (e.g., all data of a single process). For separating required entries from the other information, the function uses the filter. The values are transferred from the data structure to the output windows periodically (curve-diagram, bar-diagram) or event driven (Gantt-diagram).

6. Example

Many measurements for various applications were performed with both tools. As an example we monitored the same program (slightly different in implementation details, of course) on the two parallel machines.

The program calculates the stationary distribution of the temperature on a rectangular metal plate. The corresponding Laplace differential equation is solved iteratively using the algorithm of Gauss-Seidel. At the margins a constant temperature is stamped in. The plate is divided into strips for the calculation.

On the iPSC/860 the program was implemented on 4 nodes using the MMK programming library. On each node one task responsible for calculating the stripe´s values was mapped. Value exchange is done by mailboxes. Results are sent to a mailbox on node 0 where they are received from the MMK host task that is executed on the SUN workstation. The host task animates the results (using colours for the different temperatures).

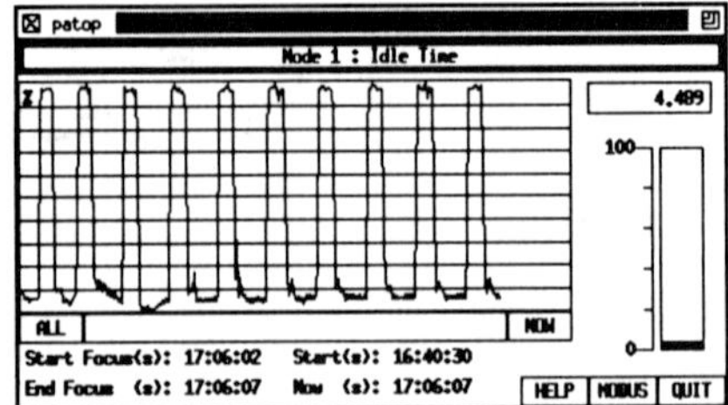

Figure 6.1. Histogram showing Node 1 Idle Time

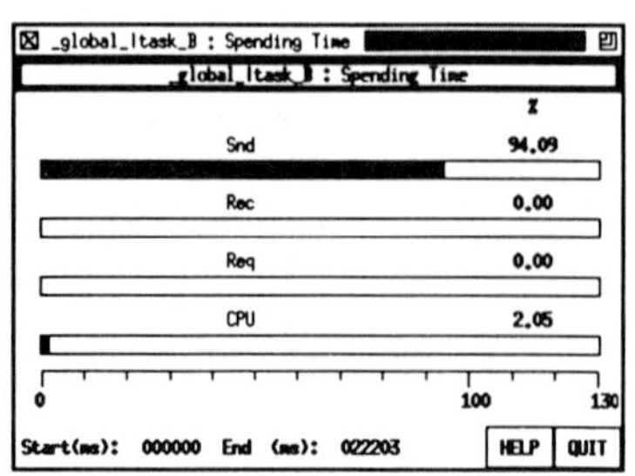

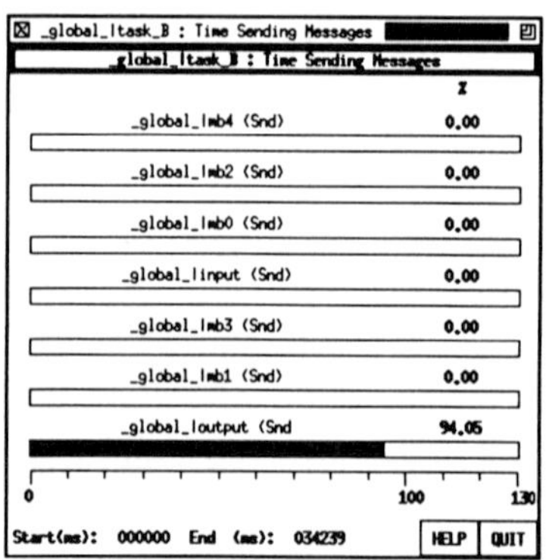

a) Activities of Task_B

b) Delay of Task_B at Different Mailboxes

Figure 6.2. Bargraphs of Task_B

Pictures 6.1, 6.2 show the metrics measured with PATOP on the iPSC/860 implementation. Picture 6.1 is a histogram of the idle time on node 1. It can be seen that there are very active and almost idle periods. The bargraph diagram of figure 6.2 a shows that node 1 mostly waits (idle periods) and is ready to send data to mailboxes. In figure 6.2 b note that the output mailbox is responsible for blocking the send operations of the task. Thus the reason for the program´s poor performance on the iPSC/860 is the low bandwidth of the communication link with the host workstation. This problem could be solved by using a faster communication link or by data compression algorithms.

On the transputer system (DAMP), neighbouring nodes were connected by one link to enable the exchange of the margin values from the single stripes (32 stripes for 32 used processors). Via a separate network of links, the results were sent to another transputer (node 0) responsible for the graphical output.

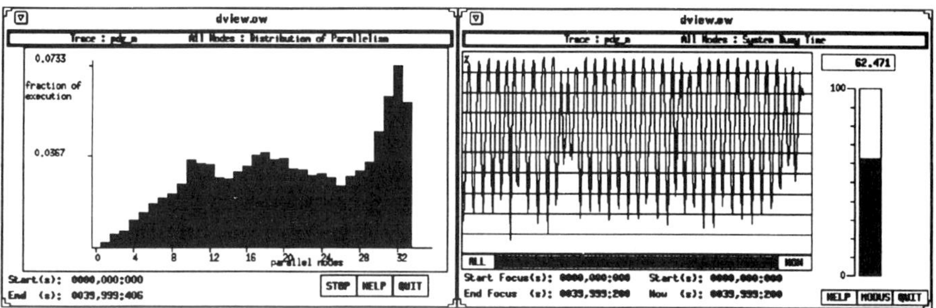

a) Distribution of Parallelism b) System Load

Figure 6.3. Output Windows of ΔVIEW

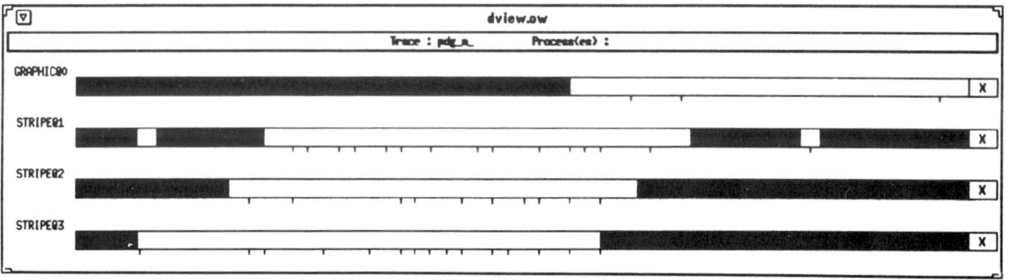

Figure 6.4. Gantt-chart of Several Nodes (black = node busy, white = node idle)

Figure 6.3 displays some output windows of ΔVIEW. The histogram "Distribution of Parallelism" (figure 6.3.a) shows that all 33 processors were working in parallel during only 7% of the execution time. The poor performance (62% average load) emerges because the system load broke in periodically (figure 6.3.b). A more detailed view into the states of different nodes with the Gantt-chart (figure 6.4, for this overview all processes on a node are combined) reveals the reason of this: At certain instants the calculation of the stripes was interrupted, because the nodes had to wait until the graphical output was finished.

The bottleneck was removed by changing the output strategy (insertion of a time shift mechanism for sending the results). This way the average load was increased to more than 90%.

This example elucidates how PATOP and ΔVIEW can be used in an interactive top down manner to locate the origins of performance bottlenecks.

7. Concluding Remarks

This article describes how the performance analysis tool PATOP was ported to a new environment different in some important details. Although other target systems (multi-transputer systems instead of Intel hypercubes) and a distinct monitoring concept exist (off-line instead of on-line evaluation), substantial parts of PATOP have been used to build ΔVIEW, the evaluation tool of the DELTA-T project. The reason is that PATOP's modular structure contains a definite interface between target system dependent and target system independent parts.

During use, the programmers profited by the hierarchical approach to performance debugging supported by the tools. Bottlenecks in program execution were rapidly detected and improvements were made by iterative proceedings.

The further work of both departments (in this context) will concentrate on developing new output forms and the adaptation to the next generation of transputers (T9000).

References

[BaM91] A. Bauch, E. Maehle: Self-Diagnosis, Reconfiguration and Recovery in the Dynamical Reconfigurable Multiprocessor System DAMP, Proc. FTCS 91, Informatik Fachberichte 283, 18 - 29, Springer-Verlag, Berlin 1991

[BBM91] A. Bauch, R. Braam, E. Maehle: DAMP - A Dynamic Reconfigurable Multiprocessor System With a Distributed Switching Network. Proc. EDMCC2, Lecture Notes in Comp. Science 487, 495-504, Springer-Verlag, Berlin 1991

[BeL90] T. Bemmerl, T. Ludwig: MMK - A Distributed Operating System Kernel with Integrated Dynamic Loadbalancing. Proc. CONPAR 90-VAPP IV, Lecture Notes in Computer Science 457, 744 - 755, Springer-Verlag, Berlin, 1990

[Bem90] T. Bemmerl: The TOPSYS Architecture. Proc. CONPAR 90-VAPP IV, Lecture Notes in Comp. Science 457, 732-743, Springer-Verlag, Berlin, 1990

[BHL90] T. Bemmerl, O. Hansen, T. Ludwig: PATOP for Performance Tuning of Parallel Programs. Proc. CONPAR 90-VAPP IV, Lecture Notes in Comp. Science 457, 840-851, Springer-Verlag, Berlin 1990

[BiO91] B. Bieker, W. Obelöer: Leistungsmessung von Transputersystemen, Proc. TAT 91, Springer Verlag, Berlin 1992

[FLM89] R.J. Fowler, T.J. LeBlanc, J.M. Mellor-Crummey: An integrated approach to parallel program debugging and performance analysis on largescale multiprocessors. ACM SIGPLAN Notices, vol. 24, no. 1, 183-194, January 1989.

[FLM92] R. Funke, R. Lüling, B. Monien, F. Lücking, H. Blanke-Bohne: An optimized reconfigurable architecture for Transputer networks. Proc. 25th Hawaii Int. Conference on System Science, Vol. 1, 237-245, 1992

[Hoa78] C.A. Hoare: Com. Sequential Processes. CACM Vol. 21, Nr. 8, 666-677, 1978

[INM88] Transputer Reference Manual. Prentice Hall, New York, 1988

[MaO91] E. Maehle, W. Obelöer: Monitoring-Werkzeuge zur Leistungsmessung in Multi-Transputersystemen. Proc. 2. Int. Fachmesse und Kongreß für RISC/Transputer-Architekturen und Anwendungen, 609-619, VDE-Verlag, Berlin 1991

[MCN90] A. Mink, R. Carpenter, G. Nacht, J. Roberts: Multiprocessor Performance-Measurement Instrumentation. IEEE Computer, vol. 23, no. 9, 63 - 75, 1990.

[MiY87] B.P. Miller, C.Q. Yang: IPS: An Interactive and Automatic Performance Measurement Tool for Parallel and Distributed Programs. Proc. of 7th Int. Conference on Distributed Comp. Systems, Berlin, IEEE Computer Society Press, Washington D.C., 482 - 489, 1987.

[Moh90] B. Mohr: Performance Evaluation of Parallel Programs in Parallel and Distributed Systems. Proc. CONPAR 90-VAPP IV, Lecture Notes in Comp. Science 457, 176 - 187, Springer-Verlag, Berlin 1990

PROGRAMMING ENVIRONMENTS FOR PARALLEL COMPUTING
N. Topham, R. Ibbett and T. Bemmerl (Editors)
Elsevier Science Publishers B.V. (North-Holland)
1992 IFIP

Building Synthetic Parallel Programs: The Project *ALPES*

João Paulo Kitajima and Brigitte Plateau[a]

[a] LGI/IMAG - Calcul Parallèle - 46, av. Félix Viallet - 38031 - Grenoble CEDEX - France - (e-mail: {kitajima,plateau}@imag.fr)

Abstract

This paper presents a proposal of a description language developed in order to describe the temporal behavior of parallel programs during execution. From such a description, a synthetic parallel program (composed of a set of message-passing tasks) is automatically generated for execution on a Transputer[1]-based machine (the *Meganode*[2]). The proposed language is oriented towards the performance evaluation of software and hardware designs. Preliminary experiments are carried out. This work is part of the project *ALPES*.

Keyword Codes: C.4; D.2.2; I.6.0
Keywords: Performance of Systems; Tools and Techniques; Simulation and Modeling, General

1. The Project *ALPES*

ALPES (*AL*gorithms, *P*arallelism and *E*valuation of *S*ystems) is a project concerning the development of an environment for the performance evaluation of parallel applications. The aim is to evaluate the implementation (e.g., strategies for task mapping, scheduling, message routing, dynamic topology reconfiguration, etc ...) of different parallel programs on different target machines.

The proposed environment does not tackle the problem of algorithm parallelization. The starting point of *ALPES* is indeed a parallel program model, expected to be as flexible as possible, allowing the representation of computation and communication requirements at run-time, as well as other characteristics (such as memory demand) which eventually affect program performance. This model is the *application profile* and is expected to be able to represent a large number of applications in the scientific domain. Note that we deal with a model of the application and not with the application itself.

The target machine is modeled in the *architecture profile*. Not only the physical aspects are represented (e.g., number and speed of processors, memory size, topology) but also execution kernel characteristics (multitasking, queue sizes). The main intention is to evaluate the performance of distributed memory multiprocessors, but the model is intended to be as flexible as possible in order to evaluate other kind of parallel architectures (e.g., clusters of shared memory multiprocessors connected by a message passing network). Like

[1]INMOS trademark
[2]Telmat trademark

for the application profile, it is not interesting to describe exhaustively the target machine, but to use instead a model of the architecture, taking into account relevant features for performance.

Given the model of the parallel application and the model of the parallel machine, it is necessary to specify strategies which direct the implementation of the application model on the architecture model. It is intended to use strategies (e.g., heuristics) developed elsewhere or possibly new strategies developed inside the project. This set of implementation specifications is described in the *implementation strategy profile.*

Knowing the program model, the architecture model and the implementation strategies, the environment is able to emulate the *quantitative* behavior of the modeled program on the modeled architecture with the modeled strategies. In order to effectively use the multiprocessor available (a reconfigurable machine with 128 Transputers called *Meganode* [16]), the analysis of these three profiles generates a synthetic parallel program which "emulates" the combined modeled objects (it should be clear that "emulation" here is taken in a restrictive sense: only quantitative aspects are emulated). At the same time, traces of this execution are recorded in order to evaluate the performance of an implementation strategy or of an architectural feature. The interest is not only in criteria like the execution time but also the target machine resource utilization. The traced measures should be utilized (in a feedback fashion) by the user of the environment to enable the comparison between different strategies and eventually to improve and tune some parameters. As commented above, all this information may also affect the algorithm design because they allow the comparison of different parallelization schemes (for the environment, each scheme is represented by a different parallel program model). For example, granularity may be adjusted for performance optimization.

2. Describing Parallel Applications: a Brief Survey

The first stage of the research in *ALPES* is to define a methodology for characterizing parallel applications. The most popular models found in the literature are those related to the *scheduling* [6] and *mapping* [3] problems. Classical scheduling models are Directed Acyclic Graphs (DAGs), where the vertices correspond to sequential computations and the arcs, to precedence relations. Execution times are associated to the computations. These execution times may be deterministic [6] or random [10]. When the execution times of all computations are identical, the model is said to be a Unit Execution Time (UET) model. Recent work extends scheduling models by adding communication costs (in general, message sizes) to the arcs [13, 24], logical behavior to the arcs (AND/OR) [12], probabilities of occurrence of a communication [23] and additional resource requirements (e.g., memory) [8]. Examples of extended scheduling models are GMB [9], Petri Nets [18], ELGDF [8] and Paralex [17].

Another paradigm of representation is for the mapping problem. A parallel application is described as a set of tasks (sequential computations) that exchange data according to a communication pattern. The model is also a directed graph, but the arcs represent communication and not precedence relation. When all the communications are bidirectional, the graph becomes undirected. Also, execution costs are associated to the tasks and communication costs to the arcs (edges) [21, 3, 10].

3. The Parallel Application Description Language

In *ALPES*, the first version of the language for describing parallel applications behavior is basically a language to express an extended DAG, as in the previous references. The host programming language used is the standard *C* [14]. Models, tasks and communications are stored as structures. Ad-hoc types are created: `Model`, `Task` and `Comm`.

3.1. The Basic Language

Two different mutual-exclusive models can be described in *ALPES*: *scheduling* and *mapping* graphs. The object of type `Model` has two attributes: a *name* (a string) and a *type* (scheduling or mapping). It is important to remark that other modeling methodologies are acceptable. In this sense, the application description technique is also a parameter for the tool.

The scheduling graph type, called *precedence task graph*, allows the representation of precedence dependencies between tasks. Tasks (vertices) are characterized by a number of *basic operations* (a fixed number, a result of a random function or even a value that is function of the attributes of other tasks or communications), by the *type of logic of its inputs* and by the *type of logic of its outputs.* For input, the types currently supported are `AND`, `OR` and `ROOT`. If a task has an `AND` input condition, this task executes only when all the inputs have messages. The `OR` condition models the Occam2[3] `ALT` instruction: the task begins to execute when one of its inputs contains a message. If more than one input have a message, one of them is chosen at random. `ROOT` means that the task has no inputs. For the output logic, the currently supported logic operators are `AND` and `LEAF`. If the output logic is an `AND`, at the end of the task, all outputs are activated with messages. `LEAF` means that the task has no outputs. A next improvement of the language is to define an output logic that is deterministic, according to the result of an `ALT` input.

A communication is characterized by the *message size* (also a constant, a result of a random function or a function of a variable of the description–program), by the *name of the task that activates this communication* and by the *name of the task destination.*

For example, to describe the precedence task graph of the Back Substitution algorithm [2], the following "program" is obtained:

```
#include "alpes.h"       /* ALPES header with type definitions, constants,
                            etc...*/
#define M_SIZE 5         /* system size: corresponds to n */

/* back substitution -- scheduling */
/* ==================================================== */
/* This description corresponds to the back substitution */
/* algorithm. The array "grid" corresponds to the  tasks */
/* of the substitution(the tasks of the  triangle in the */
/* Figure 2). Half of these tasks are not used. The task */
/* "root" starts the algorithm, computing the  value  of */
/* x1. "root_grid" is the array with the  communications */
/* between "root" and the first  line of "grid".  "pass" */
/* is the array with the communications of the substitu- */
/* tion.                                                 */
```

[3]INMOS trademark

```
/* ======================================================= */

Model m;    /* model variable */
Task  grid[M_SIZE-1][M_SIZE-1], root;
Comm  root_grid[M_SIZE-1], pass[M_SIZE-2][2*(M_SIZE-2)];
int   i,j;

void main()
  {
     init_def_appli ();    /* initialize description */

     create_model (&m, "m01", SCHE);  /* model parameters */

     create_task (&root, 1, ROOT, AND);  /* root task parameters */
     for (i=M_SIZE-2;i>=0;i--)           /* grid tasks parameters */
        for (j=0;j<=i;j++)
           if ((j == 0) && (i == 0))
              create_task (&grid[M_SIZE-2-i][j], 1, AND, ROOT);
           else
              create_task (&grid[M_SIZE-2-i][j], 1, AND, AND);

     for (i=0;i<M_SIZE-1;i++)      /* root-grid parameters */
        create_comm (&root_grid[i], 1, &root, &grid[0][i]);

     for (i=0;i<M_SIZE-2;i++)      /* intra-grid comm. parameters */
        for (j=0;j<M_SIZE-2-i;j++)
           create_comm (&pass[i][j], 1, &grid[i][0],
                                        &grid[i+1][j]);

     for (i=0;i<M_SIZE-2;i++)      /* vert. communications */
        for (j=M_SIZE-2-i;j<2*(M_SIZE-2-i);j++)
           create_comm (&pass[i][j], 1, &grid[i][j-((M_SIZE-2-i)-1)],
                                        &grid[i+1][j-(M_SIZE-2-i)]);

     fini_def_appli ();
  }
```

The mapping representation does not model precedence relations but only communication relations. They are known also as *task communication graphs*. A task in this model is only characterized by the *number of operations*.

Communications in the task communication graph are characterized by a *message size*, a *task sender*, a *task receiver* and a *communication phase specification*. In task communication graphs, communications can occur in different moments of time. So, it is necessary to include in the model the information about the message send time and its reception time. So, between two tasks, distinct communications may happen, each one in a different phase. For example, the n-body problem [15] is described below:

```
#include "alpes.h"

#define BODY_NUMBER 7    /* number of bodies */
#define COMPUTE_1   10   /* computation time between two ring
    communications */
```

```
#define COMPUTE_2   20   /* computation time after chordal
    communication */
#define PRECISION   5    /* number of iterations */
#define RING        ((BODY_NUMBER-1)/2) /* number of ring comms.
   per iteration */
#define MSGSIZE     10   /* message size */

/* n-body problem */
/* ==================================================== */
/* The "body" array contains the body tasks. The  "ring" */
/* array models the ring comms.:(for each body, for ea-  */
/* ch iteration, RING times)."chordal" models the chor-  */
/* dal communications (one per body and per iteration).  */
/* ==================================================== */

Model m;
Comm  ring    [BODY_NUMBER][PRECISION][RING],
      chordal [BODY_NUMBER][PRECISION];
Task  body    [BODY_NUMBER];
int   i, j, k;

void main()
  {
     init_def_appli ();

     create_model (&m, "m01", MAP);

     for (i=0;i<BODY_NUMBER;i++)   /* comm creation */
         for (j=0;j<PRECISION;j++)
             {
                for (k=0;k<RING;k++)
                    create_comm(&ring[i][j][k],
                                MSGSIZE,
                                &body[i],
                                &body[(i+1)%BODY_NUMBER],
                                (j*((RING*COMPUTE_1)+COMPUTE_2))+
                                     (k*COMPUTE_1), /* phase */
                                (j*((RING*COMPUTE_1)+COMPUTE_2))+
                                     (k*COMPUTE_1));
                    create_comm(&chordal[i][j],
                                MSGSIZE,
                                &body[i],
                                &body[(i+(BODY_NUMBER+1)/2)%BODY_NUMBER],
                                (j*COMPUTE_2)+((j+1)*(RING*COMPUTE_1)),
                                (j*COMPUTE_2)+((j+1)*(RING*COMPUTE_1)));
                                /* phase */
             }

     for (i=0;i<7;i++)             /* task creation */
         create_task (&body[i], ((RING*COMPUTE_1)*PRECISION)+
                                 (PRECISION*COMPUTE_2));

     fini_def_appli ();
  }
```

This program is comparable to the description using *LaRCS* (*La*nguage for *R*egular *C*ommunication *S*tructures), a formal description language used in the *OREGAMI* environment [15].

3.2. Other Language Features

Some additional features are currently being implemented: communications with associated probabilities of occurrence in precedence graphs (a probability associated with an arc), communications based on the result of an `OR` (`ALT`) input, hierarchical descriptions, macros describing regular structures (rings, grids, trees), description of application memory requirements, support for other parallel programming paradigms (Linda [5], Strand [11]). We are also studying the possibility of using *C++* [22] and a graphic interface.

3.3. The Automatic Generator of Synthetic Applications

Using the parallel application description, different actions can be performed. For example, in the *PPSE* environment [7], scheduling heuristics are applied to the description (taken into account a target machine description). Another approach is to simulate the execution of the application on a sequential machine. This is the choice done by *MIMD* [20]. In *ALPES*, from the application description, a synthetic parallel program is generated. According to Poplawski [19], synthetic programs have many-fold applications: quantification of the performance of parallel programs on parallel architectures, utilization as "prototype for alternate implementations of an algorithm" and "prediction of the behavior and performance of programs or new hypothetical architectures". Poplawski proposes three methods for the generation of synthetic jobs: *from scratch*, *from an existing program* and *from observed behavior*. The *ALPES* approach is the generation of a synthetic program from *a model* of parallel application: this model may come from an existing program or may be built before writing a real program (in order to validate different parallelization schemes).

The automatic generated parallel synthetic program is written in a standard *C* with macros for parallelism management [4]. The automatic generator produces also an incomplete configuration file. In this file, the user has to add manually – for the time being – a mapping of task to physical processors. The synthetic program may then be executed. Traces are generated automatically with a software monitor called *TAPE* [1].

4. Experiments

Preliminary experiments were performed to verify if there are implementation aspects (e.g., synchronization problems) that may change the execution time complexity of an algorithm. The algorithm chosen is the n x n matrix multiplication AB on an n x n mesh [2]. This is a simple example used to exercise with the language constructs and to verify if the synthetic tasks are generated correctly.

In this algorithm, each processor (i, j) contains elements a_{ij} and b_{ij}. On each processor, there is a sole task (i, j) composed of three stages:

1. broadcast of the element a_{ij} to the tasks on the i-th row of the mesh,

2. broadcast of the element b_{ij} to the tasks on the j-th column of the mesh,

3. computation of the ij-th element of the product, i.e., $\sum_{m=1}^{n} a_{im} b_{mj}$.

The algorithm may be described as a *task communication graph.* The topology of this graph is equal to the topology of the parallel machine, i.e., an n x n mesh. This simplifies the mapping task-to-processor (considering that it is not still available an automatic mapper). Each task (i, j) of the graph is composed of 2 consecutive stages (see below description): the *broadcast* (through the row and through the column), modeled as the sequential execution of $n - 1$ couples of parallel send-receive (a no optimized pipelined broadcast) and the *computation* of each element (i, j) of the product (modeled as a loop of $2n - 1$ operations: n multiplications and $n - 1$ additions).

```
#include "alpes.h"
#define SIZE 8          /* matrix size */

/* O(n) matrix multiplication */
/* ===================================================== */
/* "grid" is the task array (SIZE = n).  "hor_1" is  the */
/* array of horizontal communications going to the right */
/* side. "hor_2" corresponds to the left oriented comms. */
/* "ver-1" corresponds to the going down comms. The  go- */
/* ing up comms. are modeled by "ver_2".                 */
/* ===================================================== */

Model m;
Task  grid[SIZE][SIZE];
Comm  hor_1[SIZE][SIZE-1][SIZE-1],
      hor_2[SIZE][SIZE-1][SIZE-1],
      ver_1[SIZE-1][SIZE][SIZE-1],
      ver_2[SIZE-1][SIZE][SIZE-1];
int   i, j, k;

void main()
  {
     init_def_appli ();

     create_model (&m, "m01", MAP);

     for (i=0;i<SIZE;i++)      /* task creation */
         for (j=0;j<SIZE;j++)
     create_task (&grid[i][j], (3*SIZE) - 3);

     for (i=0;i<SIZE;i++)      /* horizontal communications */
         for (j=0;j<SIZE-1;j++)
             for (k=0;k<SIZE-1;k++)
                 {
                 create_comm(&hor_1[i][j][k], 1, &grid[i][j],
                                                 &grid[i][j+1],
                                                 k, k);
                 create_comm(&hor_2[i][j][k], 1, &grid[i][j+1],
                                                 &grid[i][j],
                                                 k, k);
```

```
            }

    for (i=0;i<SIZE-1;i++)     /* vertical communications */
        for (j=0;j<SIZE;j++)
            for (k=0;k<SIZE-1;k++)
            {
            create_comm(&ver_1[i][j][k], 1, &grid[i][j],
                                            &grid[i+1][j],
                                            k, k);
            create_comm(&ver_2[i][j][k], 1, &grid[i+1][j],
                                            &grid[i][j],
                                            k, k);
            }

    fini_def_appli ();
}
```

After the above description is compiled, tasks are generated. The *Meganode* is configured as an n x n mesh and the parallel synthetic program is executed. The generated traces contain informations about task creation and destruction, thread creation and destruction and communication beginning and end. For this experiment, only the total execution time is considered. Figure 1 shows the comparison between the measures and the values produced by a theoric model obtained by linear regression. The coefficient of regression (least-square method) values 0.9955. For this range of matrix sizes, the linear complexity is still verified, even with all the overhead imposed by the implementation.

5. Conclusions

The automatic generation of synthetic parallel programs is a different approach toward the performance evaluation of parallel systems. The proposed description language does not demand sophisticated resources (just a *C* compiler). Some large applications can be described in a very compact way. The possibility of using all the capabilities of a programming language is important (e.g., loops constructors, variables, functions, etc...). Thanks to these capabilities, general models can be described representing complex program structures.

Acknowledgement

João Paulo Kitajima is supported by a grant from the CNPq/Brazil.

1 Yves Arrouye, TAPE: Un Enregistreur d'Evénements. LMC/IMAG Stage Report, 1991.

2 Dimitri P. Bertsekas and John N. Tsitsiklis. *Parallel and Distributed Computation: Numerical Methods.* Prentice-Hall, Englewood Cliffs, 1989.

3 Shahid H. Bokhari. On the mapping problem. *IEEE Transactions on Computers*, 30(3):207–214, March 1981.

4 Pascal Bouvry et al. Manuel du méganode. Rapport Technique 63, LMC – IMAG, avril 1991.

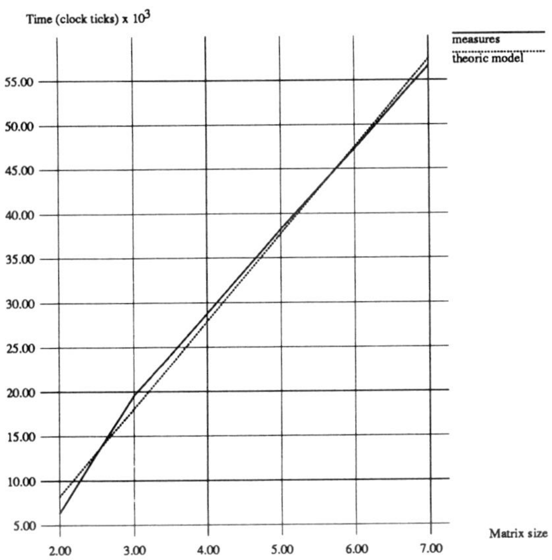

Figure 1: Experimental results for the $O(n)$ matrix multiplication.

5 Geoffrey F. Carpenter and Andrew M. Tyrrell. The use of GMB in the design of robust software for distributed systems. *Software Engineering Journal*, pages 268–282, September 1989.

6 E. G. Coffman and R. L. Graham. Optimal scheduling for two-processor systems. *Acta Informatica*, 1(3):200–213, 1972.

7 Robert W. Currey. *The Parallel Programming Support Environment.* Oregon State University, March 1990.

8 H. El-Rewini and T. Lewis. Software development in parallax: the ELGDF language. Technical Report 88-60-17, Dept. of Computer Science, Oregon State University, July 1988.

9 Gerald Estrin et al. SARA (System ARchitects Apprentice): Modeling, analysis, and simulation support for design of concurrent systems. *IEEE Transactions on Software Engineering*, 12(2):293–311, February 1986.

10 David Fernández-Baca. Allocating modules to processors in a distributed system. *IEEE Transactions on Software Engineering*, 15(11):1427–1436, November 1989.

11 Ian Foster and Stephen Taylor. *Strand: New Concepts in Parallel Programming.* Prentice-Hall, Englewood Cliffs, 1990.

12 Donald W. Gillies and Jane W.-S. Liu. Scheduling tasks with AND/OR precedence constraints. In *Parallel and Distributed Processing*, pages 394–406, Los Alamitos, California, December 1990. IEEE Computer Society, IEEE Computer Society Press.

13 J.-J. Hwang et al. Scheduling precedence graphs in systems with interprocessor com-

munication times. *SIAM J. Comput.*, pages 244–257, April 1989.

14 Brian W. Kernighan and Dennis M. Ritchie. *The C programming language.* Prentice-Hall, Englewood Cliffs, 1988.

15 Virginia M. Lo, S. Rajopadhye, S. Gupta, D. Keldsen, M. A. Mohamed, and J. Telle. OREGAMI: software tools for mapping parallel computations to parallel architectures. Technical Report TR-PPSE-90-1, OACIS, 19500 H.W. Gibbs Drive, Suite 110 - Beaverton, OR - USA, 1990.

16 Denis A. Nicole. ESPRIT project 1085: Reconfigurable transputer processor architecture. In *CONPAR88: Additional Papers.* British Computer Society, September 1988.

17 Özalp Babaŏglu et al. Paralex: an environment for parallel programming in distributed systems. Technical Report UB-LCS-91-01, University of Bologna, Italy, February 1991.

18 J. L. Peterson. *Petri net theory and the modeling of systems.* Prentice-Hall, 1981.

19 D. A. Poplawski. Synthetic models of distributed memory parallel programs. Technical Report ORNL/TM - 11634, Oak Ridge National Laboratory - Martin Marietta, ORNL - Oak Ridge, Tennessee 37831 - USA, 1990.

20 Neil Skilling. *MIMD - version 1.4.* Department of Chemical Engineering - University of Edinburgh, The Kings Buildings - Mayfield Road - Edinburgh - EH9 1HA - Scotland, February 1991.

21 Harold S. Stone and Shahid H. Bokhari. Control of distributed processes. *Computer*, pages 97–106, July 1978.

22 B. Stroustrup. *The C++ programming language.* Addison-Wesley, Reading, MA, 1986.

23 Don Towsley. Allocating programs containing branches and loops within a multiple processor system. *IEEE Transactions on Software Engineering*, 12(10):1018–1024, October 1986.

24 Min-You Wu and Daniel D. Gajski. Computer-aided programming for message-passing systems: Problems and solutions. *Proceedings of the IEEE*, 77(12):1983–1991, December 1989.

PROGRAMMING ENVIRONMENTS FOR PARALLEL COMPUTING
N. Topham, R. Ibbett and T. Bemmerl (Editors)
Elsevier Science Publishers B.V. (North-Holland)

© 1992 IFIP. All rights reserved.

Maritxu: Generic Visualisation of Highly Parallel Processing

Eugenio Zabala Richard Taylor
Adaptive Systems Engineering Group
Department of Electronics
University of York
York Y01 5DD
e-mail: ez@ohm.york.ac.uk

Abstract

This paper presents *Maritxu*, a visualisation system developed to aid in the understanding and optimisation of highly parallel computer systems. Maritxu implements a new visualisation paradigm, combining the use of colour, algorithm animation and visual overload. Maritxu adopts an integral approach to Parallel Computing by emphasising the role of the *processor* (rather than process) in performance optimisation. There are no constraints to the visualisation: network size, topology, subnetworks, icon shapes, data mapping, statistics, etc. can all be interactively defined by the user. An example of performance enhancement in a practical transputer-based EMC application is included.

Keyword Codes: C.1.2; D.2.2; H.5.2
Keywords: Multiple Data Stream Architectures; Tools and Techniques, Software Engineering; User Interfaces, Information Systems

1. Introduction

In the last few years parallel processing has become a reality affordable to many companies and institutions. Parallel processing promises enormous power at a cost - understanding. Parallel computations involve highly complex and little understood behaviour. This lack of understanding prevents efficient use of this power.

The need for support tools to analyse the dynamics of parallel computations is evident. Literature reviews show that most of the systems under development aim at *processes* [11, 3, 8] and do *not* exploit graphics [12, 8, 7]. To extract the maximum performance from processor networks, study of hardware's run-time needs to be addressed. Maritxu exploits *visual overloading* techniques [13] to provide an integral approach to the study of parallel computing. The tool is oriented towards the behaviour of the underlying hardware.

2. The Maritxu System

Maritxu is best seen as an experimenters workbench. It's aim is to *aid in the understanding of parallel computing* and to help users obtain the *best performance* out of processor networks.

The goals of the Maritxu project may be summarised as:

- provision of a tool for the run time visualisation of many models of parallel computation, focusing on the *processors*;
- processor type, network size and topology independent;
- capable of the visualisation of multiple parallel programs running simultaneously in subnetworks of a complete network;
- problem and language independent;
- capable of being run on any hardware platform that supports Unix and the X-Windows graphical system.

Maritxu integrates different techniques to meet these goals. The primary problems of visualisation are those of dimensionality and volume of data. The human visual system is best suited to assimilate this information *graphically* rather than textually [13], and *quantitative* use of colour increases the number of visual dimensions. This alone is not enough to deal with the quantity of data parallel computing provides. Maritxu relies on a technique known as '*visual overloading*', exploiting the ability of the human visual system to generalise and recognise patterns in animated images.

The best example of visual overloading is the television set: the TV displays thousands of pixels. Each isolated pixel is meaningless, whereas many pixel put together are *interpreted* by a human as image.

Maritxu emulates the TV set by presenting the user with a 2D grid of processors. This provides the user with a composite of the behaviour of the *whole network* rather than partial details. This visualisation model is scalable. In addition, Maritxu features unconstrained conventional support statistics.

Maritxu's total reliance on graphical representation has required that the display techniques be designed to exploit modern models of human perception. The assimilation of graphical data is highly dependent on its presentation, and researchers in both psychology and visual ergonomics [16] have made contributions to the display formats. For instance, Maritxu's colour-scale is a grey scale with colour hues at the bottom (blue and cyan) and the top (yellow and red) of the scale (see figure 2). This scale emphasises the non-desirable states: under and over-usage.

Maritxu differs profoundly from most visualisation systems used for studying parallel computations (such as Voyeur [12], Schedule [11], TOPSYS (PATOP) [1]) in the exploiting of graphics. Visual overloading has shown to work successfully on specialised applications such as PIE [9], the monitoring program for VICTOR 256 [15], and MatVu [2]; Maritxu attempts to provide a framework which permits the application of this technique to a greater range of problems.

'Trace files', traced on run-time from any kind of parallel network, are presented to Maritxu and displayed. The system implements the *declarative approach to visualisation* [6]. This combination makes Maritxu independent of the processor, programming language and problem. In addition, the portability of files implies that the analysis can be performed away from the parallel hardware.

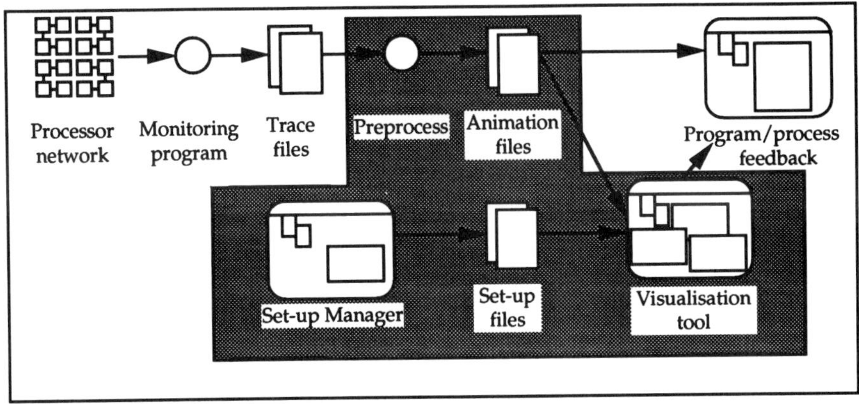

Figure 1. Functional structure

Input data *preprocessors* are provided so the 'raw data' (such as memory utilisation and processor load) extracted from the tracing can be combined, filtered and scaled. Maritxu's *Set-up Manager* allows the user to define the input data and its mapping onto icons. Furthermore, the Set-up Manager allows the user to define the icons' shape and lay-out, as well as the statistics to be gathered. This approach does not constrain the user and therefore provides an *integral* approach to the study of parallel processing.

Maritxu is environment sensitive: it adapts itself to network and screen size, implements many standard topologies and discriminates sub-networks running different programs.

3. Functional Structure

Figure 1 shows the functional structure of the Maritxu System. A *monitoring program* monitors the run-time of a *processor network* and creates *trace files.* The trace files are preprocessed resulting in *animation files.* The *Set-up Manager* saves the user's preferences in *set-up files.* The *Visualisation Tool* loads the set-up files and uses the animation files to provide animated visualisation. Afterwards, feedback goes into *program/process* analysis.

The Maritxu system includes the elements contained in the shaded area. Note that Maritxu does not include monitoring programs, however packages such as GPMS [14], OTSimul, PICL [4] or TMON [14] cover this function. The processor network is engaged only once, whereas *preprocessors*, *Set-up Manager* and *Visualisation Tool* may be reused to gain new understanding of the program.

4. Visualisation Tool

Maritxu's *Visualisation Tool* (or simply Maritxu) is a X Windows/Motif [10] based graphical user-interface. A menu bar controls cascadeable pulldown menus. Additional output (e.g. animation) is shown in dialogs that open and close dynamically.

Figure 2 is an overall view of the Visualisation Tool displaying two 4x4 subnetworks. The top line is the menu bar. The rest of the windows, from top left to bottom right, are : Work Window, Communications Length Window, colour scale, data mapping (obscured), processor specific, and subnetworks.

The Visualisation Tool displays the traced data in three *Main Windows*. Processors are represented by square nodes in a 2D grid.

- *Work Window*: displays the usage of processor resources (e.g. C.P.U. load, queues, memory usage, link communication). Every node contains various icons, each displaying a traced data item associated with the icon. Icons' colour (or grey level) represent the value measured for the data item. This window is overloaded with information changing dynamically as the parallel program trace is processed. Subnetworks are discriminated by their background pattern. The appearance and contents of the Work Window are defined by the Set-up Manager;

- *Communications Length Window*: shows the current communications (integrated over an arbitrary time scale). Coloured lines joining the communicating processors, overlap the lattice grid. The line's layout depends upon the sub/network topology. Colour is used to represent the *length* of the communication path. The display changes dynamically as the parallel program runs. Subnetworks are discriminated by their background pattern;

- *Topology Window*. This window provides support for the other two by showing the topology of the sub/network. It displays a lattice grid with lines representing the physical connections between processors. The line's layout depends upon the sub/network topology. Subnetworks are discriminated by their background pattern. Maritxu is prepared to handle switches, such as the Inmos C104 intelligent crossbar switch. This window's display is static.

Dedicated windows display statistics for each subnetwork. The *statistics* to be displayed may be gathered in two groups:

- *Static*: gather the information displayed on the Work and on the Communications Length Windows;

- *Dynamic*: show the evolution of different metrics through time, arithmetic and logical operations. The operations to perform are defined by the user via the Set-up Manager.

A set of secondary windows is dynamically opened and closed. These windows serve various purposes, including processor specification, colour legend, data mapping, data generation and preprocessing description, error, warning and help messages.

5. Set-up Manager

Maritxu's *Set-up Manger* is a X Windows/Motif based graphical user-interface. A menu bar controls cascadeable pulldown menus. Additional output (e.g. icon definition or information input) is performed using dialogs that open and close dynamically.

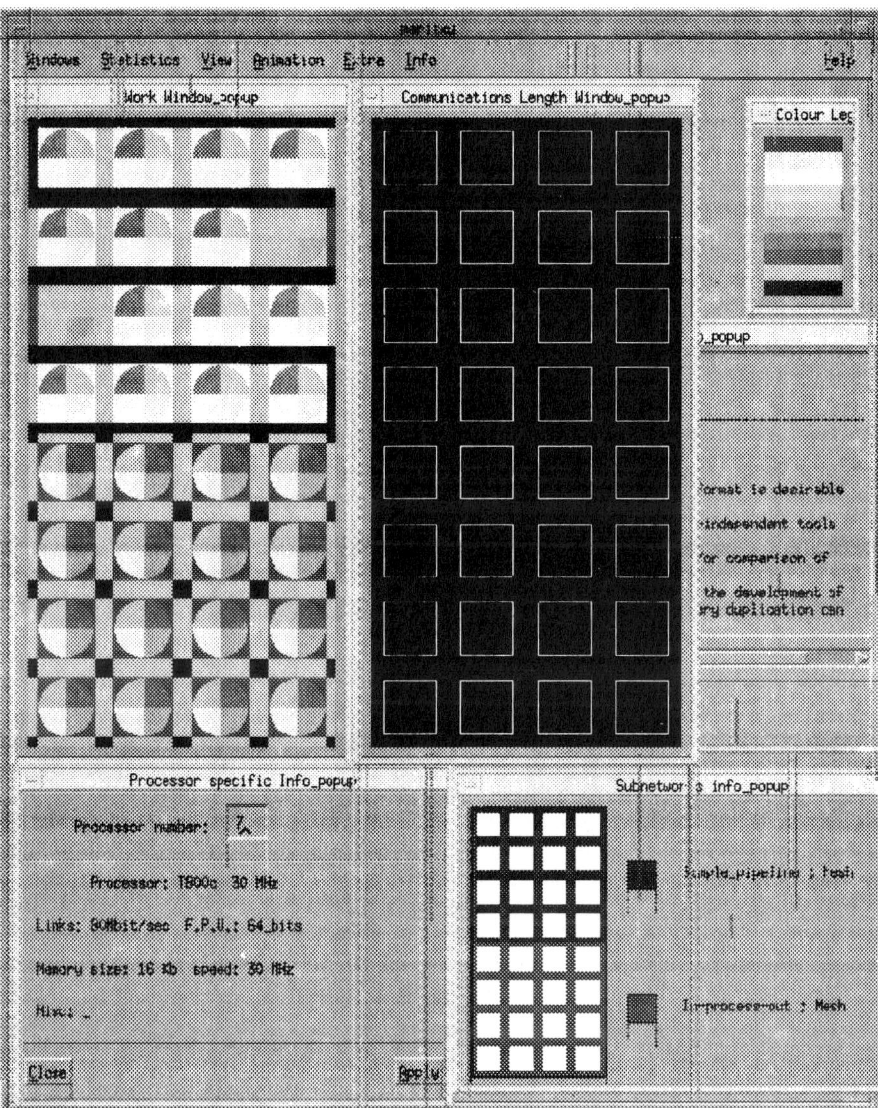

Figure 2. Overall view of the *Visualisation Tool*

The Set-up Manager allows the user to define the Visualisation Tool's parameters. This grants the system with a great deal of flexibility. The main areas the Set-up Manager covers are:

- *Icons.* Allows the definition of icons and the mapping of data into icons. Icons are defined by setting points on a magnified node, in a fashion similar to the *bitmap* program (a widespread bitmap editor for X). However, the Set-up Manager allows the *simultaneous* definition of various icons (note that this defines the icon layout as well). Another window provides the means to map traced data into the icons;
- *Topology.* Allows the creation of subnetworks and definition of their topologies. It also allows to enable and disable processors (e.g. faulty processor);
- *Input.* A browser navigates the directory hierarchy to set the files that fed Maritxu's animation;
- *Statistics.* Statistics, graphs and layout may be set per each subnetwork. Ilimitated number of arithmetics involving the traced data can be typed in; they will be gathered, and displayed by the Visualisation Tool. The graph to map each arithmetic and the graphs' layout is also defined;
- *Defaults.* Sets default for various of Maritxu's parameters, among them: input mode, motion mode and colour scale;
- *Libraries.* Provides libraries to ease and speed the use of the Set-up Manager.

6. Results

The Visualisation Tool and the Set-up Manager have been developed using *UNIX*, *C*, *X Window System* and the *OSF/Motif* widget set.

Transputer networks have been used to run the first experiments. A range of network sizes (from 4x4 to 10x10) and topologies have been studied. Figure 3 describes the icon shapes and data mapping used for the EMC study case.

The displays generated show the program structure, the load balance, the parallelism, the use of resources and context switches. Preliminary results reveal the need for buffering of communications, the inter-relation between cpu load and process queues, non-linearity of transputer 'work', and the non-linearity of process addition to the queues.

6.1. Study case: EMC

The study case is a test of a numerical EMC (Electromagnetic Compatibility) package. The part of the package being simulated is responsible for gathering together the rows of a matrix (spread across the processors), performing some simple calculations on these rows and then distributing the data through the columns of the matrix. A pseudo Occam description of the code for a single node (within a toroid) is given by

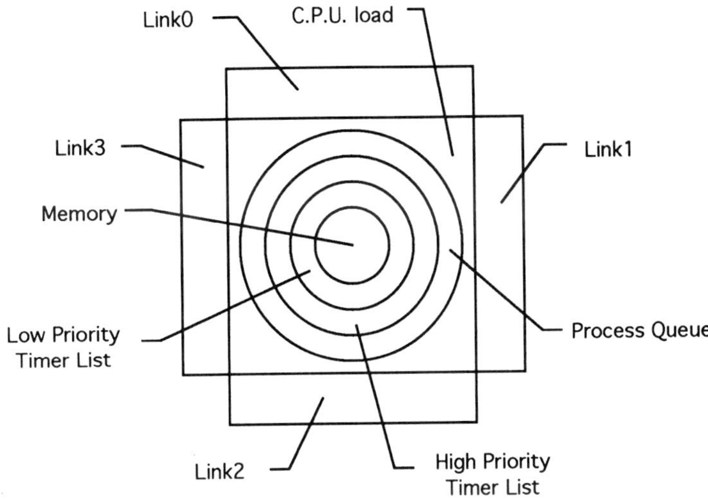

Figure 3. Mapping of traced data from the EMC package

```
SEQ
  PAR
    East ? EData
    West ? WData
  Compress(Edata,Wdata)
  Compute(Edata,Wdata)
  PAR
    South ! SData
    North ! NData
```

The sequence of figures 4, 5 and 6 shows neatly the structure of the program: load, process, broadcast. This statement fulfills one of the project's aims: to understand parallel processing in terms of what is going on in the processor network.

Furthermore, the visualisation helps to detect performance related factors: it is apparent that load drops to blue (inactivity) when a transputer is communicating. This means that the transputer is *only* communicating. This is a dramatic example of how performance is degraded due to the lack of buffering in communications in this program implementation. The program is operating as a sequence in a sequential program. By adding buffering, the transputers are capable of executing all three of these tasks in parallel. The display reveals that each task takes roughly one time unit (figures 4,5,6), accordingly by implementing communications buffering will cause the execution time to drop substantially.

Maritxu also shows at a glance, that the program is well load balanced (all the processors are showing the same behaviour) and working very hard (red colour is predominant). The process queue is blue which means that there are not many processes, therefore there are no many context switches. The computation is making intensive (yellow) use of memory.

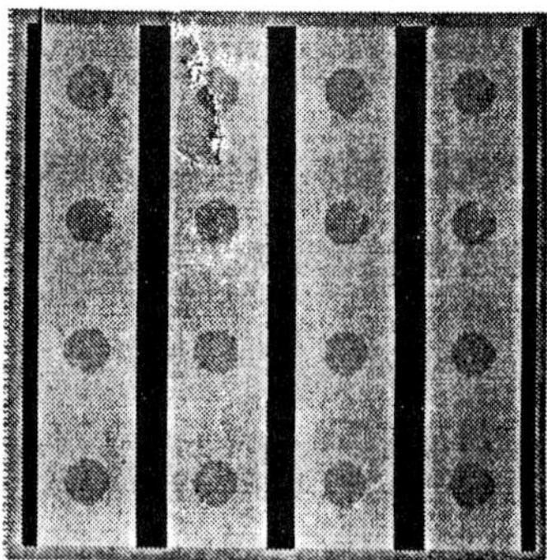

Figure 4. Time t in the sequence. The data is loaded trough the East - West links

Figure 5. Time $t+1$ in the sequence. The data is processed

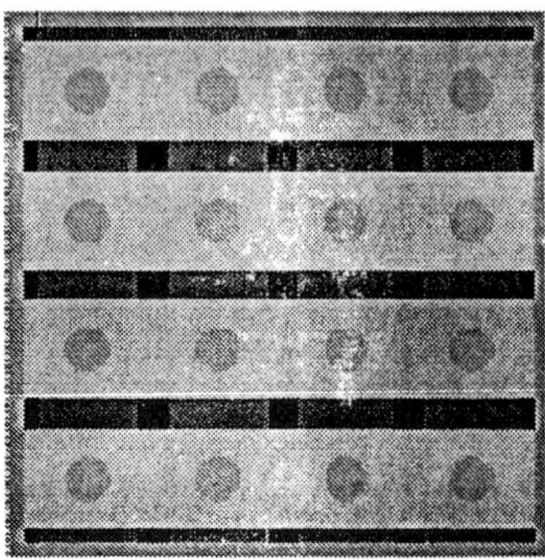

Figure 6. Time $t+2$ in the sequence. The results are sent away through the North - South links

Figure 7. Two 4x4 subnetworks: top running a pipeline, bottom running the EMC case. (Note the different icon shapes)

The fact that the program is well load balanced and that all the processors are working within 90 and 100% (red colour on a linear scale) leads to the conclusion that there is not a much better way of implementing this program - apart from buffering, of course.

7. Further Work

A *Neural Network* able to recognise static and dynamic performance degradation patterns is to be developed. An *Advanced Help* system is to be developed to suggest performance improving alternatives. A profound development in this direction could lead to a parallel computing *teaching* package. *Sonic* representation of data, and its potential for Maritxu will also be investigated.

All these 'extra' features are to be implemented as *modules* that may be added to Maritxu's kernel. All the modules integrate smoothly, so Maritxu can be tailored to specific requirements. In addition, the module strategy allows the parallel development of the extra utilities and keeps the system within manageable limits.

The subnetwork capability (figure 7) makes Maritxu suitable to analyse the effect of size and topology in performance. Maritxu is going to be 'hot tested' during the development of a highly distributed MIMD load distribution kernel [5].

8. Conclusions

The initial results have established that, even on complex and large networks, Maritxu and the theories it implements, are of substantial value in aiding the understanding of parallel computations and improving the performance of processor networks. It has justified the investment of more research efforts in this direction.

1 Hans-Jorg Beier, Thomas Bemmerl, et al. TOPSYS: Tools for parallel systems. Technical Report TUM 19013 SFB-Bericht Nr. 342/9/90 A, Institut fur informatik Technische Universitat Munchen, January 1990.
2 M W Berry. The use of matrix visualisation in algorithmic design. *Computing Systems in Engineering*, pages 63–73, April 1990.
3 Robert J Fowler, Thomas J LeBlanc, and Jhon M Mellor-Crummey. An integrated approach to parallel program debugging and performance analysis on large-scale multiprocessors. *Journal of Parallel and Distributed Computing*, pages 203–217, 1990.
4 G A Geist, M T Heath, B W Peyton, and P H Worley. A user's guide to PICL: A portable instrumented communication library. Research report ORNL/TM-11616, Oak Ridge National Laboratory, Mathematical Sciences Section, May 1991.
5 Don Goodeve and Richard Taylor. A highly distributed MIMD tasking kernel. Research report YEE6/92, Adaptive Systems Engineering Group, Electronics Department, University of York, Heslington - York YO1 5DD, England, February 1992.
6 Roman Gruia-Catalin and Kenneth C Cox. A declarative approach to visualising concurrent computations. *IEEE Computer*, pages 25–36, October 1989.
7 E Hart and S Flavell. Prototyping transputer applications. *Real-Time Systems with Transputers*, pages 241–247, September 1990.
8 P K Harter, D M Heimbigner, and R king. IDD: an interactive distributed debugger. In *Proceedings 5th International Conference on Parallel Processing*, pages 498–506, Denver, CO, 1985.
9 Ted Lehr, Zary Segall, Dalibor F Vrsalovic, Eddie Caplan, et al. Visualising performance debugging. *IEEE Computer*, pages 38–51, October 1989.
10 Open Software Foundation, editor. *OSF/Motif Style Guide*. OSF/Motif. Prentice Hall, Englewood Cliffs, New Jersey 07632, 1991. OSF/Motif Release 1.1.
11 Cherri M Pancake and Sue Utter. Models for visualisation in parallel debuggers. *Proceedings ACM*, pages 627–636, 1989.
12 David Socha, Mary L Bailey, and David Notkin. VOYEUR: Graphical views of parallel programs. *SIGPLAN Notices*, pages 206–215, January 1989.
13 David Travis. *Effective colour displays: theory and practice*. Computer and people series. London, Academic Press, 1991.
14 Maurice van Riek and Bernard Tourancheau. A general approach to the monitoring of distributed memory machines. Research report 91-28, Laboratoire de l'Informatique du Parallelisme, Ecole Normale Superieure de Lyon, October 1991.
15 W W Wickle, D G Shea, E Ma, et al. The IBM Victor multiprocessor project. In *Proceedings of the 4th International Conference on Hypercubes*, pages 201–207, March 1989.
16 John Wilson and Peter Thompson. Use of colour in computer visualisations. Personal communication, June 1991. Psychology Department University of York.

PROGRAMMING ENVIRONMENTS FOR PARALLEL COMPUTING
N. Topham, R. Ibbett and T. Bemmerl (Editors)
Elsevier Science Publishers B.V. (North-Holland)

© 1992 IFIP. All rights reserved.

Communicating Through Shared Objects

David P. Mallon
Peter M. Dew

Parallel Programming Group, School of Computer Studies, Leeds University, England

Abstract

In this paper a model for interprocess communication is presented that sits between the abstractions of message passing and shared memory. Its purpose is to provide a shared variable abstraction which exhibits performance and scalability characteristics similar to those of message passing. In the model, interprocess communication occurs through shared instances of abstract data types; for example, shared queues or trees. Abstract data appears to provide a flexible and expressive means of interprocess communication, through which radically different programming models can be integrated.

Keyword Codes: D.1.3; D.4.4
Keywords: Concurrent Programming; Communications Management

1. Introduction

This paper presents a new model for interprocess communication called *Shared Objects*. The model falls somewhere between the traditional extremes of message passing and shared variables, and is based on shared abstract data types. Its purpose is to provide a shared variable abstraction in distributed memory machines which maintains the performance and scalability characteristics of message passing, rather than those usually associated with virtual shared memory.

Whilst a shared memory abstraction is desirable in many parallel programs, the expense of building this is often too high [7]. If the programmer undertakes the task, the effort required to build the program greatly increases—and the program becomes more complex. If the system undertakes the task, only 'general purpose' shared memory abstractions can be provided. Kai Li's Virtual Memory system [10] for example, provides a memory abstraction similar to real shared memory and can support arbitrary shared data structures. However, accommodating the general case often implies accommodating the worst case; general caching and synchronisation techniques have to be employed since nothing is known of user data structures in advance.

Shared Objects (SO) is different because it doesn't provide support for general shared data structures. Instead, specific abstract data types—for example; trees, queues, grids, lists and bags—are provided which, although physically distributed around the system, appear as autonomous, concurrently accessible objects.

Shared objects is different from other hybrid systems; for example, Linda [12], Emerald [4], Orca [9] and CMU's Concurrent Objects [13], because it is machine rather than application oriented. It is concerned with providing an efficient low level abstraction for shared data management. Most hybrid systems are aimed at providing high level programming abstractions which simplify the intellectual task of parallel programming by hiding complex details or becoming application or methodology specific. For example, Linda provides the 'generative communication model' of tuple space to decouple processes in time and space.

The computational model provided by shared objects is presented in §2, along with a number of examples of its use. §3 describes the implementation of the system, and in particular, the element distribution strategy employed by objects. In §4, the project status is presented, and some consideration is given to the future of SO given current hardware trends.

2. Shared Objects

In *Shared Objects* a parallel program is a collection of sequential threads of execution called processes which communicate through shared abstract data types called objects[1].

Programs are written in a conventional sequential language such as *C* or *fortran*, and linked to a pre-defined library of shared abstract data types. The types are instantiated at run-time and accessed via an explicit call interface.

A contiguous shared address space spans all processes in the system; at each location an instance of one of SO's pre-defined types may be created. This contrasts with the associative memory of Linda which addresses data via structured naming, and with conventional models of shared memory which provide a contiguous (or sometimes segmented) address space of words.

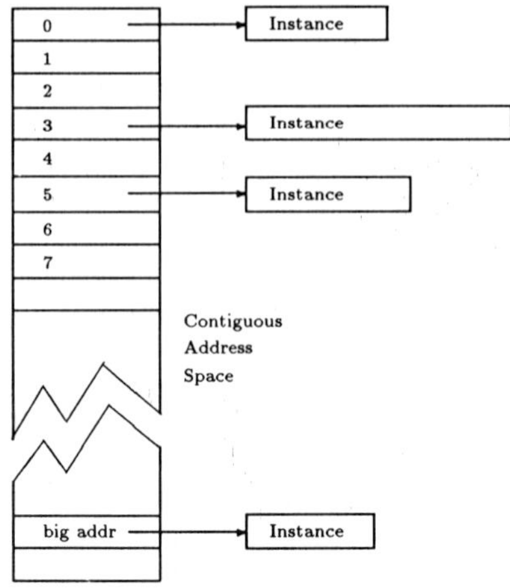

Figure 1: SO's Shared Address Space

Shared objects are instantiated and destroyed by calls to *Create* and *Destroy* respectively. When creating an object the programmer specifies the type and shared address of

[1]This is exactly the same model proposed for CMU's Concurrent Objects [13]; a system based on communication primitives from the Mach operating system.

the object. For example, placing an instance of the 'Queue' data type at shared address *102*. The address is a unique *identifier* for the instance, and must be used whenever a process wishes to interact with it.

Figure 1 shows SO's contiguous address space with objects instantiated at addresses 0, 3, 5, and near the top of memory. Since the memory is logically shared, it looks the same to all processes. Any process may create an instance at any free address; and once the instance exists, any process can access, modify or destroy it.

Processes interact with objects by message passing. Each object type provides an explicit call interface through which processes invoke methods. For example, the Queue data type provides methods to *enqueue* and *dequeue* elements and the Stack data type to *push* and *pop* elements. Other object types define 'Lists', 'Grids', 'Trees', 'Bags', and single elements called 'Items'.

In the following sub-section, a message passing system is presented to demonstrate how programmers create and interact with shared objects. Later examples show how the more complex types supported by SO may be used.

2.1. A Message Passing System

Message passing systems, ignoring various functional and stylistic differences, essentially consist of shared queues and a name-space associating the queues with specific processes [5, 6]. The queues are shared since any process can write to them, although they are often physically located on one node and only readable by one process. The name-space is usually representative of the communication model provided; for example, logical port names, channel names or process identities.

It is simple to build a variety of message passing systems using SO. For example, Queues can be instantiated for each process (or port) in the system, and a mapping established between the user's name-space and SO's address space. Figure 2 shows a system in which four queues have been instantiated in a system containing four processes. There is no relationship between the processes and queues; any process can read or write any queue. However, if the processes are known to the application by the identifiers {0, 1, 2, 3}, and the queues exist at shared addresses {0, 1, 2, 3}, then the application can make the obvious mapping between them. That is, process 1 'receives messages' from queue 1, and process 2 from queue 2; and any process wishing to 'send' to process 1, enqueues the data at queue 1.

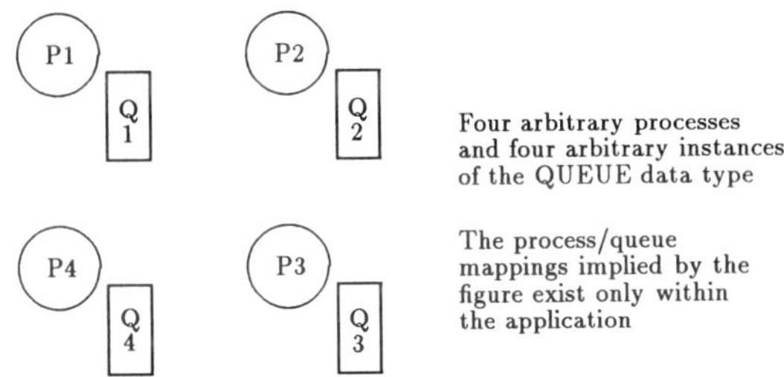

Figure 2: Message Passing using Queues

This mapping is simple. The complexity of a mapping depends upon the name-space required, which itself depends upon the desired communications abstraction. It may also depend upon orthogonal issues such as the process name-space.

Consider, for example, a system in which processes are identified by a pair consisting of a node identifier (NID) and process identifier (PID). Since processes are uniquely identified by the tuple (NID,PID), it may be desirable to use this as the communications name-space. Given that the maximum number of processes per node is MPN, then the addresses of the queues for each process may be determined from:

```
address = NID * MPN + PID
```

The code to implement an asynchronous message passing system using NID/PID addressing is shown below. `init()` is called by each process once to create an 'associated' communications queue. `send()` is called whenever a process wishes to send a message to another process, `recv()` is called whenever a process wishes to receive a message.

```
/* initialise system */
        int init () {
                return Create (my_nid * MPN + my_pid, QUEUE);
        }

/* send message */
        int send (int nid, int pid, void *buffer, int length) {
                return Enq (nid * MPN + pid, buffer, length);
        }

/* recv message */
        int recv (void *buffer, int length) {
                static int my_address = my_nid * MPN + my_pid;
                return BDeq (my_address, buffer, length);
        }
```

The variables `my_nid` and `my_pid` are assumed to have been established by (say) the process management system. The variable `my_address` is the address of the message queue associated with this process (computed once in `recv` for efficiency).

Every process wishing to receive messages must first call `init()` to create their associated shared queue. This is the target for other processes wishing to send them messages. Processes send messages by calling `send()` with the appropriate (NID,PID) tuple identifying the destination process. `send()` maps the tuple onto the address of the shared queue associated with the destination, and enqueues the message there. Processes receive messages by calling `recv()`. `recv()` attempts to dequeue a message from the calling process's associated queue; if one is available it is returned, otherwise the function blocks until one becomes available.

The program uses two methods from SO's Queue abstract data type. The Queue data type exhibits the usual *first-in/first-out* behaviour expected of a FIFO queue. Elements are added to the tail of the queue and removed from the head, but it is not possible to add or remove elements from any other point in the structure. Part of the interface for the Queue is summarised below.

```
int Enq (int address, void *data, int length)
int Deq (int address, void *data, int length)
int BDeq (int address, void *data, int length)
```

`Enq` copies the element referenced by *data* of size *length* into the queue instance at *address*. `Deq` removes an element from the queue at *address* if one is available, otherwise it returns 'empty queue'. `BDeq` is similar to `Deq` except that it blocks if the queue is empty, until an element is available.

SO can supports a simple message passing system by instantiating queues for each process in the system. Variant message passing systems which associate priorities with messages or, conversely, which have no requirements on message delivery order at all, may be implemented using the PriQueue and Bag data types respectively. The one-to-one process/queue mapping described here is only an example; if it is sensible to have multiple queues associated with some processes and have none with others, then this is just as easy to arrange. (For example, multiple queues per process could be used to implements *typed* message passing.) Also note that there is nothing special about Queues; all object instances are addressed in the same way, and any number of any type may be coincident within one program.

2.2. Shared Variables

The discussion so far has concentrated on the Queue data type, and briefly mentioned the PriQueue and Bag types. As with all types in SO, instances of these are physically distributed around the system; but are logically, autonomous shared structures. Although Queues, PriQueues, Bags and indeed Stacks may be concurrently read and written by multiple processes, they have a stronger association with message passing that they do with shared memory. This is because data 'files-in' to and 'files-out' of these structures, rather than being randomly 'placed-in' and 'removed-from'

The Grid, Tree, Item and List data types support random access to stored data. The Item data type is simple one element; the List and Grid types are 1 and 2 dimensional static arrays respectively. Trees are n-ary, although upper bounds may be specified on the number of branches per node and maximum tree depth.

This section concentrates on the Grid data type. It is one of the more powerful types supported by SO and is particularly useful for numerical applications involved in matrix manipulations.

2.2.1. The Grid Abstract Data Type

A Grid is a two dimensional data structure that exhibits the behaviour of a 2D static array—as found in high-level programming language such as C or Pascal.

Grid objects are unlike most other SO data structures in that their bounds are fixed. When instantiated, the number of rows and columns, and maximum element size (for example, doubles are 8 bytes) must be given. Fixed bounds are necessary so that element locations may be uniquely identified. If they were dynamic, like a Queue for example, then the result of removing an element (perhaps from one of the rows) would break the regular structure of the Grid.

The Grid data structure—like all other data types—is shared and amenable to concurrent access; processes may read and write the same or different elements simultaneously.

When two processes attempt to concurrently write to the same location, without attempting to synchronise the operations, the resulting value (the latest write) is unknown.

When instantiated, all elements of a Grid are *unset*; the content of each location is not simply undefined, but is without value. If a process attempts to read an unset location, then an error is returned. However, if a blocking read is attempted, then the process is suspended until the location is set—that is, assigned a value. This property of synchronising through Grid elements is particularly useful for program flow control and 'Multireel' operations (see below).

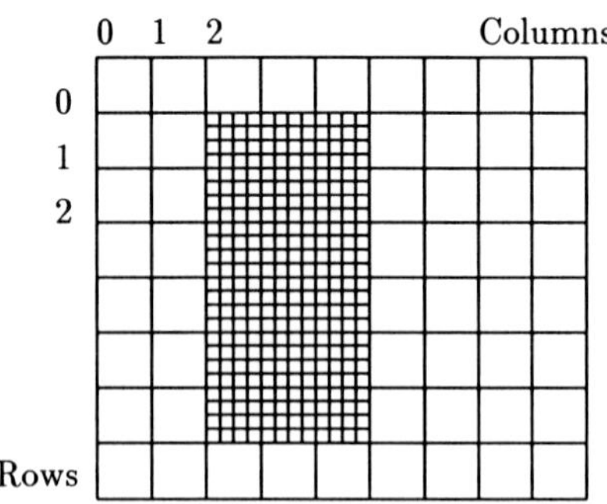

Figure 3: A Shared Grid

Functions supported by the Grid data type usually operate over an area of the grid rather that specific elements. Figure 3. illustrates a grid where the shaded region identifies the area over which an operation is applied. The region is defined by a start point *row, col*, with extents along the row *row_cnt* and column *col_cnt.*

```
int Write (address, row, row_cnt, col, col_cnt, data)
int Read (address, row, row_cnt, col, col_cnt, data)
int Remove (address, row, row_cnt, col, col_cnt, data)
int Multireel (address, row, row_cnt, col, col_cnt, function, result)
int BRead (address, row, row_cnt, col, col_cnt, data)
int BRemove (address, row, row_cnt, col, col_cnt, data)
int BMultireel (address, row, row_cnt, col, col_cnt, function, result)
int Swap_Row (address, row_a, row_b)
int Swap_Col (address, col_a, col_b)
int Set (address, row, row_cnt, col, col_cnt, value)
int Unset (address, row, row_cnt, col, col_cnt)

void *data, *result, *value
int address, row, col, row_cnt, col_cnt, row_a, row_b, function
```

`Write` copies the matrix in *data* from the calling process's address space into the Grid at *address.* Sufficient data will be copied to fill the defined region, overwriting existing data. `Read` and `Remove` copy a matrix out of the Grid into the process's address space. `Remove` also changes the state of the copied region to unset. `BRead` and `BRemove` are blocking read equivalents—they block the calling process until all of the elements requested have a value (are set), and then read or remove the region. The swap operations swap entire rows or columns; and the set and unset operations explicitly assign values to, or remove values from, regions of the Grid. The **Multireel** function is a reduction operation over a specified region of the grid. It can determine the maximum or minimum value within the region, or return the sum or product of all the elements contained therein.

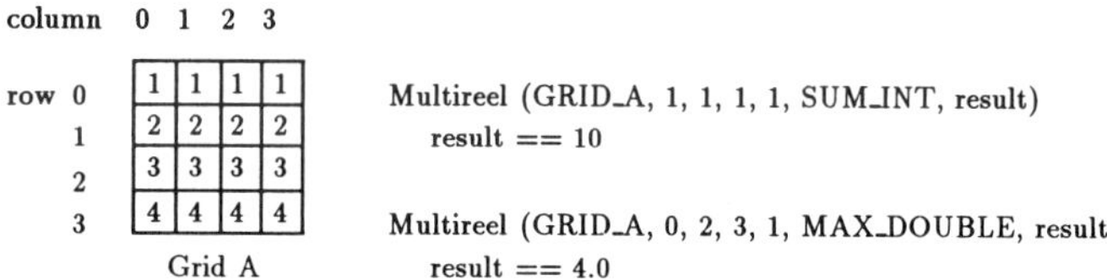

Figure 4: Using Multireel with a GRID

Figure 5 illustrates **Multireel** being used to find the sum and maximum of specified regions. The region is indicated by a start coordinate, and row and column extents. Thus, the specification {1,1,1,1} describes the region from {1,1} to {2,2} in the Grid.

2.2.2. A Numerical Application

The Grid data type is currently being used at Leeds to implement a numerical algorithm for LU decomposition [3]. The details of the algorithm are not important, only the requirements it places upon SO. During the course of the algorithm, rows must be 'reduced' to determine the largest value, and then re-organised with the pivotal row swapped to the top of the matrix. The current solution employs two Grid instances, one for the initial matrix, and the other for the solution.

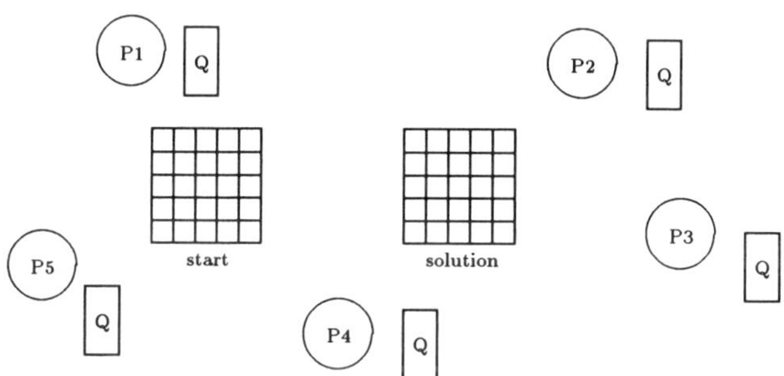

Figure 5: LU Decomposition for Shared Objects

Each process (indicated by circles) has an associated queue so that control information can be distributed to the nodes. The addresses of the two grid instances may be hardwired into the program, or propagated to all processes via the communications queues. Computation starts by each process creating its associated queue, and then waiting for a START message. This is generated by a 'controlling' process once it has created the Grids and loaded the start grid with the initial matrix.

To maximise parallelism each process will then try to work on a portion of the matrix without interfering with other parts; for example, reduce rows to find maximum values.

Processes requiring the results of other computations must wait for these to be generated, usually by waiting on the location(s) in which the results will be placed. That is, using the tagged (set and unset) facility of the Grids.

In the code fragment below, a 'multireeling' process is blocked until all the elements in the specified range have values; that is, until the row of 10 elements starting at {0, 0} are set. The process is then resumed and passed the result of the operation, in this case a summation. The elements in the row are generated in parallel by a set of processes. Each perform some computation and place the result in a corresponding grid location.

```
/* synchronisation using tagged memory */
        Multireel (GRID, 0, 0, 0, 9, SUM_INT, result)

/* process producing row element 4 ... */
        while (!done) {
                res = compute()
                Write (GRID, 0, 4, 0, 0, res);
        }

/* process producing row element 5... */
        while (!done) {
                res = compute()
                Write (GRID, 0, 5, 0, 0, res);
        }
```

Grids are particularly efficient when operations (such as Multireel) are performed because the entire data set on which they operate is stored in the instance. Several reductions across a shared region (which may actually be across the processor network) can be performed together, thus increasing the granularity of communications. Earlier work with an experimental message passing system [6] indicated that the fine communication granularity of the Multireel operation limited its ability to scale. Grids efficiently support row/column swapping, since this equates to pointer manipulation plus a little data relocation if it is later required. The Grid is also expressive, not only due to the general utility of having a shared object, but because tagged locations avoid explicit synchronisation.

2.3. Bags and Balancing Bags

The final abstract type to be considered is the Balancing Bag. Bags are unordered collections of elements exhibiting an any-in/any-out behaviour. There is no inherent structure, and therefore Bags are used whenever element order is not important.

Balancing Bags are similar to Bags, except that 'any-out' is *most suitable out* and depends on the location and current load of the reading process. The balancing bag is a back end for task load balancing systems. Based on knowledge of the relative computational complexity of one element (task) compared with another, the Balancing Bag migrates elements around the system. It is up to the application to partition the work into discrete tasks, and to associate with each a relative complexity number. The system works particularly well when *divide-and-conquer* is used to recursively partition the problem. Where several task types are identified, multiple Balancing Bags may be used.

Balancing Bags work by migrating large tasks (elements with big complexity values) around the network in preference to small tasks. Large tasks are usually associated with large amounts of data and are more likely to give rise to sub-tasks. Thus Balancing Bags attempt to maximise data locality and minimise communication.

3. Implementation

The primary objective for SO is to provide support for shared data structures on distributed memory machines, with performance and scalability similar to message passing. To achieve this, SO restricts support to a few specific data types, and optimally implements each based upon their particular access, synchronisation and structural requirements. Central to the performance of all data types is the strategy employed to distribute object elements around the network. Elements must be distributed in such a fashion that they can be quickly located when requested by processes, without recourse to centralised services which may otherwise impair the systems ability to scale.

3.1. Object Distribution Strategy

Object instances are physically distributed around the system. A single instance may grow to utilise all of the available system memory, supporting data structures too large to reside on any single processor. Object instances are logically shared. Therefore any process in the system may place an element into any instance, or request an element from any instance. This leads to the difficult question of where should elements *actually* be stored when placed into an object, and where should the system look when they are requested from an object?

The distribution strategy is based upon run-time heuristics of the application's communication patterns. If only one process has placed elements into a particular instance, then it is 'likely' that this process will place the next element. Similarly, if only one process removes an element from the instance, then it is most likely that this process will remove the next element. Where several processes interact with an instance, then the extent of their interactions results in a set of probabilities for the next interaction.

Knowledge of object interactions is maintained locally by each processor. There is no central information. When elements are first placed into an object they reside on the calling process's node. Then, according to local communication heuristics, they are moved towards the node at which they are most likely to be requested. Thus a presure map of sorts is established, migrating elements towards the focal point of where they are most often accessed. Against this presure a repelling force is introduced as the memory utilisation of nodes increase. Thus, elements fan-out around the focal point until they eventually fill the entire system memory.

The advantages of localised heuristics is that where regular communication patterns prevail good performance may be achieved. However, where communication is irregular (or where it appears irregular) the network may start thrashing.

4. Conclusion

Shared Objects provides data structures to support a variety of message passing abstractions and to support shared variables. Objects are not instantiated on particular nodes, but are physically distributed around the system, and logically accessible by shared addresses. Mechanisms support concurrent access and synchronisation—usually in keeping with the abstract data—and techniques are employed to eliminate bottlenecks (central controllers) and minimise communication overheads by reducing all such operations (ie, combine several dequeues into one). Some object types are sophisticated; for example, Balancing Bags back-end many load balancing algorithms by handling task distribution, and Grids provide multireel operations on rows, columns or any sub-grid. In effect, SO provides a unifying structure in which message passing, shared variables and load balancing are integrated within a single model.

SO is limited in that it provides few shared data types, and does not provide a means for programmers to define their own. This situation may be eased by providing a generic graph data type from which more general structures can be refined. However, whatever data types are supported by SO, the overriding goal is to ensure that implementations can exhibit good performance and are scalable. SO is also limited in that unlike shared memory (and languages as opposed to libraries) the programmer must still linearise parts of local data structures in order to move them into shared memory. However, this limitation may have the positive side effect of increasing the sizes of messages when communicating with objects, and hence of increasing the granularity of interprocess communications. In any case, in situations in which SO is used as a compiler target (rather than being accessed directly from an application library) the interface is hidden.

In the current state of hardware technology, SO offers an abstraction for shared memory in which programming flexibility is traded for performance and scalability. In the future, it is likely that hardware caching, hashed addressing and two-phase routing [2]; combined with parallel slackness in the application [8, 1], will make virtual shared memory systems a feasible solution. In such systems, fundamental shared data types (such as Queues, Bags and Grids) supported by SO will still provide a powerful and expressive programming tool. Work at Leeds University is investigating implementations of SO on current and future parallel machines; with scalability, absolute performance and predicatable performance as central issues.

5. Acknowledgements

The support of the UK Science and Engineering Research Council and IBM UK Scientific Centre is gratefully acknowledged.

1 Nash J., *A General Purpose Programming Interface for the XPRAM Abstract Machine Model*, Technical Report, University of Leeds, 1991.

2 May D., *Towards General Purpose Parallel Computers*, INMOS Report, October 1989.

3 van de Vorst J.G.G., and Bisseling R.H., *Parallel LU decomposition with partial pivoting on a mesh network of transputers*, In G.A. van Zee and J.G.G. van de Vorst, eds, Lecture Notes in Computer Science 384, Springer Verlag, 1988.

4 Black A., Hutchinson N., Jul E., and Levy H., *Object Structure in the Emerald System*, In proceedings of the Object Oriented Programming Systems, Languages and Applications, Vol 21, No 11, pp78-86, 1986.

5 Davy J.R., Mallon D.P., Hillen S., Dew P.M., *Towards Message Passing Standards : A User's Perspective*, Technical Report 91, University of Leeds, 1990.

6 Mallon D.P., Hillen S., *Issues of Multireel on the MPS*, Technical Report 90, University of Leeds, 1991.

7 Lee R.L., Yew P-C., Lawrie D.H., *Multiprocessor Cache Design Considerations*, In Proceedings of the 14th Annual International Symposium on Computer Architecture, pp253-262, 1987.

8 Valiant L.G., *Bulk Synchronous Parallel Computers*, Technical Report TR-08-89, Aiken Computation Laboratory, Harvard University, 1989.

9 Bal H.E., Tanenbaum A.S., *Distributed Programming with Shared Data*, In Proceedings of the International Conference on Computer Languages, IEEE Computer Society, pp82-91, October 1988.

10 Li K., *Shared Virtual Memory on Loosely Coupled Multiprocessors*, Ph.D. Dissertation, RR-492, Yale University, New Haven, CT, September 1986.

11 Kruskal C.P., Rudolph L., Snir M., *The Power of the Parallel Prefix*, IEEE Transactions on Computers, Vol c-34, No 10, pp965-968, October 1985.

12 Gelernter D., *Generative Communication in Linda*, ACM Transactions on Programming Languages and Systems, Vol 7, NO 1, pp80-112, January 1985.

13 Wing M. J., Gong C., *A Simulator for Concurrent Objects*, Technical Report CMU-CS-90-150, Carnegie Mellon University, July 1990.

PROGRAMMING ENVIRONMENTS FOR PARALLEL COMPUTING
N. Topham, R. Ibbett and T. Bemmerl (Editors)
Elsevier Science Publishers B.V. (North-Holland)
1992 IFIP

A Synchronous Model for Static Optimizations of Multicomputer Programs

Salvatore Orlando[ab]
Marco Vanneschi[a]

[a] Dipartimento di Informatica, Università di Pisa, Corso Italia, 40 – 56125 Pisa - Italy, e-mail: {orlando,vannesch}@di.unipi.it

[b] Pisa Science Center, Hewlett Packard Laboratories, Corso Italia, 115 – 56125 Pisa - Italy, e-mail: orlando@pisa1.italy.hp.com

Abstract

In this paper a *synchronous execution model* for multicomputers is proposed. It is aimed at making easier the ***static optimization*** of ***CSP-like*** concurrent programs. The synchronous model, called SYMPLE (SYnchronous Model for ParalleL execution based upon Elementary steps), requires that all processes that make up a concurrent program execute fixed-length elementary steps in a lockstep-ed way. The optimization techniques here defined are applied to CSP-like programs running according to SYMPLE. They reorder communications and computations within each process to reduce the time waiting for synchronization, and produce the migration of computations to reduce idle time intervals. The optimized programs can even be executed in an asynchronous way, provided that synchronous communication primitives are used.

Keyword Codes: C.1.2; D.1.3; D.2.2
Keywords: Multiple Data Stream Architectures (Multiprocessors); Concurrent Programming; Tools and Techniques

1. Introduction

Distributed memory, message-passing, MIMD parallel systems (*multicomputer*) are considered very promising because of their scalability and good performance/cost ratio. Furthermore, many applications have been successfully implemented on them. However, proper programming environments are needed to *efficiently program* such machines, and to *optimize* a program with respect to a specific target architecture, especially in the area of general-purpose, parallel machines [11, 12, 2].

While the tuning and the mapping of parallel programs for improving performance and efficiency is currently made by the programmer, the design of proper static optimizing tools is regarded as very difficult, because many parameters must be taken simultaneously into account, and the program behavior is very complex to be statically analyzed.

We argue that the complexity of analyzing and optimizing parallel programs comes from considering an *asynchronous execution* model in the design of optimizing tools. In fact, according to the asynchronous model, every process refers to its own local time, and all parallel activities may proceed at different speeds. Thus, many distinct behaviors can be observed for the same program, and one could deduce that a static optimizing tool cannot be devised because of the complexity of this analysis.

To make it possible the definition of static analyses and optimizing strategies, we propose a *synchronous execution model* for multicomputers. Since most of the languages used to program such systems are based on the CSP model [7, 8], we refer to this class of languages to describe our techniques.

The features of the synchronous model we propose have been inspired by two compiler-oriented architecture classes, RISC computers [5] and VLIW machines [4]. The former class emphasizes the simplicity of the instruction set, which makes the generation of code easier and code optimization more effective for a compiler. The latter proposes a synchronous execution model for a set of processing units. This model allows new parallelizing compiling techniques to be defined. Along with the synchronous model, we define a synchronous CSP-like concurrent language. We assume that a CSP asynchronous program is first compiled into this synchronous language. For this language we are able to define a simple static analysis and devise a proper optimizing technique.

The optimized program we obtain can also be executed in asynchronous mode, because the necessary synchronization is guaranteed by adopting synchronous communication primitives.

2. SYMPLE, a synchronous execution model for multicomputers

The synchronous execution model we propose is called SYMPLE (SYnchronous Model for ParalleL execution based upon Elementary steps). A collection of communicating sequential processes running according to SYMPLE can simultaneously and cyclically execute elementary steps including:

i) an *internal computation phase*, composed of elementary instructions referring to the local environment of each process, and

ii) a *local communication phase*, which only involves processes mapped on neighboring processing nodes (PNs), i.e. nodes that are directly connected.

Δ_c is the duration of any computation phase, while Δ_{io} is the duration of any communication phase. These durations are the same for all the processes, so that the execution goes on in *lockstep*.

A list of sequential instructions can belong to a computation phase if and only if the execution of all these instructions does not take a larger time than Δ_c. A communication between processes mapped onto neighboring PNs can be completed within Δ_{io} only if the size of the data to be sent is not larger than the maximum size fixed a priori by the model. Communications that

- involve processes not mapped onto neighboring PNs, or
- require the transmission of data whose size is larger than the maximum size allowed by SYMPLE,

take several communication phases to be completed. However, several messages can be sent and received by one process during the same phase. In fact, several messages can be transmitted over the same link if the size of all the data to be sent is less than or equal to the maximum size fixed by SYMPLE. Furthermore, several messages can be sent and received over distinct links.

SYMPLE allows a basic communication form to occur within a communication phase, i.e. point-to-point, synchronous, and between processes mapped onto neighboring PNs. Messages exchanged between processes that are allocated to non-neighboring PNs take more communication phases to be *routed.*

The alternative choice of allowing communications involving non-neighboring PNs to be completed during a single communication phase [9], also produces the lengthening of the communication phase itself, and may lead to inefficient implementations for those programs that instead allow communication locality to be exploited.

The RISC-like features of SYMPLE are related to the reduced set of communication forms allowed, and to the possibility of providing more complex communication forms by combining the basic communication primitives supplied by the model.

2.1. CSP processes running according to SYMPLE

If the execution model is SYMPLE, all the processes composing a concurrent program exhibit an alternate execution of computation and communication phases, whatever execution *trace* (stream of sequential instructions and communication primitives) they follow. We propose a CSP-like language, called *CSP-SY*, designed to directly program a system adopting SYMPLE as execution model. Since the subdivision in phases is reflected in the constructs of the language, a tool is necessary to transform an asynchronous CSP program into a *CSP-SY* program. In fact computation and communication phases must be built out of a collections of commands able to be executed within the corresponding time intervals (Δ_c and Δ_{io}) fixed by the model. A *CSP-SY* program must be mapped so that communicating processes are allocated to neighboring PNs. As a consequence, if an unregular process network must be mapped on a physical network having a regular topology, some router processes may be added to transform it into a regular process network. Our analysis and optimization technique are applied to the process networks so obtained. The detailed syntax and semantics of the language are presented in [14]. Here, we only give an informal description of *CSP-SY*, which should become clearer when specific examples will be presented.

A *CSP-SY* program consists of a collections of parallel processes. The parallel command cannot be nested, except for modeling the parallel execution of more communication commands within a single communication phase. The syntax of these communication command is the same as CSP, where the commands are characterized by message-type constructors. The symbol *nio* is used to model an empty communication phase, i.e. a time period (Δ_{io}) during which a process does not send nor receive any message.

As regards the computation phases, they have been defined as a sequential execution of statements only involving the local environment of the processes. Their execution must take a time less than or equal to Δ_c. The time taken to execute every sequential statement is considered to be known and depends on the specific sequential processor adopted. The symbol *nop* is used to denote an empty computation phase, i.e. a time period (Δ_c) during which a process remains idle.

Moreover, all the computations have to be performed within the computation phases. Thus, the arguments of the output commands are to be variables, since the burden of evaluating the expressions have to be moved to the preceding computation phases. In the same way and for the same reason, all the logical predicates, which appear in *if-then-else* and *while* constructs, as well as in the global guards of *alternative/repetitive commands*, are supposed to be Boolean variables.

3. Static analysis of synchronous concurrent programs

We present an automatic *static analysis* able to deduce the behavior of *CSP-SY* programs. In the next section effective *optimization techniques*, improving the overall performance of a concurrent program, are also proposed.

The optimizations are based upon the *data-flow analysis* of the phases composing every process and the synchronous analysis of the behavior of the concurrent program. In fact, the data-flow analysis shows when *code motions* and *code migrations* can be performed without changing the semantics of the program. The synchronous analysis shows instead when such optimizations improve the overall performance.

In order to statically analyze the behavior of a *CSP-SY* concurrent program, every process is characterized by means of a finite automaton (FA). Each automaton identifies all the possible execution sequences of the associated process with respect to the global time of the system. The FAs modeling the processes of a concurrent program can be merged to build a *joint FA*, provided that all the *CSP-SY* processes modeled by these FAs are mapped onto neighboring PNs. The new joint FA models the behavior of all the processes, and points out the phases during which the processes may be idle due to waiting for synchronization. The optimization techniques are applied to the joint FA so obtained. These modeling techniques have been inspired by a static analysis [10] for *real-time* concurrent programs.

For the sake of brevity, in this paper we do not show how such FAs can be obtained, and how they can be merged. The complete formal analysis can be found in [14].

3.1. Processes characterized by FAs

The FA associated with every process P_i is derived from a regular expression. The symbols of this expression belong to an alphabet denoted by Σ_i. The events represented by the symbols in Σ_i are computation and communication phases of process P_i.

As regards the computation phases, the symbols adopted are alphanumeric labels. As an example, the phases belonging to process P_i will be denoted by a_i, b_i, c_i, d_i, etc. To simplify the presentation, we utilize the same labels to represent the computation phases in the *CSP-SY* programs. Along with the *nop* symbol, these labels make up the alphabet Σ_{C_i}.

As regards the communication phases, we need symbols to represent not only phases during which a communication can occur, but also phases during which a communication cannot occur because the partner process is not ready for the synchronization. Along with the *nio* symbol, these symbols makes up Σ_{IO_i}.

The symbols belonging to Σ_{IO_i} depend on the specific processes with which process P_i exchanges messages. To specify the composition of Σ_{IO_i}, we need define the alphabet $\Sigma_{I/O}$, which introduces the symbols adopted to describe the communications between pairs of processes. Let $[P_1 \parallel .. \parallel P_N]$ be a concurrent program including N parallel processes. The alphabet $\Sigma_{I/O}$ is constituted by the following records:

- $< i, j, constr, ! > \in \Sigma_{I/O}$ if there exists a communication phase in process P_i during which P_i executes an output command of the form $P_j!constr(...)$;
- $< i, j, constr, ? > \in \Sigma_{I/O}$ if there exists a communication phase in process P_j during which P_j executes an input command of the form $P_i?constr(...)$;

To describe a communication phase of process P_i during which one or more input/output commands are completed, we use symbols belonging to $COMM_i$, which is defined as follows:

$$COMM_i = \{< i, j, constr, ! > \in \Sigma_{I/O} \mid i \neq j\} \cup \{< j, i, constr, ? > \in \Sigma_{I/O} \mid i \neq j\}.$$

To describe a generic process P_i that wishes to communicate with another process during a given phase, i.e. to denote a communication phase that should be modeled by $D \in COMM_i$ and that cannot be completed because the partner process is not ready for synchronization, the following symbol is used:

$$R(D), \qquad \textit{where R stands for Ready}.$$

The complete definition of the alphabet Σ_{IO_i} is given by:

$$\Sigma_{IO_i} = \{nio\} \cup COMM_i \cup R(COMM_i),$$

where $R(COMM_i) = \{R(D) \mid D \in COMM_i\}$.

The communication phases of process P_i are represented either by nio or by subsets of

$$COMM_i \cup R(COMM_i)\ ^1.$$

As an example, if process P_i has to execute the phase $[P_j\ !\ constr_1(e) \parallel P_y\ ?\ constr_2(x)]$, and both the communications are completed within only one communication phase, then such an event will be represented by the subset $\{ < i, j, constr_1, ! >, < y, i, constr_2, ? > \}$.

Finally, we can define the alphabet Σ_i:

$$\Sigma_i = \Sigma_{C_i} \cup \Sigma_{IO_i}.$$

3.1.1. Association of regular expressions with the language constructs

Rewriting rules are defined to associate regular expressions with the various language constructs. The symbols of these expressions belong to the alphabets defined above. By using these associations and the structural induction, a regular expression can be associated with every sequential process. Such expression describes the behavior of the process with respect to the global environment.

As an example, the following is the regular expressions associated with a communication phase of a generic process P_i:

$$L(P_j!constr(e)) = (R(< i, j, constr, ! >)\ nop)^* \ < i, j, constr, ! >,$$

where $L(S)$ is a function that associates regular expressions with the command list S of a generic process. The expression before models a generic process P_i that either synchronizes with process P_j without further delays, or waits for synchronization for a

[1] To simplify the notation, subsets of one element ($\{el\}$) are represented by the element itself (el)

time that is a multiple of $(\Delta_c + \Delta_{io})$. While process P_i waits for synchronization, the PN onto which P_i has been mapped remains idle (P_i executes *nop* empty phases).

An example of a regular expression associated with a compound communication phase (composed of *several input/output commands*) of a generic process P_i is the following:

$$
\begin{aligned}
&\boldsymbol{L}([P_j\,!\,constr_1(e)\;\;||\;\;P_h\,?\,constr_2(x)]) = \\
&(\;\{R(<i,j,constr_1,!>),\;R(<h,i,constr_2,?>)\}\;\;nop\;)^* \\
&(\quad \{<i,j,constr_1,!>,\;<h,i,constr_2,?>\}\;+ \\
&\qquad +\;(\;\{<i,j,constr_1,!>,\;R(<h,i,constr_2,?>)\}\;nop\;\boldsymbol{L}(P_h?constr_2(x))\;)\;+ \\
&\qquad +\;(\;\{<h,i,constr_2,?>,\;R(<i,j,constr_1,!>)\}\;nop\;\boldsymbol{L}(P_j?constr_1(e))\;) \\
&)
\end{aligned}
$$

3.1.2. Generation of the FA associated with a single process

The FA that models every process P_i can be obtained from the regular expression $\boldsymbol{L}(P_i)$ by exploiting well-known algorithms [1]. The ε-transitions must be removed from such FAs. In such a way, the length of every sequence accepted by an ε-free automaton corresponds to the time taken for its execution (in terms of Δ_c and Δ_{io}).

Distinct processes may terminate at distinct time instants, so that the lengths of their execution sequences may be different. Hence, we introduce the symbol τ_c, which models an empty computation phase, and the symbol τ_{io}, which models an empty communication phase. Such symbols are used to model the termination of a process. They capture the behavior of the clock that continues to run even though the process is terminated.

3.2. Parallel composition

The FAs modeling the processes of a concurrent program can be *composed* in parallel to obtain a *joint FA*. Such an FA models all the possible combinations of execution sequences of the processes. Obviously, it is possible that execution sequences belonging to distinct processes cannot be composed, even though each sequence is separately accepted by the FA characterizing each process. Only if execution sequences can be composed, they are called *consistent* and are accepted by the joint FA. Two sequences are consistent iff they model the simultaneous execution of corresponding input/output commands, and do not model unnecessary waiting, i.e. two processes that wait for two corresponding input/output commands at the same time. With respect to the consistency of two execution sequences, the symbols τ_c and τ_{io} are analogous to *nop* (empty computation phase) and *nio* (empty communication phase), respectively.

The algorithm to merge the FAs associated with the processes composed in parallel is similar to that described in [10]. It uses the notion of *consistency* of distinct execution sequences that has been given informally before. In fact, the joint FA so obtained models each and every *consistent* combination of execution sequences belonging to the modeled processes.

3.2.1. Joint FAs of deterministic programs

We show an example of composition of FAs associated with deterministic *CSP-SY* processes. The concurrent program is the following:

```
P:: [P1 || P2]      P1:: a1;                  P2:: a2;
                         P2?constr(e);              nio;
                         b1;                        b2;
                         nio;                       nio;
                                                    c2;
                                                    P1!constr(x);
                                                    d2;
                                                    nio;
```

The transition sets corresponding to the FAs modeling the processes P_1 and P_2 are T_1 and T_2, respectively:

$$\begin{aligned} T_1 = \; \{ & [1,\ a_1,\ 2], [2,\ R(<2,1,constr,?>),\ 3], [3, nop, 2], [2,\ <2,1,constr,?>,\ 4], \\ & [4,\ b_1,\ 5], [5,\ nio,\ 6], [6,\ \tau_c,\ 7], [7,\ \tau_{io},\ 6] \}. \end{aligned}$$

$$\begin{aligned} T_2 = \; \{ & [1,\ a_2,\ 2], [2,\ nio,\ 3], [3,\ b_2,\ 4], [4,\ nio,\ 5], [5,\ c_2,\ 6], [6,\ R(<2,1,constr,!>),\ 7], \\ & [7,\ nop,\ 6], [6,\ <2,1,constr,!>,\ 8], [8,\ d_2,\ 9], [9,\ nio,\ 10], [10,\ \tau_c,\ 11], [11,\ \tau_{io},\ 10] \}. \end{aligned}$$

In both transition sets state 1 is the initial one, while 6 and 10 are the final states of T_1 and T_2, respectively. The transition set T of the *joint FA* obtained through composition is the following:

$$\begin{aligned} T = \; \{ & [(1,1),\ (a_1,a_2),\ (2,2)], [(2,2),\ (R(<2,1,constr,?>),nio),\ (3,3)], [(3,3),\ (nop,b_2),\ (2,4)], \\ & [(2,4),\ (R(<2,1,constr,?>),nio),\ (3,5)], [(3,5),\ (nop,c_2),\ (2,6)], \\ & [(2,6),\ (<2,1,constr,?>,<2,1,constr,!>),\ (4,8)], [(4,8),\ (b_1,d_2),\ (5,9)], \\ & [(5,9),\ (nio,nio),\ (6,10)], [(6,10),\ (\tau_c,\tau_c),\ (7,11)], [(7,11),\ (\tau_{io},\tau_{io}),\ (6,10)] \}. \end{aligned}$$

While the alphabets of T_1 and T_2 are Σ_1 and Σ_2 respectively, the new alphabet of T is $\Sigma_1 \times \Sigma_2$. The ith component $(i = 1,2)$ of a symbol $s \in \Sigma_1 \times \Sigma_2$ corresponds to an action performed by process P_i. Moreover, given N_1 and N_2, defined as the sets of states of T_1 and T_2 respectively, the set of states N of T is characterized by the relationship $N \subseteq N_1 \times N_2$. The cardinality of N is usually much less than the cardinality of $N_1 \times N_2$. This is due to the synchronous model adopted, which does not produce the explosion of the number of states in the parallel composition.

The joint FA shows when the processes wait for synchronization. Looking at the transition set T, we can notice that process P_1, after the execution of the computation phases a_1, corresponding to $[(1,1),\ (a_1,a_2),\ (2,2)]$, will execute two *empty computation phases* (nop), corresponding to $[(3,3),\ (nop,b_2),\ (2,4)]$ and $[(3,5),\ (nop,c_2),\ (2,6)]$.

Before illustrating the parallel composition of *nondeterministic* programs, i.e. programs whose processes make local and global choices, we show the issues in deriving the FAs to be associated with each nondeterministic process.

3.2.2. Modeling local nondeterminism

Local nondeterminism is introduced by the constructs *if-then-else* and *while*. The syntax of these constructs is similar to *alternative* and *repetitive* constructs, where the guards are only local and correspond to mutually exclusive predicates.

As we will see in the following, the information concerning *Boolean variables* and *conditions* are included in the FA associated with each process. This information is used by the optimization technique.

As an example, Fig. 1 shows a process P_i characterized by some *local choices*. The same figure also illustrates the transition set T_i of the FA modeling process P_i. New

```
Pi:: ai;
     *[bool1i -> nio;
                 bi;
                 nio;
                 [bool2i    -> ci;
                               nio;
                 []~bool2i  -> di;
                               nio;
                 ]
     ei;
     Pj!consr(x);
     fi;
     ]
     nio;
```

T_i = {
[1, a_i, 2] : //,
[2, nio, 3] : /$bool1_i$/,
[2, nio, 10] : / $\sim$ $bool1_i$/,
[3, b_i, 4] : //,
[4, nio, 5] : //,
[5, c_i, 6] : /$bool2_i$/,
[6, nio, 7] : //,
[5, d_i, 11] : / $\sim$ $bool2_i$/,
[11, nio, 7] : //,
[7, e_i, 8] : //,
[8, $< i, j, constr, ! >$, 9] : //,
[8, $R(< i, j, constr, ! >)$, 12] : //,
[12, nop, 8] : //,
[9, f_i, 2] : //,
[10, τ_c, 13] : //,
[13, τ_{io}, 10] : //
}.

Figure 1. A process P_i making local choices, and the transitions of the corresponding FA.

symbols are now associated with every transition. The new symbols, which are shown on the right side of the transitions belonging to T_i, correspond to the Boolean conditions that must hold to execute the associated transition. The two transitions [2, *nio*, 3] and [2, *nio*, 10] only differ in being associated with distinct Boolean conditions. Process P_i will execute the phase corresponding to the transition [2, *nio*, 3] only if the Boolean expression $bool1_i$ will be equal to *true*, while it will execute the other phase, corresponding to [2, *nio*, 10], only if $bool1_i$ will be equal to *false*. The states 2 and 5 are called *local choice states*.

Many transitions are associated with empty conditions (//). This means that the selection of these transitions does not depends on any local choice.

3.2.3. Modeling global and global+local nondeterminism

Global nondeterminism is introduced by *alternative* and *repetitive* commands with input guards only.

The regular expression associated with an alternative command has to model the waiting for synchronization on all the guards, as well as the success of one of the guards and the execution of the corresponding command list. We do not model the failure of a global guard due to the termination of the partner process (distributed termination). The failure of a guard may only depends on the local Boolean part of the guard.

The expression associated with a repetitive command, which is syntactically equivalent to a star (*) concatenated to an alternative command, is instead the Kleene closure of the expression modeling the alternative command.

To associate regular expression with an alternative/repetitive command whose guards include Boolean variables (global+local nondeterminism), we have to distinguish among the various subsets of guards on which the command may wait for synchronization. The guards making up these subsets depend on the values Boolean variables associated with the guards. As an example, consider the following process, where b_j is a Boolean

$T_i = \{$

$[1,\ a_i,\ 2]$ $: //,$

$[2,$
$\{R(<j,i,constr_j,?>),$ $: /b_j/,$
$R(<h,i,constr_h,?>)\},$
$3]$

$[2,\ <j,i,constr_j,?>,\ 4]$ $: /b_j/,$

$[2,\ <h,i,constr_h,?>,\ 5]$ $: /b_j/,$

$[3,\ nop,\ 6]$ $: //,$

$[6,$
$\{R(<j,i,constr_j,?>),$ $: //,$
$R(<h,i,constr_h,?>)\},$
$3]$

$[6,\ <j,i,constr_j,?>,\ 4]$ $: //,$

$[6,\ <h,i,constr_h,?>,\ 5]$ $: //,$

$[4,\ c_i,\ 10]$ $: //,$

$[5,\ d_i,\ 10]$ $: //,$

$[2,\ R(<h,i,constr_h,?>),\ 7]$ $: /\sim b_j/,$

$[2,\ <h,i,constr_h,?>,\ 9]$ $: /\sim b_j/,$

$[7,\ nop,\ 8]$ $: //,$

$[8,\ R(<h,i,constr_h,?>),\ 7]$ $: //,$

$[8,\ <h,i,constr_h,?>,\ 9]$ $: //,$

$[9,\ d_i,\ 10]$ $: //,$

$[10,\ nio,\ 11]$ $: //,$

$[11,\ \tau_c,\ 12]$ $: //,$

$[12,\ \tau_{io},\ 11]$ $: //$

$\}.$

Figure 2. Transition set of the FA modeling the nondeterministic process P_i.

variable:

```
Pi:: ai;
     [  bj; Pj?constrj(x) -> ci;
     [] Ph?constrh(z)     -> di;
     ]
     nio;
```

Fig. 2 shows the transition set of the FA that models P_i. Notice that the transition group that goes from transition $[2, \ldots, 3]$ to transition $[5, \ldots, 10]$ models the behavior of the alternative command in case b_j is equal to *true*. Conversely, the group that goes from $[2, \ldots, 7]$ to $[9, \ldots, 10]$ models the alternative command in case b_j is equal to *false*. Nonempty conditions are associated with only the transitions going out from the state 2, i.e. such a state corresponds to the check of the local conditions and to the selection of a given group of transitions.

3.2.4. Joint FAs of nondeterministic programs

When processes that perform local choices are composed in parallel, the merging algorithm has to take into account the local conditions associated with the transitions. The conditions are to be considered when two (or more) transitions turn out to be consistent, and their composition becomes a new transition of the joint FA. Consider $[j_1,\ C_1,\ k_1] \in T_1$ and $[j_2, C_2,\ k_2] \in T_2$, where T_1 and T_2 are the transition sets of two FAs. Suppose that the conditions associated with the two transitions are $/bool_1/$ and $/bool_2/$, respectively. If $\mathcal{C}_1$ and $\mathcal{C}_2$ are consistent, then $[(j_1, j_2),\ (C_1, C_2),\ (k_1, k_2)]$ will be a new transition of the joint FA, while $/bool_1/bool_2/$ will be the corresponding composite condition.

When two (or more) FAs associated with processes characterized by global nondeterminism are merged, it is possible that this global nondeterminism is removed. This occurs when no global guards of the same alternative/repetitive command can simultaneously be verified (during the same communication phase). On the other hand, nondeterminism continues to be present in the joint FA in case more global guards of an alternative/repetitive command become verified at the same time, i.e. when more

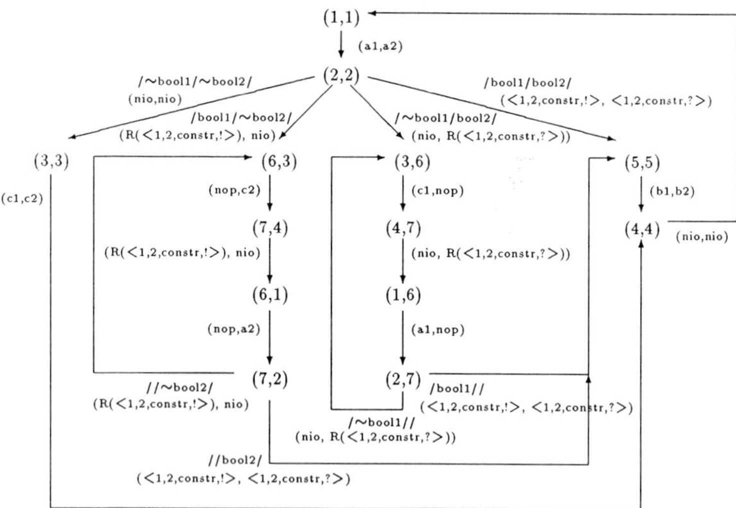

Figure 3. Joint FA modeling two loop-processes.

messages arrive at one process during the same communication phase. In this case, the receiving process has to make a global choice, and the joint FA reflects this choice by means of more transitions that go out from the same state and are associated with the same composite condition, i.e. such a state does not correspond to a local choice. Since our purpose is the exploitation of the joint FA to optimize a *specific implementation of the concurrent program*, we can remove from the joint FA part of the transitions modeling global nondeterminism. Thus, once removed global nondeterminism from the joint FAs, no differences exist between the joint FAs modeling global and local nondeterminism.

4. Optimization of *CSP-SY* programs

The optimizations of *CSP-SY* programs are basically of two types:

- one is concerned with the modification of the original control flow within a single process to reduce delays for synchronization, i.e. to reduce idle periods;
- the other is concerned with the migration of computation phases from processes that have phases that can be executed in parallel, to processes that are idle.

Both optimizations are based on the *data-flow analysis* of the phases making up each process. Data-flow analysis needs to determine whether phases can be moved within the same process as well as between distinct processes without changing the semantics of the program.

Given an execution trace of a process, the data-flow analysis [1, 15] produces a *data-dependency direct acyclic graphs* (DAGs). The analysis is applied to the elementary instructions composing each computation phase, and to the input/output commands making up the communications phases. As regards the input/output commands, every input command is considered as a new assignment of the target variable, and every output command as a new use of the variable containing the value to be sent to the other process. The nodes of the DAGs so produced correspond to computation phases and input/output commands. Moreover, also local choice nodes and some specific dependency relationships are to be represented in the DAGs.

4.1. Deterministic programs

The basic technique can be easily understood if we consider two deterministic *CSP-SY* processes, which communicate each other and are mapped on neighboring PNs. The technique consists of the following steps

- a data-flow graph is generated for each process, where each node corresponds to either a computation phase or an input/output command;
- the traces of the two processes are re-built trying to obtain traces whose lengths are smaller than the length of the transition sequence obtained by merging the FAs associated with the processes. The computation/communication phases of these traces are thought of as temporal slots in which the optimization technique has to insert the nodes belonging to the data-flow graphs.

A node belonging to a data-flow graph of a process can be inserted into the temporal slot of that process if all its predecessors in the graph have been inserted into previous slots. A node having such characteristics is called *free* node.

Corresponding communication commands must be inserted into slots representing simultaneous communication phases of the processes. More communication commands can be inserted within a single phase if they are executable within the Δ_{io} interval [2].

nio and *nop* phases are inserted when no communication commands and no communication phases, respectively, exist among the free nodes of the data-flow graph. A *migration* of a computation phase may occur in case no free nodes exist in the graph associated with a process (and thus a *nop* phase should be inserted in the corresponding slot), but there exist a free node in the data-flow graph associated with the other process.

An analogy is possible between this technique, and the *list scheduling* algorithm used in [3] to build a VLIW program. The *Trace Scheduling* technique tries to build some very long instructions (that corresponds to our temporal slots), but it considers sequential programs, whose instructions refers to a single environment. Conversely, we have more processes, each with its own environment, so that when the various computation phases and input/output commands are assigned to the temporal slots, we have to take into account that they refer to distinct environments. Thus, when we assign a computation phase c_i of a process P_i to a slot of another process P_j (*migration*), it is possible that some portions of the environment of P_i, namely $inp(c_i)$, must be communicated to P_j (to be accessed by the migrated phase), as well as some portions of the environment modified by the migrated phase, namely $out(c_i)$, must be returned to process P_i (to be accessed by following phases). This means that, in order to perform the migration, some new input/output commands must be inserted into both processes.

[2]Such message-passing optimization minimizes the number of synchronizations required, because concatenates multiple short messages to be sent to the same process

4.2. Nondeterministic programs: *MultiTrace Scheduling*

While the optimization technique above can be applied to deterministic processes to produce optimized programs, we have to take into account the local choices made by the processes when nondeterministic programs are considered.

A similar problem is faced by the *Trace Scheduling* techniques, that

- tries to pick the most frequently executed trace from all the traces that a *sequential* program may follows due to its local choices (*conditional branches*), and
- applies an optimization technique devised for programs without local choices.

In that case, the selection of the most likely trace of a sequential program is performed by exploiting the *control flow graph* associated with the sequential program as well as some *profiling information.* In our case we have more processes, each one performing local choices. In order to apply the same optimization technique presented in Sec. 4.1, we have to select a combination of the most likely traces followed by each process. For this reason, our optimization technique has been called *MultiTrace Scheduling.* For the selection we exploit the joint FA produced by our static analysis, as well as some profiling information about the execution probability of the combinations of traces. Such combinations of traces are modeled by a sequences of transitions of the joint FA.

4.3. An example of optimization

In order to describe the optimization technique, consider the following two loop-processes, communicating each other:

```
P1 :: *[TRUE -> a1;                         P2 :: *[TRUE -> a2;
               [bool1  -> P2!constr(x);                    [bool2  -> P1!constr(y);
                          b1;                                         b2;
               []~bool1-> nio;                             []~bool2-> nio;
                          c1;                                         c2;
               ]                                           ]
               nio;                                        nio;
      ]                                           ]
```

The diagram of the joint FA that models this *CSP-SY* program is shown in Fig. 3. The diagram shows all the conditions associated with the transitions of the FA except for empty conditions. We can notice that both processes do not execute empty computation phases (*nop*) only when either the condition $\sim bool_1 \wedge \sim bool_2$ or the condition $bool_1 \wedge bool_2$ is verified. This corresponds to the selection of either the transition $[(2,2),\ldots,(5,5)]$ or the transition $[(2,2),\ldots,(3,3)]$. Conversely, when either the transition $[(2,2),\ldots,(6,3)]$ or the transition $[(2,2),\ldots,(3,6)]$ is selected, one of the two process waits for synchronization. Specifically, the loops

$$(6,3) \rightarrow (7,4) \rightarrow (6,1) \rightarrow (7,2) \rightarrow (6,3) \quad \text{and} \quad (3,6) \rightarrow (4,7) \rightarrow (1,6) \rightarrow (2,7) \rightarrow (3,6)$$

correspond to waiting cycles of P_1 and P_2, respectively.

MultiTrace Scheduling technique exploits this diagram for the optimization. In fact, the technique

- selects one transition sequence that is regarded as the most likely to be executed,
- produces an optimized transition sequence,
- inserts this new sequence into the initial joint FA, adding some *bookkeeping* code,
- repeats the previous three steps for another un-optimized transition sequence, until no un-optimized sequences exist in the joint FA,
- produces the new processes from the optimized joint FA.

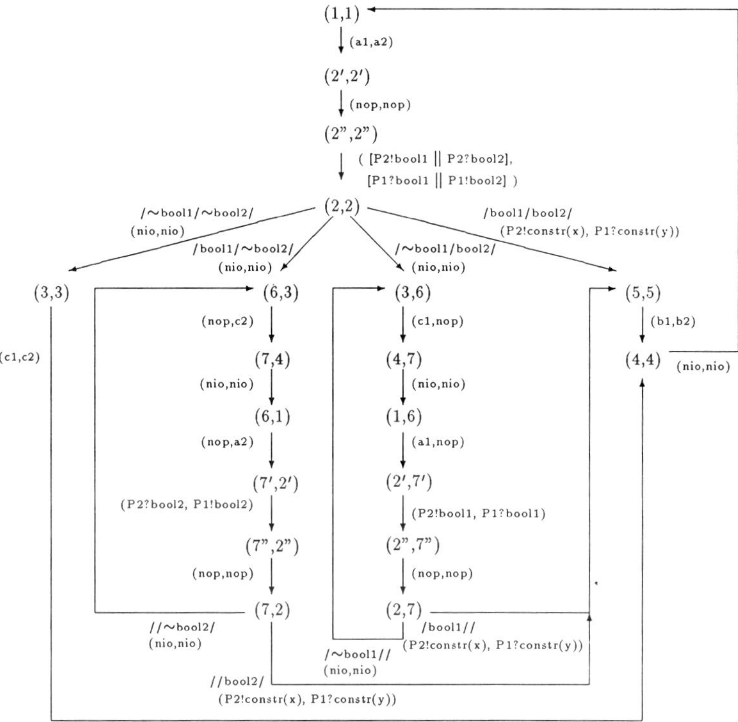

Figure 4. Joint FA with spreading out of local choices.

After the optimizations have been applied to the joint FA, the new processes can be derived from the optimized joint FA. This is carried out by generating the FA associated with every process. These new FAs are obtained by making the projection of the symbols labeling the transitions of the joint FA with respect to each component.

In applying our technique, we have to take into account the presence of *composite conditions*. Each condition is a *global information* that is to be shared by all processes before applying the above optimizations. The sharing is necessary because when a given combination of traces is optimized, some new communication may be inserted to obtain the migration of some computation phases.

Since composite conditions are shared by all the processes, such conditions continue to be associated with the transitions of the projected FAs. Hence, all the optimized processes,which may be easily obtained from the projected FAs, will perform simultaneously their choices on the basis of the shared knowledge of the composite conditions.

Fig. 4 shows a solution for the problem of sharing composite conditions [3]. The values

[3]Notice that, in this new diagram, the symbols representing the success of a given communication and the waiting for synchronization have been substituted by the corresponding input/output commands and by empty phases (*nio*), respectively.

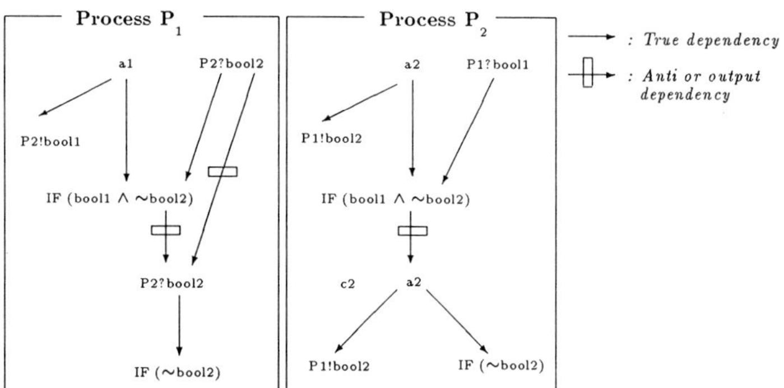

Figure 5. Data flow graphs of the traces to be optimized.

of the Boolean variables entailing the local choices have been spread out by means of new SYMPLE input/output commands. These commands have been inserted before the states corresponding to the global choices. Now, the *MultiTrace Scheduling* can be applied. The new communications we have inserted can be optimized as normal communication primitives.

Suppose the following transition sequence is regarded as the most frequently executed:

$$(1,1) \rightarrow (2',2') \rightarrow (2",2") \rightarrow (2,2) \rightarrow (6,3) \rightarrow (7,4) \rightarrow$$
$$(6,1) \rightarrow (7',2') \rightarrow (7",2") \rightarrow (7,2) \rightarrow (6,3)$$

The data-flow graphs of the two traces corresponding to this sequence are shown in Fig. 5. Notice that c_2 and a_2 can be executed in parallel. Moreover, $bool_1$ and $bool_2$ are assigned by the phases a_1 and a_2, respectively. Since the above transition sequence models a waiting cycle of process P_1, all the sequence can be shortened if the computation phase c_2 is executed by P_1 (*migration*). In fact, looking at the optimized FA shown in Fig. 6, the new transition sequence produced by the optimization technique is:

$$(N1) \rightarrow (N2) \rightarrow (N3) \rightarrow (N4) \rightarrow (N5) \rightarrow (N4)$$

Notice that, since a_2 is now executed by process P_1 (transition $[(N5),\ldots,(N4)]$), the boolean variable $bool_2$ is no longer sent from P_2 to P_1. On the contrary, its new value must be communicated by P_1 to P_2 together with the other data contained in $out(a_2)$. The length of the new transition sequence is considerably reduced. Notice that the time taken to execute the new loop

$$(N4) \rightarrow (N5) \rightarrow (N4)$$

is $(\Delta_c + \Delta_{io})$, while the time taken to execute the loop

$$(6,3) \rightarrow (7,4) \rightarrow (6,1) \rightarrow (7,2) \rightarrow (6,3)$$

of the initial FA was $2(\Delta_c + \Delta_{io})$. If this loop is executed very frequently, this optimized version of the program runs in a time that is about 50% of the time taken by the initial program.

Some *bookkeeping* transitions have been inserted in this new FA to reconnect the optimized transition sequence to the rest of the transitions. As an example, consider the transition $[N3,\ldots,B1]$. This transition has been added because the conditional test

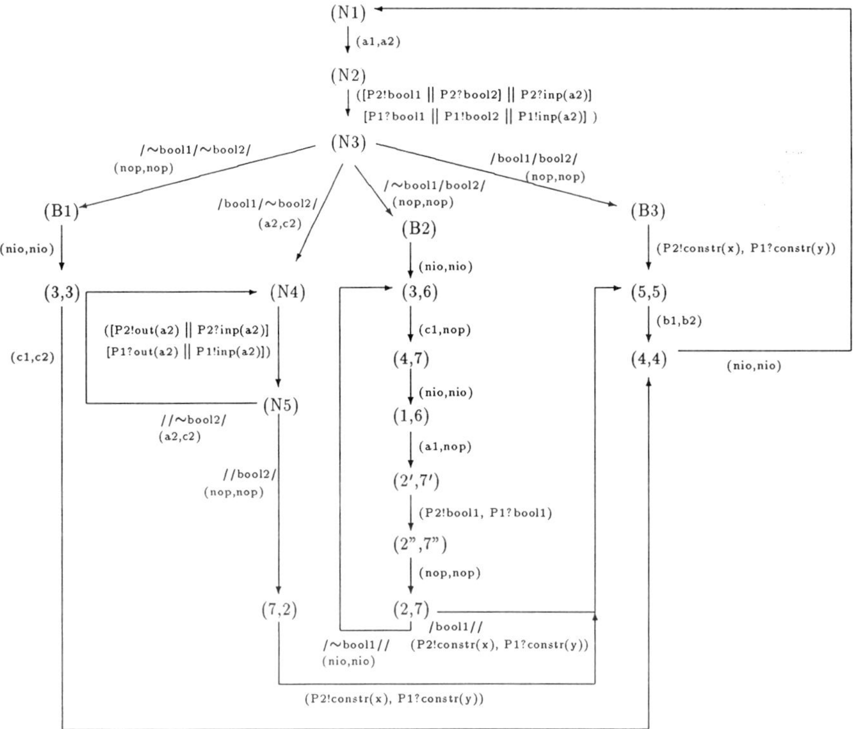

Figure 6. Joint FA after the optimization of the most frequent combination of traces.

has been moved before a computation phase instead of a communication phase.

4.4. Global states vs local communications

In the example above, the problem of sharing composite conditions has been solved by inserting some new SYMPLE communications to spread out the various Boolean variables entailing each composite condition. Then such new input/output commands have been optimized as normal communication commands. This method works well if we have a complete connection between all the PNs of the system. If this is not the case, local communications do not suffice for broadcasting values to all the processes. In fact, the form of communication that in this case is required is *global*, while SYMPLE only allows *local* communications. A solution might be to provide a specific *global synchronization phase* in the model. Notice that the amount of information to be exchanged is very limited (e.g. one bit), so that the phase can be carried out with low overhead. The time instants when each global synchronization phase should occur can be determined on the basis of the joint FA. For instance, looking at the FA of Fig. 3, such a synchronization should take place just after the computation phase corresponding to the transition $[(1,1),\ldots,(2,2)]$.

In the next section we present an example of *CSP-SY* program in which some routing processes have been inserted to deliver non local communications. Thus, the target system does not have a completely connected interconnection network, so that we need a global synchronization phase to share the global conditions.

4.5. Another example: a processor farm

The program we describe is built out of an Emitter process, which sends some tasks to two Worker processes, and a Collector process, which receives the output from the two Worker processes. The corresponding process network with the Router processes is shown in Fig. 7. Notice that we have two Routers (*RE*) to deliver messages from the Emitter to the Workers, and two other Routers (*RC*) to deliver messages from the Workers to the Collector. The mapping of the processes to the PNs of the system is also shown, where each PN is denoted by a distinct number. Moreover, the allocation of the channels to the links of the system is shown.

A set of libraries might be supplied to avoid directly programming the routing code. A different library call might be furnished for each pattern of parallelism [6], and for each physical topology we have at disposal. For instance, in the case of the program above, the pattern of parallelism exploited is the so-called *processor farm*, while the topology on which the program can be mapped is a *mesh*.

The code of the processes shown in Fig. 7 is the following:

```
PROGRAM :: [E || RE1 || RE2 || W1 || W2 || RC1 || RC2 || C]

E::init;
   *[~end -> RE1!task(T);
             prod;
   ]
   nio;

C::init;
   *[RC2?res(RES) -> collect;
   ]

Wi::init;
    REi?task(X);
    *[TRUE->ai;              /* Computation */
            nio;
            bi;              /* Computation */
            nio;
            ci;              /* Computation */
            nio;
            di;              /* Computation */
            nio;
            ei;              /* Computation */
            [REi?task(X) || RCi!res(RES)]
    ]

RE1::init;
     E?task(X);
     nop;
     *[TRUE->[E?task(Y)||RE2!task(X)]
             nop;
             [E?task(X)||W1!task(Y)]
             nop;
     ]

RC1::init;
     W1?res(X);
     nop;
     *[TRUE->[W1?res(Y) || RC2!res(X)]
             nop;
             [W1?res(X) || RC2!res(Y)]
             nop;
     ]

RE2::init;
     RE1?task(X);
     nop;
     *[TRUE->[RE1?task(Y)||W2!task(X)]
             nop;
             [RE1?task(X)||W2!task(Y)]
             nop;
     ]

RC2::init;
     Wi?res(X);
     nop;
     *[TRUE->[RC1?res(Y) || C!res(X)]
             nop;
             [W2?res(X) || C!res(Y)]
             nop;
     ]
```

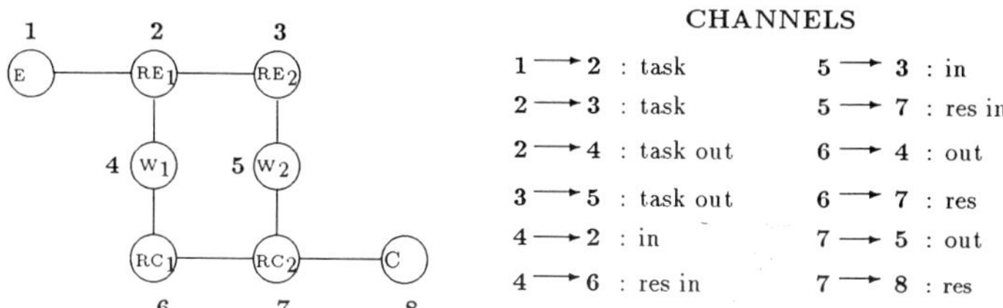

Figure 7. Process network of a processor farm, with the mapping of processes and channels.

Notice that the channels that are associated with the type constructors *in* and *out*, and that are shown in Fig. 7, do not belong to the original program. As we will see in the following, they are introduced by our optimization techniques to perform some code migrations.

The joint FA obtained by merging the FAs associated to every process has 106 states. In order to perform our optimizations, we have to pay attention to the most likely transition sequence of this new FA. This sequence is shown in the following. It corresponds to the case in which the Emitter has tasks to be processed, both Workers are processing some tasks, while the Collector is receiving the results of the elaboration of some tasks.

```
[(17),
    (nop,
    nop,
    nop,
    a1,
    a2,
    nop,
    nop,
    nop),
(18)] : /////////

[(18),
    (P2!task(T),
    [P1?task(Y) || P3!task(X)],
    P2?task(X),
    nio,
    nio,
    P7!res(X),
    [P6?res(Y) || P8!res(X)],
    P7?res(RES)),
(19)] : /////////

[(19),
    (prod,
    nop,
    nop,
    b1,
    b2,
    nop,
    nop,
    collect),
(20)] : /////////

[(20),
    (nio,
    nio,
    nio,
    nio,
    nio,
    nio,
    P8!res(Y),
    P7?res(RES)),
(9, 14, 7, 7, 7, 10, 17, 5)] : /end////////

[(20),
    (P2!task(T),
    P1?task(X),
    nio,
    nio,
    nio,
    nio,
    P8!res(Y),
    P7?res(RES)),
(21)] : /~end////////

[(21),
    (prod,
    nop,
    nop,
    c1,
    c2,
    nop,
    nop,
    collect),
(22)] : /////////

[(22),
    (nio,
    nio,
    nio,
    nio,
    nio,
    nio,
    nio,
    nio),
(23)] : /////////

[(23),
    (nop,
    nop,
    nop,
    d1,
    d2,
    nop,
    nop,
    nop),
(24)] : /////////

[(24),
    (nio,
    nio,
    nio,
    nio,
    nio,
    nio,
    nio,
    nio),
(25)] : /////////
```

```
[(25),
    (nop,
    nop,
    nop,
    e1,
    e2,
    nop,
    nop,
    nop),
(26)] : /////////

[(26),
    (nio,
    P4!task(Y),
    P5!task(X),
    [P2?task(X) || P6!res(RES)],
    [P3?task(X) || P7!res(RES)],
    P4?res(Y),
    P5?res(X),
    nio),
(27)] : /////////

[(27),
    (nop,
    nop,
    nop,
    a1,
    a2,
    nop,
    nop,
    nop),
(28)] : /////////

[(28),
    (P2!task(T),
    [P1?task(Y) || P3!task(X)],
    P2?task(Y),
    nio,
    nio,
    P7!res(Y),
    [P6?res(Y) || P8!res(X)],
    P7?res(RES)),
(29)] : /////////

[(29),
    (prod,
    nop,
    nop,
    b1,
    b2,
    nop,
    nop,
    collect),
(30)] : /////////

[(30),
    (nio,
    nio,
    nio,
    nio,
    nio,
    nio,
    P8!res(Y),
    P7?res(RES)),
(9, 14, 14, 7, 7, 17, 17, 5)] : /end///////

[(30),
    (P2!task(T),
    P1?task(X),
    nio,
    nio,
    nio,
    nio,
    P8!res(Y),
    P7?res(RES)),
(31)] : /~end///////

[(31),
    (prod,
    nop,
    nop,
    c1,
    c2,
    nop,
    nop,
    collect),
(32)] : /////////

[(32),
    (nio,
    nio,
    nio,
    nio,
    nio,
    nio,
    nio,
    nio),
(33)] : /////////

[(33),
    (nop,
    nop,
    nop,
    d1,
    d2,
    nop,
    nop,
    nop),
(34)] : /////////

[(34),
    (nio,
    nio,
    nio,
    nio,
    nio,
    nio,
    nio,
    nio),
(35)] : /////////

[(35),
    (nop,
    nop,
    nop,
    e1,
    e2,
    nop,
    nop,
    nop),
(36)] : /////////

[(36),
    (nio,
    P4!task(Y),
    P5!task(Y),
    [P2?task(X) || P6!res(RES)],
    [P3?task(X) || P7!res(RES)],
    P4?res(X),
    P5?res(X),
    nio),
(37)] : /////////

[(37),
    (nop,
    nop,
    nop,
    a1,
    a2,
    nop,
    nop,
    nop),
(18)] : /////////
```

Notice that this transition sequence corresponds to a loop (from the transition [18, ..., 19] to the transition [37, ..., 18]). The processes spend most of their execution time in this loop until a termination condition occurs.

The states of these transitions have been renamed to simplify the presentation. Since the loop begins at the state 18, the processes execute 18 transition before entering the loop. The only states that conserve the original names (obtained as Cartesian product of the states of the FAs that have been merged) are the *off–trace* branch, i.e.

the transitions selected for the condition $/end////////$. Moreover, the *nio* symbols have been substituted for the symbols corresponding to waiting for synchronization ($R(\ldots)$), while the synchronization symbols have been replaced with the corresponding input/output commands.

As the Trace Scheduling technique, *MultiTrace Scheduling* tries to optimize the inner loops first. Hence, considering the loop in the transition sequence above, we have to determine the data-flow graph for every trace executed by the processes involved. Such data flow graphs are shown in Fig. 8.

Picking the phases and the input/output commands off the graphs, our technique rebuilds the elementary steps of the processes involved, and performs some code migrations. Some new channels (*in* and *out*) are placed between some *neighboring* PNs for allowing such migrations. Since in this case we have not a complete connection among the nodes of our architecture, we cannot spread out the local choices by using the local communications of SYMPLE. Thus, in the optimized traces, the choices on the global conditions will be performed simultaneously by all the processes involved, but a *global synchronization phase* has to occur before to make known to all the processes the values of the Boolean variables entailing such choices.

The new traces obtained by our optimization technique are shown in Fig. 9.

The entries of the table correspond to either computation or communication phases. Such entries, which are denoted by labels Ti, $i \in \{1,\ldots,12\}$, will become new transactions of the optimized joint FA. In fact, Fig. 10 shows the new transition sequence that will replace the original transition loop (from $[18,\ldots,19]$ to $[37,\ldots,18]$). No bookkeeping code needs in this case, because neither computation phases nor input/output commands have been moved either before or after the local choices.

The new loop is 12 transition long, while the original one was 20 transitions long. In case this loop is executed for enough times, we obtain a reduction of the overall execution time by about 60%. Such an optimization has been possible because some of the computation phases of the Workers can be executed in parallel. Thus, some of these phases have been migrated to the neighboring, idle, Router processes.

5. Conclusion

A synchronous execution model has been introduced. It allows the static analysis of a CSP-like program and a specific optimization technique to be devised. Such a technique restructures the sequential processes allocated to the PNs of a multicomputer by statically inserting code for the migration of sub-tasks from one process to a neighboring idle process.

The optimization technique, called *MultiTrace Scheduling*, is an extension of *Trace Scheduling*. It tries to compact (shorten) a combination of possible traces followed by different process, while *Trace Scheduling* compacts a trace belonging to a single sequential process.

MultiTrace Scheduling can be thought as of a parallelizing strategy, since migrations occur only when a process has more sub-tasks that can be executed in parallel. On the other hand, it performs a static load-balancing between neighboring processes. Other models perform this kind of "local" load-balancing in a dynamic way [13]. The technique

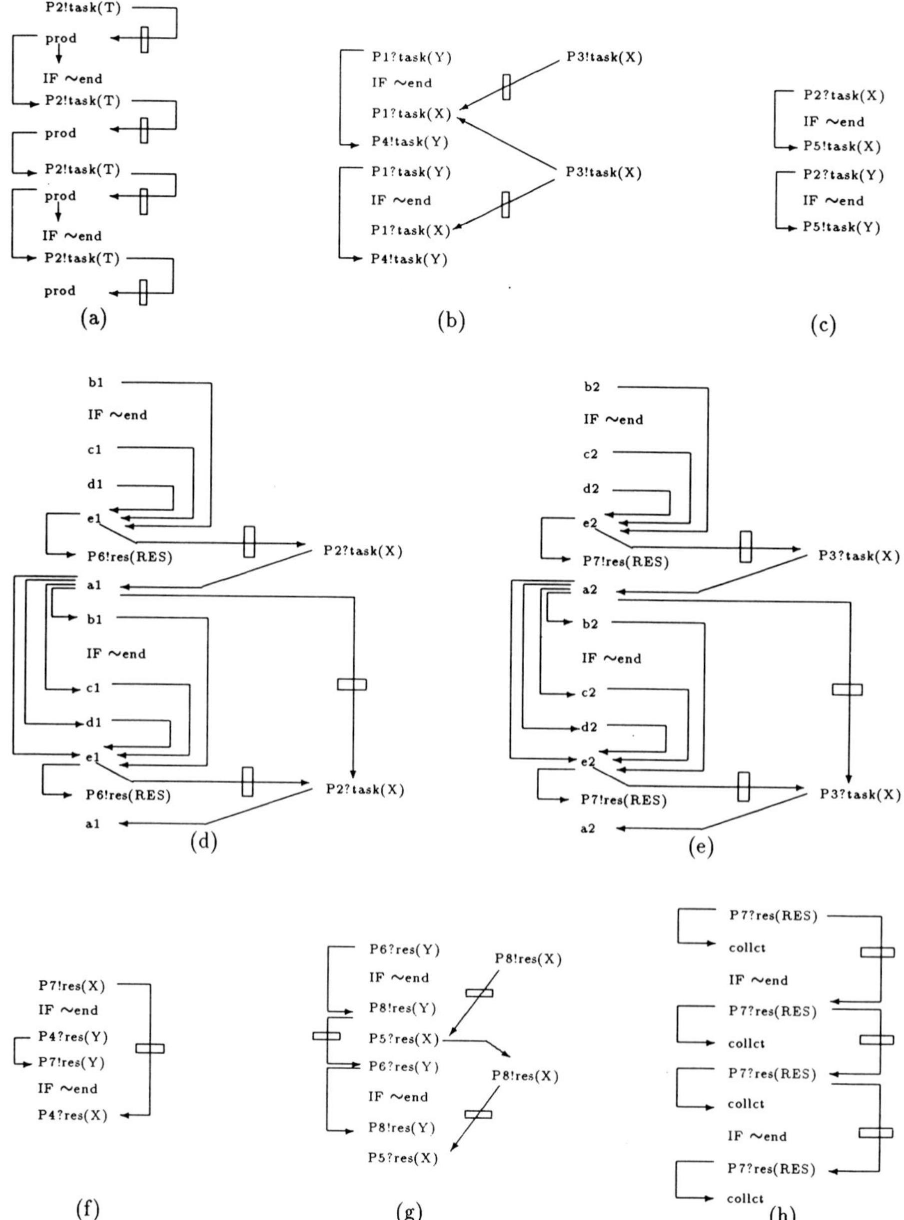

Figure 8. Data flow graphs of the most likely traces of process P1 (a), process P2 (b), process P3 (c), etc.

	P1	P2	P3	P4	P5	P6	P7	P8
T1	P2!task(T)	P1?task(Y) P3!task(X) P4?in(c1)	P2?task(X) P5?in(c2)	P2!in(c1) P6!in(d1)	P7!res(X) P3!in(c2) P7!in(d2)	P6?res(Y) P4?in(d1)	P8!res(X) P5?in(d2)	P7?res(RES)
T2	prod	c1	c2	b1	b2	d1	d2	collect
choice	IF ~ end	IF ~ end	IF ~ end	IF ~ end	IF ~ end	IF ~ end	IF ~ end	IF ~ end
T3	P2!task(T)	P1?task(X) P4!out(c1)	P5!out(c2)	P2?out(c1) P6?out(d1)	P3?in(c2) P7?out(d2)	P4!out(d1)	P8!res(Y) P5!out(d2)	P7?res(RES)
T4	prod			e1	e2			collect
T5		P3!task(X) P4!task(Y)	P2?task(Y) P5!task(X)	P2?task(X) P6!res(RES)	P3?task(X) P7!res(RES)	P4?res(Y)	P5?res(X)	
T6				a1	a2			
T7	P2!task(T)	P1?task(Y) P4?in(c1)	P5?in(c2)	P2!in(c1) P6!in(d1)	P3!in(c2) P7!in(d2)	P7!res(Y) P4?in(d1)	P6?res(Y) P8!res(X) P5?in(d2)	P7?res(RES)
T8	prod	c1	c2	b1	b2	d1	d2	collect
choice	IF ~ end	IF ~ end	IF ~ end	IF ~ end	IF ~ end	IF ~ end	IF ~ end	IF ~ end
T9	P2!task(T)	P1?task(X) P4!out(c1)	P5!out(c2)	P2?out(c1) P6?out(d1)	P3?in(c2) P7?out(d2)	P4!out(d1)	P8!res(Y) P5!out(d2)	P7?res(RES)
T10	prod			e1	e2			collect
T11		P4!task(Y)	P5!task(Y)	P2?task(X) P6!res(RES)	P3?task(X) P7!res(RES)	P4?res(X)	P5?res(X)	
T12				a1	a2			

Figure 9. New traces for the most likely transaction sequence.

$\big[(18),\ \mathbf{T1},\ (N1)\big]$: $/////////$
$\big[(N1),\ \mathbf{T2},\ (N2)\big]$: $/////////$
$\big[(N2),\ \mathbf{T3},\ (N3)\big]$: $/\sim end///////$
$\big[(N2),$
$(nio,$
$nio,$
$nio,$
$nio,$
$nio,$
$nio,$
$P8!res(Y),$
$P7?res(RES)),$
$(9,14,7,7,7,10,17,5)\big]$: $/end///////$
$\big[(N3),\ \mathbf{T4},\ (N4)\big]$: $/////////$
$\big[(N4),\ \mathbf{T5},\ (N5)\big]$: $/////////$
$\big[(N5),\ \mathbf{T6},\ (N6)\big]$: $/////////$

$\big[(N6),\ \mathbf{T7},\ (N7)\big]$: $/////////$
$\big[(N7),\ \mathbf{T8},\ (N8)\big]$: $/////////$
$\big[(N8),\ \mathbf{T9},\ (N9)\big]$: $/\sim end///////$
$\big[(N8),$
$(nio,$
$nio,$
$nio,$
$nio,$
$nio,$
$nio,$
$P8!res(Y),$
$P7?res(RES)),$
$(9,14,14,7,7,17,17,5)\big]$: $/end///////$
$\big[(N9),\ \mathbf{T10},\ (N10)\big]$: $/////////$
$\big[(N10),\ \mathbf{T11},\ (N11)\big]$: $/////////$
$\big[(N11),\ \mathbf{T12},\ (18)\big]$: $/////////$

Figure 10. Optimized transition sequence.

can be extended to also produce the migration of computation phases to PNs onto which no processes of the concurrent program has been mapped.

While the analysis of the program is synchronous, the optimized processes can be executed without synchronizing the clocks of the PNs involved. The necessary synchronization can be obtained by employing synchronous input/output primitives. The asynchronous model must be used when we cannot determine the exact length of the computation phases but only an average. This may occur, for instance, in presence of caching.

1 A. V. Aho, R. Sethi, and J. D. Ullman. *Compilers: Principles, Techniques and Tools.* Addison-Wesley, 1986.

2 M. Danelutto, R. Di Meglio, Orlando S., and Vanneschi M. A Methodology for the Development and the Support of Massively Parallel Programs. In *Proc. of the EIT Workshop on Parallel and Distributed Systems*, Florence, Italy, September 1991. To be published in FGCS journal.

3 J.A. Fisher. Trace Scheduling: A Technique for Global Microcode Compaction. *IEEE Transactions on Computers*, C-30(7):478–490, July 1981.

4 J.A. Fisher. The VLIW Machine: A Multiprocessor for Compiling Scientific Code. *IEEE Computer*, 17(7):45–53, July 1984.

5 J.L. Hennessy and D.A. Patterson. *Computer Architecture: a Quantitative Approach.* Morgan Kaufmann Publisher, San Mateo, California, 1990.

6 A.J.G. Hey. Experiment in MIMD Parallelism. In *Proc. of Int. Conf. PARLE '89*, pages 28–42, Eindhoven, The Netherlands, June 1989. LNCS 366 Spinger-Verlag.

7 C.A.R. Hoare. Communicating Sequential Processes. *Communications of the ACM*, 21(8):666–677, August 1978.

8 C.A.R. Hoare. *Communicating Sequential Processes.* Prentice-Hall International, 1985.

9 L. Lamport. Using Time Instead of Timeout for Fault-Tolerant Distributed Systems. *ACM Transactions on Programming Languages and Systems*, 6(2):254–280, April 1984.

10 L.Y. Liu and R.K. Shyamasundar. Static Analysis of Real-Time Distributed Systems. *IEEE Transactions on Software Engineering*, 16(4):373–388, April 1990.

11 D. May. Toward General Purpose Parallel Computers. Presented at the CRAI Spring International Seminar on Higly Parallel Processing, Capri, May 1990.

12 D. May. Transputer and Routers: Component for Concurrent Machines. Presented at the CRAI Spring International Seminar on Higly Parallel Processing, Capri, May 1990.

13 D.L. McBurney and M.R. Sleep. Transputer-Based Experiments with ZAPP architecture. In *Proc. of Int. Conf. PARLE '87*, pages 242–259, Eindhoven, The Netherlands, 1987. LNCS 258-259 Spinger-Verlag.

14 S. Orlando. *Exploiting Synchronous Models for Distributed Memory Multiprocessor Architectures.* PhD thesis, Dipartimento di Informatica, Università di Pisa - Italy, March 1991. TD-3/91.

15 D.A. Padua, D.J. Kuck, and D.H. Lawrie. High-Speed Multiprocessors and Compilation Techniques. *IEEE Transactions on Computers*, C-29(9):763–776, September 1980.

PROGRAMMING ENVIRONMENTS FOR PARALLEL COMPUTING
N. Topham, R. Ibbett and T. Bemmerl (Editors)
Elsevier Science Publishers B.V. (North-Holland)

© 1992 IFIP. All rights reserved.

A System for Building Scalable Parallel Applications

Simon Dobson*
Andy Wellings

Department of Computer Science, University of York, Heslington, York YO1 5DD, UK.

Abstract

One of the major problems with programming scalable multicomputer systems is defining appropriate abstractions for the programmer. In order to allow applications to scale their resource consumption according to run-time conditions, we propose a view of a scalable system which treats memory as a collection of programmer-defined and -extensible data structures. These structures may be transparently distributed across the nodes of the system while still presenting a single-entity abstraction to the programmer. The implementation of such structures, as a kernel for a programming environment, are presented, along with examples of their use.

1. Introduction

Experience has shown that the effective use of parallel systems often forces programmers to deal with low-level architecture-specific features of particular hardware platforms and communications protocols: this both reduces the portability of software and increases the burden on the programmer. This situation is exacerbated by *scalable* parallel systems, where the machine's underlying hardware resources may change dynamically. What is needed is an environment in which a high-level view of the scalable computer – having global memory and unlimited parallelism – is mapped transparently onto the underlying multicomputer architecture.

This paper describes a programming environment designed specifically for exploiting the potential of highly parallel, highly scalable computers. Section two describes some of the problems encountered when attempting to design a programming environment for a scalable computer, and suggests that the major problem is essentially one of hiding the underlying disjoint memory architecture. In order to solve this problem, section three proposes the use of "scalable memory" built from high-level data structures which can transparently span processing nodes. Section four discusses the use of such memories to automatically regulate concurrency. Section five contains some examples of our system in use, whilst section six presents our conclusions.

2. Scalable Computing

We will first define what is meant by scalability, in terms of architectures, operating systems, and applications, and then discuss some of the problems which it introduces.

---

* Supported by a research studentship from the UK Science and Engineering Research Council.

2.1. What is Scalability?

A *scalable* computer is a machine to which additional memory and processors may be added so tha the machine's power may be increased (or decreased) as desired. Although shared-memory multiprocessors may be described as scalable, contention for the shared memory places a limit on th number of processors which may be used. Workstations connected by a broadcast network are similarl limited by the saturation point of the shared communications medium. Multicomputers – collections o processor-memory pairs connected by a sparse point-to-point network – offer a better solution, as they have no globally-shared resources to place an upper-bound on their size.

Operating system and programming environment design are often seen as exercises in abstraction For a scalable system, this suggests that the physical resources of the machine are hidden from users an programmers – doing otherwise means that programs must be re-written (or at least re-compiled) if th system's resources are changed. A scalable operating system abstracts away from notions of proces location, and allows applications composed of a number of processes to take advantage of the system' inherent parallelism.

2.2. Problems of Scalability

For the applications programmer, writing a program which can take advantage of whateve resources are available at run-time is a great challenge. It effectively implies a very flexible attitud towards *entity*, *memory* and *process* management.

Entity Management

Entity management – how elements of a system's software are named and accessed – must tak account of the distributed nature of the underlying hardware. It is desirable to abstract away from th physical locations of such *software resources*, allowing different resources to interact regardless of thei relative locations. This permits remote resources to be manipulated in an identical fashion to local ones and relieves the programmer of the need to manage data locality explicitly. Techniques for achievin such *location transparency* vary from the channel abstraction of Occam[19] to the shared tuple space o Linda[1].

An approach which is gaining popularity is the *virtual object space*[18], which uses object-oriente techniques to name and manipulate software resources. Object names allow objects to be located an accessed regardless of their location in the network. Objects are then the unit of distribution, with eac object residing on exactly one node at any time (although objects may migrate between nodes in som systems, notably [13]).

Memory Management

In discussing memory management, one must consider two distinct ideas: the way in which loca memory is managed, and the way in which these local memories are used collectively.

Local memory is bounded, and this introduces problems of managing single entities which are large than a single local memory. The use of techniques such as distributed shared virtual memory[15] – i which physical memories are used as caches for virtual pages stored on disc – introduces consistenc and scalability problems, and for this reason many systems keep to a *real memory* architecture Nonetheless, it is obviously desirable to allow applications to use the system's memory as a single uni without worrying about its topology and distribution, as this allows these architectural features to b changed without impacting on correctly-written applications.

Process Management

Since an application has no information at compile-time about the processing requirements which will be available at run-time, concurrency regulation – deciding how many processes to create for a particular task, and where to locate them – is difficult. In the multiple-worker style of concurrency, for example, it would be advantageous to allow the system to determine the number of workers to create: this number could then be tailored to run-time conditions, such as how many processors the application is using.

2.3. Phoenix: an Environment for Scalable Parallel Programming

We have developed a scalable parallel operating system nucleus called *Wisdom*[3,20,21,22], and are now developing a programming environment called *Phoenix*[1] for use within it. The aim of Phoenix is to encourage and simplify the task of writing highly parallel, highly scalable, general-purpose applications. It takes the form of an object-oriented class library and associated supporting tools.

In order to support scalability, Phoenix views "memory" as being a set of high-level *typed memory modules* which the programmer may instantiate as required, independent of the underlying network architecture[6]. These modules appear to the programmer as familiar data structures: whilst objects remain the units of *distribution*, the memory modules are the units of *aggregation*. Any memory module may be as large as desired, unconstrained by local memory sizes: a large structure will distribute itself as necessary according to run-time conditions whilst still behaving as a single object from clients' viewpoints. Concurrency regulation occurs through these modules, with multiple worker processes being attached to memories. The processes are then replicated according to the distribution of the memory. It is thus possible to create and manipulate structures of an arbitrary size, and to process them in parallel, without being concerned with the exact mechanism or policy of their distribution – although the policy may be tailored if required to suit particular applications.

The remainder of this paper describes the mechanisms used to realise these ideas.

3. Scalable Memory

The implementation of scalable memory essentially involves the hiding of exactly *what* data is located in exactly *which* physical address space. Furthermore, it is essential that the contents of memory are structured in a meaningful (to the programmer) manner, and that the hiding of location does not destroy the performance of the application.

3.1. Data Structuring

It is first worth considering exactly what form of data structuring is used within typical distributed applications. This then allows us to provide, at the base level of the programming environment, the most useful structures as fully distributed, scalable modules, whilst making it easy for programmers to expand the basic forms into specialised application-level structures. Since we are considering general-purpose computing, we cannot restrict our considerations to a particular programming domain: we must instead consider the whole range of applications which are (or might benefit from being) run on parallel machines.

We would contend that, whilst there are as many types of data structuring as there are programs, three forms of large-scale data structure predominate: arrays, associative memories and graphs.

---

[1] In mythology, the Phoenix is the keeper of Wisdom.

3.2. Requirements

All data structures in our system share a common set of requirements, although the exact manner in which these requirements are achieved differs between different categories of structure. The overall aims may be given as follows:

- a *single object* abstraction, so a structure may be treated as a single logical unit;
- *transparent distribution*, so the distributed nature of a structure, and the locations of its elements, do not interfere with algorithms (although they may be controlled if necessary);
- *unbounded size*, so that a structure may be as large as the application requires, unconstrained by the size of individual node memories.
- *variable size*, so a structure's use of storage is governed by the number of elements which it contains: small structures to not use storage unnecessarily;
- *lack of bottlenecks*, so parallel access is possible without too much interference between activities;
- *strong typing* to prevent abuse of structures; and
- *easy extension* to encourage re-use of existing code and to simplify the construction of application-specific structures.

In order to implement such structures, we have developed a model of large data aggregates called the *partitioned object model*[8], together with a number of implementation techniques specific to each category of memory discussed above.

3.3. A Partitioned Model of Objects

The partitioned object model is founded on the observation that, whilst data aggregations are best considered as objects like any other, they differ from "simple" objects (such as integers, points *et cetera*) in possessing a highly organised and regular internal structure. Our model utilises this feature to control the distribution (or *partitioning*) of data between various host nodes in a manner which is transparent to clients of the structure. In this way, a single logical software resource may be composed from a number of objects[7] in a manner which is largely invisible to applications programmers.

A Basic Distributed Object Model

The basic object model used by Phoenix is very simple. The system itself is written in a dialect of C++[24] which has been extended to deal with distribution and concurrency: we therefore take the C++ model of objects as our base.

Object names take the form of communications capabilities, so that a capability uniquely identifies an object anywhere in the network. This allows two objects to interact regardless of their relative locations. The fact that objects may reside on different nodes introduces some additional restrictions: specifically, instance variables should not be accessible from outside the object. An object resides on exactly one node[2].

---

[2]We do not outlaw object migration, although our current implementation does not provide this feature.

Object interactions take the form of calls to methods. Method invocation is performed exactly as expected, using remote procedure call[5] techniques to translate C++-style calls into request-and-reply message transfers. It follows the same semantics as in C++, but is extended with the notion of an *asynchronous* method which never returns and does not block the caller. Asynchronous methods are represented by the pseudo-type `async`: the asynchronous nature of a method is defined by the object's class, and it is not possible to call an arbitrary method asynchronously (thus removing the need for "future" returned values[12,16]).

Objects are multi-threaded, so several method calls may be active at any time within a single object. Support is provided for intra-object concurrency control using "lock" objects, which are a fusion of ideas from the Arjuna[23] and DRAGOON[2] projects allowing concurrency control *via* deontic logic.

The Phoenix class library is formed from a single tree, with the root being the class `Object`. All `Objects` thus share a common core protocol: amongst the functions provided are equality testing and copy generation, which call virtual functions defined by the programmer for each sub-class. Little use is made of multiple inheritance.

An Overview of Partitioning

Partitioned structures are "collections" in the Smalltalk sense[11], representing what would normally be termed data structures. Each structure is a software resource whose purpose is to allow access to other objects (its *elements*) according to some meaningful protocol.

A *partitioned collection* is a collection whose size is not constrained by the size of a single node memory. It is composed of a number of smaller *component* objects, each holding a small number of the full collection's elements. These components are distributed between nodes, and are linked by a tree of *partition* objects which manage distribution. The components form the leaves of the tree, the partitions the branches, so every component is attached to exactly one partition object.

The tree may be fixed, or may vary with time. For an array, whose size is fixed at its creation, the tree will be created and will never change; for associative memories and graphs, the number and arrangement of both partition and component objects will change as elements are added and removed.

A partitioned collection has the property that any component acts as a *pseudonym* for the entire collection. A request for any element of the structure may be addressed to any component, with the same result: alternatively, all components can deal with exactly the same set of requests. Accesses to local and remote data are identical, with the only difference being that the time taken to satisfy requests for remote data will be longer than for local data. Thus the collection behaves as a single resource, even though it is composed of a number of independent objects. A generic partition tree is shown in figure 1.

Requests for data are satisfied by a process termed *resolution*. When a request is sent to a component (by another object or by a sub-class), it is checked to see whether it can be satisfied locally. If it can, then servicing occurs locally; if not, the details of the requested element are passed to the partition. The partition then makes use of a distributed algorithm to locate the component which *can* service the request locally, and the original request is forwarded *in toto* to this component. There is no requirement for global locking, so several requests may be active within the structure at any one time – only if two requests access the the same object will concurrency control become necessary.

There is thus a very clear division of responsibility: components perform data processing, whilst partitions perform data location. A component's knowledge of distribution is limited to a single "locality" test, with the partition being free to use any policy for distribution it wishes; conversely, a partition only sees enough of requests to perform resolution, and does not perform any data processing. It is a simple matter to use a specialised partition sub-class to tailor distribution of data, or to sub-class a component class to provide advanced processing.

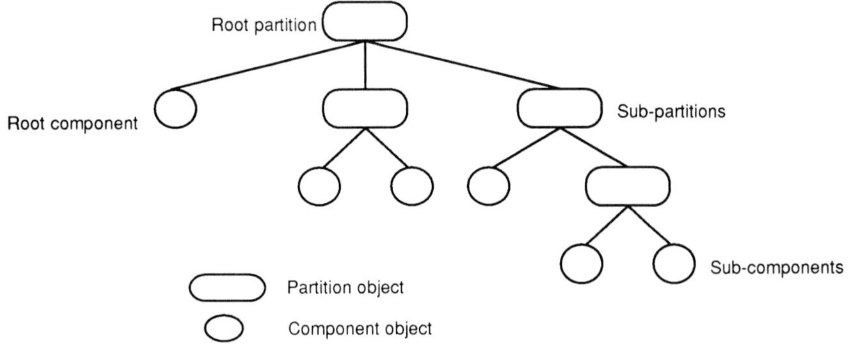

Figure 1: A generic partition tree

3.3.1. Some Partitioning Techniques

As already stated, we consider three categories of structures – arrays, associative memories, an graphs – to be fundamental. However, the internal structures of these categories is obviously ver different. Within the framework of partitioned collections, we have therefore developed appropriat category-specific implementation techniques. Care has been taken to ensure that a clean interface i retained between sub-classes, and between collection and partition objects, to maximise the possibilitie for code and design re-use.

Arrays

An array represents a bounded discrete n-space. It may thus be defined by a "region" specifying it boundaries. It may further be observed that such a region may be built from a number of smalle regions, which together define the same space. Partitioning an array is a matter of dividing the "global" region into a number of smaller sub-regions, distributing them, and creating a component array for each

The partitioning process occurs when an array is first created, with the first component generating partition object. The partition splits the global region into a number of smaller sub-regions, each o which will eventually be used by a component to define its local storage.

The partition determines which regions to hold locally, and how many sub-partitions to create. I then creates the sub-partitions and divides the remaining sub-regions between them. The sub-partition will then in turn keep some regions and generate further sub-partitions, until the process bottoms-ou with a partition retaining all sub-regions itself. A partition thus knows all the regions which are hel below it in the tree. A component is generated for each locally-held region, with the size of the arra being taken from its region.

A `Region` is an object representing a small region of an array's space. It is capable of "flattening a point into an offset, allowing multi-dimensional regions to be stored in simple linear arrays. Th protocol for the `Region` class is shown in figure 2. The important functions provided by `Region` ar defined as virtual member functions, so that they may be over-ridden in sub-classes to provid specialised `Regions`.

```
class Region : public Object {
  ...
public:
  Region( Point ll, Point our );

  virtual int Size( void );
  virtual boolean Contains( Point p );
  virtual int Flatten( Point p );
  virtual Point Expand( int i );
  virtual int Split( int md, Region **&subRegions );
};
```

Figure 2: The Region protocol

Resolution makes use of the fact that every element which might be requested is a member of exactly one region, and a partition can determine which object – locally-held component or sub-partition – a region was assigned to, if any. Elements are addressed using "points" within a region. Hence a request to locate a particular element proceeds as follows: the partition's region table is searched to locate the region containing the requested point. If this region maps onto a locally-held component, resolution has succeeded; if it maps onto a sub-partition, the request is forwarded to this partition for further resolution; if a region cannot be found, it may be assumed to be serviceable higher-up the tree and may be forwarded to the parent partition for further resolution.

Associative Memories

An associative memory is based around the principle of hashing. However, in a scalable environment, the standard hashing techniques do not work as the number of "buckets" of data is fixed, as is a bucket's size. What is required is an "extensible" hashing algorithm, and a suitable algorithm has been derived from similar methods used in storage management applications (for instance [9,10,14,17]). In effect, an associative memory is composed of a variable population of buckets, whose number varies as the structure grows or shrinks whilst maintaining the validity of keys.

When initially created, an associative memory will consist of a single bucket into which all elements are placed. When the bucket become full, it is split. A prefix of the hash key (say two bits) is taken, a partition with the correct number of new buckets created (three in this case, yielding four in combination with the original), and the elements of the split bucket divided between the new buckets. All these buckets share a common prefix of the hash key, but have a different two-bit suffix.

This process of splitting a full bucket occurs recursively: every time a bucket become full, another prefix of the key is consumed to re-distribute the elements. Conversely, if a number of buckets are empty, they may join to form a single bucket. The depth of the partition tree (and hence the size of the collection) may thus vary dynamically according to the number of elements in the structure.

Resolution occurs by examining the hash key of the sought element and determining its prefix. If this prefix is held locally, the sought element should be local; if not, the key is passed to the partition. This may then determine, from comparison of the key prefix with its own, whether the bucket containing this key is above or below in the tree, and forward or resolve the request accordingly. This comparison of hash keys requires no global information about the collection and so is a completely distributed algorithm.

Graphs

A graph is composed of a number of nodes, connected by arcs. Retrieval of elements is based on traversal of arcs from another, already-known node. Partitioning, in this case, is simply a matter of ensuring that nodes are evenly distributed; resolution is automatic, and requires no intervention by the partition.

Nodes are connected by arcs, which may be labelled and may have an associated direction. Node creation occurs by taking an existing node and generating an arc to a new, non-existent node. The calling node's partition object will then determine the location for the new node and perform creation and arc linking.

3.3.2. Affecting Distribution

The manner in which elements of a distributed application are mapped onto the underlying processing nodes has a major impact on performance, but is in many sense a peripheral issue: a distributed object-oriented program will work no matter how this mapping occurs, but some configurations will be more efficient than others.

The partitoning process allows programers to ignore the manner in which components are mapped onto nodes, or allows them to implement "designer" strategies for particular applications. There is, however, a third alternative: by allowing programs to acquire some of their distribution parameters at run-time, a particular partitioning strategy may be "fine tuned" simply by supplying different parameters.

We have implemented this option by providing a *property sheet*. This is a set of name-value pairs which may be interpreted as directives about how to partition a collection (or any other run-time property, for that matter). The intention is to place in the property sheet information which may affect the *distribution* of a program without affecting its *semantics*. Properties may be specified on a system-wide, per-class or per-instance basis, allowing a very fine degree of control to be exercised over an application.

Typical properties used at present control the width and depth of the partition tree, the number of elements held in each component, the "eagerness" with which the partition tree grows *et cetera*. Changing these parameters can drastically alter the distribution pattern of a collection without altering its code or semantics.

4. Processing in a Scalable Environment

The problems of concurrency *control* are well-understood, but concurrency *regulation* – determining how many processes to create for a given task, and where – has received far less attention.

We take the view that we may use our scalable memory to regulate our scalable processing. The basis for this assumption is that, in the partitioned model, a larger structure is distributed more widely (amongst more components and on more nodes) than a smaller structure, and the amount of data to be processed is a good metric for determining the amount of concurrency to employ.

4.1. What is a Process?

Within our object model, a method may be called asynchronously and give rise to a parallel thread of activity. This however is a rather unstructured view of concurrency: it is easy to see that unrestrained use of such methods could result in a serious danger of deadlock, interference, race conditions *et alia*.

```
class Activity : public Object {
private:
  ...

protected:
  virtual void Body( void );

  Activity( Collection *c, Group *g );

public:
  void SetAttachment( Collection *c );
  Collection *GetAttachment( void );

  async Start( void );
};
```

Figure 3: The Activity class protocol

In order to impose a structure onto processing, we define an `Activity` class of object. `Activity` objects are *in no way* privileged over other objects: they simply possess a protocol and support for attachment to our scalable memory modules. The basic protocol for activities is shown in figure 3. The `Body()` member is over-ridden in each sub-class to define the process' actions.

Such processes are intended to function in a "multiple worker" style of concurrent processing. That is to say, a number of worker tasks are each assigned a disjoint part of a data set, which they transform in some way. This transformation may require access to the data allocated to other workers. Concurrency regulation, then, is the task of determining how many workers to create, and where. There must also be support to enable a worker to determine its part of the overall data set.

4.2. Attachment and Concurrency Regulation

At the most basic level, a "process" accesses a "memory" in order to acquire (and possibly change) data. Since we support the notion of multiple memories (partitioned collections), a process must be *attached* to the particular structure which it is to process.

Attachment consists of informing the memory that an activity is to be attached to it. In general, the memory will then replicate the given process, once per component, with each replica being passed the name of the component with which it is co-located. The effect of this strategy is that as many processes will be created as there are components of a structure. The names of these replicas are collected into a `Group` object, which is a sub-class of `Activity` and allows all the replicas to be manipulated *en masse*. Activities notify their `Group` of state changes such as termination, making it possible to perform synchronisation.

In terms of programming style, processing a partitioned collection consists of instantiating a single process of the appropriate class and attaching it to the desired collection. From an activity's viewpoint, it will have access to the entire partitioned collection, using the same syntax, *via* the component to which it is attached. Since it must only actually process the local part of the component, there must be a method by which it can obtain the local data. For this purpose, all partitioned collections support the notion of *iteration*: a process may acquire the "first" item in a component and repeatedly request the "next" until the component is fully processed. For generality it is also possible to iterate globally across the entire collection. Component classes may also define alternative ways to acces local data – for example by allowing clients of an array to access the local Region.

```
class ObjectArray : public Array {
private:
  ...

protected:
  /* internal storage management */
  virtual void BasicAtPut( Point p, void  *o );
  virtual void BasicAt( Point p, void *o );

  /* resolution */
  virtual Array *BasicResolve( Point p );

public:
  Array( Region *gr );

  void SetLocalRegion( Region *lr );
  Region *GetLocalRegion( void );

  /* bounds and locality testing */
  boolean IsHeldLocally( Point p );
  boolean CanResolve( Point p );

  /* user-level access routines */
  void AtPut( Point p, Object *o );
  void AtCopy( Point p, Object *o );
  Object *At( Point p );

  /* partitioning */
  Partition *GetPartition( void );
  virtual void Initialise( Object *o =nil );

  /* concurrency */
  Group *Attach( Activity act );
  void AttachStartAndAwait( Activity *act );
  void AttachAndStart( Activity *act );
};
```

Figure 4: The ObjectArray class protocol, slightly compressed

If a process accesses only the local data, it will make maximum use of the principle of locality of reference no remote access to data will occur, hence no network traffic and no interference with other processes. In practice it is often necessary for a process, whilst dealing with local data, to make reference to other areas of the structure. Because of the transparency of access to data in partitioned collections, these accesses have exactly the same syntax and semantics as local accesses: remoteness has a *performance* aspect, but no *semantic* effect.

5. Examples

We are currently finishing the implementation of the Phoenix prototype, and are starting its evaluation *via* a series of example applications. The purpose of the evaluation is four-fold: to show that the "data-based" style of programming is indeed suitable for scalable systems; to ensure that the partitioning techniques we have developed are indeed scalable in real cases; to determine exactly how much performance is sacrificed by using resolution; and to investigate the effects of different distribution policies on test applications. We are also interested in the uses of caching the results of recent resolutions in order to accelerate the resolution process (using the techniques developed by Austin[4]).

We will now present examples of Phoenix code. The code is slightly simplified over that found in the actual system: the class protocols have been stripped-down to essentials, and the syntax used is "pure" C++ rather than the slightly embellished code required by our (primitive) RPC manager. We have also "flattened" the inheritance tree to remove abstract classes.

The two examples show the basic use of partitioning from a client's viewpoint, and the considerations in creating specialised collections and distributions. Both take the form of a cellular automaton simulation[25], which are discrete simulations based around arrays, with each element in the array representing a "cell." The values of the cells are updated through time, with each cell being updated according to the values of itself and its near-neighbours. They thus exhibit substantial locality of reference, and so are well-suited to execution within our environment. Automata of the form shown here are used extensively in electric field simulations.

Basic Partitioning

The skeleton protocol for an array of objects, `ObjectArray`, is shown in figure 4. For the sake of brevity we have compressed the class hierarchy, placing some functions (which are inherited from abstract superclasses in Phoenix) into a single class definition – the use of abstract superclasses maximises the possibilities for re-use and re-definition, at the expense of a proliferation of class definitions.

Clients call the `Array()` constructor to create an instance of the array. The `Initialise()` member is then called to perform the partitioning operation: the result is that the initial array instance is augmented by a partition tree and additionalcomponents. The original instance will have the same status as any other component, and will hold a small number of elements. Access to the collection may then occur through this component.

Each element of the array, in our example, is an instance of class `Cell`. A cell's value changes according to the current simulation time:

```
class Cell : public Object {
private:
  ...

public:
  Cell( int history );

  float GetValueAt( int t );
  void SetValueAt( int t, float v );
};
```

We will assume that the `GetValueAt()` operation will block until the value of the cell for the requested time is available. A cellular automaton is constructed by creating an array and initialising it with cells. The cell values are initially zero, with two high-value "peaks" being placed manually towards the centre of the model. This may be accomplished as follows:

```
Array *a;    Cell *cell;
Point p(2, 0, 0), q(2, 10000, 10000);
Region *r =new Region(p, q);

cell=new Cell;   cell->SetValueAt(0, 0.0);
a=new Array(r);   a->Initialise(cell);

cell->SetValueAt(0, 5000.0);
p.Is(100, 5000);   a->AtCopy(p, cell);
p.Is(9900, 5000);   a->AtCopy(p, cell);
```

In this code fragment, a `Cell` is first created and initialised to have a value of zero at time zero. An `Array` is then created using the `new` operator, and it partitoned by the call to `Initialise()`. This operation will both diistribute the array's storage and initialise each element with a copy of the given `Cell`. The two peaks are inserted by placing copies of the appropriate-valued `Cell` into the array where desired – the first probably local, the second almost certainly remote.

Internally, the access routines `AtPut()`, `AtCopy()` and `At()` perform resolution to acquire the holder of the possibly remote elements. The resolution takes the form of a locality test possibly followed by a call to the partition object and a re-direction of the request, with "hidden" functions being called to manipulate local storage (the `BasicAt()` and `BasicAtPut()` routines in the class description):

```
void ObjectArray::AtPut( Point p, Object *o ) {
 ObjectArray *a;

 a=(ObjectArray *) BasicResolve(p);
 if(a==this) {
  /* store element locally */
  BasicAtPut(p, &o);
 } else {
  /* forward request to appropriate component */
  c->AtPut(p, o);
 }
}
```

Different sub-classes may use storage representations without affecting the user-level routine, simply by over-riding the basic storage manipulation functions.

Concurrency

Sequential access, whilst managing distribution, does not fully utilise the potential parallelism of partitioning. If parallel processing is required, a process object must be instantiated and attached to the collection. The `Body()` routine of such a task is shown below:

```
void CellActivity::Body( void ) {
 Array *a =(Array *) GetAttachment();
 Region *r =a->GetLocalRegion();
 Point p(2), q(2), dp(2);
 Iterator iter =r->NewIterator();
 int x, y;   int t;
 float value;
 Cell *cell, *n;

 for(t=0; t<simTime; t++) {
  p=r->First(iter);
  while(!p.Undefined()) {
   cell=a->At(p);   value=0.0;
   for(x=-1; x<=1; i++)
    for(y=-1; y<=1; y++) {
     dp.Is(x, y);   q=p;   q.Add(dp);
     n=a->At(q);
     if(n!=nil) value+=n->GetValueAt(t);
    }

   cell->SetValueAt(t+1, value/9);
   p=r->Next(iter);
  }
 }
}
```

At each time step, a cell's value for the next step is set to the average of its neighbour's values, with n activity dealing with the local elements of the component to which it is attached. Instances of the ctivity may be attached to a structure and started in parallel:

```
a->AttachStartAndAwait(new CellActivity);
```

In this example, the caller will block until all the workers have finished: by using the ttachAndStart() routine instead of AttachStartAndAwait(), the activities could left to xecute independently. Both these routines are simplifications of the Attach() routine, which returns ne Group of activities being used by the collection. The process bodies will then execute until the imulation time ends, whereupon the array may be queried to determine the values of the cells.

It should be noted that there is no explicit statement anywhere as to the distribution of the Array or s to the amount of concurrent activity deployed to process it. It is the system's responsibility to ensure nat these factors are dealt with.

xtensibility

A class library is only useful if it easily extensible, so programmers can create new structures from ne supplied infrastructure. Furthermore, it is vital that programmers writing dedicated Phoenix ollections are freed from low-level distribution concerns – this is as important for sub-classes as for xternal clients.

The important point is that, in many respects, a sub-class behaves *exactly* as a client, and may hence se the parent's public interface. This means that distribution is transparent to sub-classes of collection lasses, as much as to clients. The only time when a sub-class needs to be concerned with distribution is vhen it uses "covert" knowledge to manipulate its parent's internal data structures in the interests of erformance.

As an example, we will derive a "well-behaved" sub-class of `ObjectArray` tailored towards our cellular automaton. It defines an additional function which calculates the average values of cells around a particular cell, freeing client objects of the need to perform averaging from outside:

```
class CellArray : public ObjectArray {
public:
 CellArray( Region *gr );

 float GetAverageOf( Point p );
};

float CellArray::GetAverageOf( Point p ) {
 int x, y;   float value;
 Point dp(2), q(2);   Cell *cell;

 value=0.0;
 for(x=-1; x<=1; i++)
  for(y=-1; y<=1; y++) {
   dp.Is(x, y);   q=p;   q.Add(dp);
   cell=At(q);
   if(cell!=nil) value+=cell->GetValueAt(t);
  }

 return value/9;
}
```

This new sub-class makes use of the standard `At()` routine, which handles all resolution. The `GetAverage()` routine simply uses this routine to access the data it requires, without any knowledge of distribution.

It is similarly quite simple to use a novel partitioning strategy. For arrays, one may use a sub-class of `Region` which, for example, defines a hexagonal region (useful in some other kinds of cellular automata). By defining appropriate virtual members for the new region (as illustrated in figure 2), it may be used to distribute an `Array` without any intervention on the part of the collection class – although the data held locally by each component will change.

In a similar way one might also generate specialised partition sub-classes for particular applications. An example might be an `Array` partition which maps components onto an *nxm* mesh, one per processor, exactly as might occur using a traditional data mapping tool.

Constraints of space prevent us from discussing these points more fully: however the partitioned model, by breaking-down the responsibilities of classes between data manipulation and distribution, simplifies the task of creating distributed applications without preventing the knowledgeable programmer from fully controlling an application's mapping onto the hardware.

6. Conclusion

From the outset we have been considering the use of parallel computers as *general-purpose* computing engines, rather than as supercomputers. We believe that scalable parallel machines built from "off the shelf" components promise to make supercomputer levels of performance available to a wider class of users than is currently possible – but for this to occur, the programming interfaces to such machines must be simplified.

We have described a programming environment whose main goal is to allow applications to exploit the scalability of the underlying parallel machine. It approaches this by hiding the disjoint-memory topology of the machine behind behind a set of scalable distributed data structures. These structures may be used both to arrange objects in memory and to regulate concurrency, without the programmer being forced to consider either the exact distribution used or the amount of concurrency to deploy. Run-time properties of objects allow the details of distribution – the size of components and the like – to be tailored to improve performance without re-compilation.

By separating the concerns of data *versus* distribution management through the use of parallel class hierachies, our system allows one aspect of an application to be changed without affecting the other. This means that programs may be written and debugged before their exact distribution is decided upon.

We are currently proceeding with the evaluation of Phoenix to determine both its efficiency and appropriateness to general-purpose scalable parallel programming. Proposed future work involves the investigation of different partitioning strategies and their dynamics, especially in the case where several structures interact by sharing a set of processors. We are also interested in the effects of placing processes themselves into partitioned collections, using the collections as a process as well as data structuring technique.

We believe that scalable systems offer major advantages for available, high-performance computing in the future, and that the key to their successful exploitation lies in providing high-level views of their capabilities. Partitioning is an attempt to provide these features.

7. References

[1] Sudhir Ahuja, N. Carriero and D. Gelernter, "*Linda and friends*", IEEE Computer **19**(8) (August 1986), pp. 26-34.

[2] Colin Atkinson, *Object-oriented reuse, concurrency and distribution*, Addison-Wesley, 1991.

[3] Paul B. Austin, Kevin A. Murray and Andy J. Wellings, "*The design of an operating system for a scalable parallel computing engine*", SOFTWARE – practice and experience **21**(10) (October 1991), pp. 989-1013.

[4] Paul B. Austin, Kevin A. Murray and Andy J. Wellings, "*File system caching in large point-to-point networks*", Software engineering journal **7**(1) (January 1992), pp. 65-80.

[5] A.D. Birrell and B.J. Nelson, "*Implementing remote procedure call*", ACM Transactions on computer systems **2**(1) (February 1984), pp. 39-59.

[6] David Bruce, "*A strongly-typed approach to parallel systems*", pp. 57-59 in Collected position papers of the BCS workshop on abstract machine models for highly parallel computers, volume 2, University of Leeds, 25-27th March, 1991.

[7] Andrew A. Chien and William J. Dally, "*Concurrent Aggregates*", ACM SIGPLAN Notices **25**(3) (March 1990), pp. 187-196. Proceedings of the 2nd ACM symposium on principles and practice of parallel programming.

[8] Simon A. Dobson and Andy J. Wellings, "*Programming highly parallel general-purpose applications (extended abstract)*", pp. 49-56 in Collected position papers of the BCS workshop on abstract machine models for highly parallel computers, volume 2, University of Leeds, 25-27th March, 1991.

[9] R. Fagin, J. Nievergelt, N. Pippenger and H.R. Strong, "*Extendible hashing: a fast access method for dynamic files*", ACM Transactions of database systems **4**(3) (September 1979), pp. 315-344.

[10] E. Fredkin, "*Trie memory*", Communications of the ACM **3**(9) (September 1960), pp. 439-499.

[11] Adele Goldberg and David Robson, "Smalltalk-80: the language and its implementation", Addison-Wesley, 1985.

[12] R.H. Halstead, "*MultiLisp: a language for concurrent symbolic computation*", ACM Transactions on programming languages and systems **7**(4) (October 1985), pp. 501-538.

[13] E. Jul, H. Levy, N. Hutchinson and A. Black, "*Fine-grained mobility in the Emerald system*", ACM Transactions on computer systems **6**(1) (February 1988), pp. 109-133.

[14] Per-Åke Larson, "*Dynamic hashing*", BIT **18** (1978), pp. 184-201.

[15] Kai Li, "*Shared virtual memory on loosely coupled multiprocessors*", Department of computer science, Yale University, September 1986. Ph.D. dissertation.

[16] B. Liskov and L. Shira, "*Promises: linguistic support for efficient asynchronous procedure calls*", ACM SIGPLAN Notices **23**(7) (July 1988). Proceedings of the ACM conference on programming language design and implementation.

[17] Witold Litwin, "*Virtual hashing: a dynamically changing hashing*", pp. 517-523 in Proceedings of the 4th international conference on very large data bases, 1978.

[18] S.E. Lucco, "*Parallel programming in a virtual object space*", ACM SIGPLAN Notices **22**(12) (December 1987), pp. 26-34. Proceedings of OOPSLA '87.

[19] David May, "*Occam-2 language definition*", Inmos, 13 February 1987.

[20] Kevin A. Murray and Andy J. Wellings, "*Issues in the design of a distributed operating system for a network of Transputers*", Microprocessing and microprogramming **24**(1-5) (1988), pp. 169 178.

[21] Kevin A. Murray and Andy J. Wellings, "*Wisdom: a distributed operating system for Transputers*", Computer systems science and engineering **5**(1) (January 1990), pp. 13-20.

[22] Kevin A. Murray, "*Wisdom: the foundation of a scalable parallel operating system*", Department of Computer Science, University of York, February 1990. Ph.D. dissertation.

[23] Graham D. Parrington, "*Management of concurrency in a reliable object-oriented computing system*", Computing laboratory, University of Newcastle upon Tyne, July 1988. Ph.D. dissertation.

[24] Bjarne Stroustrup, "*The C++ programming language*", Addison-Wesley, 1987.

[25] Greg Wilson, "*The life and times of cellular automata*", New Scientist (8th October 1988), pp. 44-47.

PROGRAMMING ENVIRONMENTS FOR PARALLEL COMPUTING
N. Topham, R. Ibbett and T. Bemmerl (Editors)
Elsevier Science Publishers B.V. (North-Holland)

© 1992 IFIP. All rights reserved.

A New Programming Model for Massively Parallel Systems

W.K. Giloi, A. Schramm, W. Schröder–Preikschat
GMD Research Center for Innovative Computer Systems and Technology at the Technical University of Berlin
Hardenbergplatz 2
D–1000 Berlin 12
Germany
e–mail: w.giloi@compnet.com

Abstract

New, very important application paradigms call for the development of massively parallel MIMD computer systems with a very large number of processors [1]. These systems are by nature distributed memory systems in which the nodes communicate through message passing. Recently, new kinds of hierarchical interconnection structures have evolved that combine economy of realization with the high connectivity required for massively parallel systems [2]. In order to provide for the necessary scalability of massively parallel systems, new programming models must be developed that allow programming to take place at a sufficiently high level of abstraction as needed to make such systems programmable and manageable. Moreover, the level of abstraction must allow application programs to be written independently of the actual size of the system. In this paper we present the new programming model for massively parallel distributed memory systems called the *virtual processor model.* This programming methodology eliminates the restrictions of other models with respect to the degree of parallelism and the connectivity of the interconnection structure. Therefore, it allows the user to write parallel programs in an application–oriented, fine–grain fashion, in which the message–passing mechanisms are hidden from the user. The aggregation of a virtual processor topology into executable threads of code and the mapping of these threads onto the physical resources of the system can be performed by the compiler. The compiler also takes care of synchronization, which is required only once per iteration as opposed to once per communication or process invocation. The concepts of an object–oriented implementation of the virtual processor model and its implications on the system architecture, the operating system, and the compilers are discussed. As a means for an efficient implementation, the notions of featherweight processes and featherweight communication are introduced

Keywords: *massively parallel system, programming model, virtual processor model, featherweight processes, featherweight communication, family of operating system kernels, object–oriented implementation.*

1. INTRODUCTION

Massively parallel systems are computers with a very large number of processors. What is "very large", however, is strongly dictated by the technology available. So far, Thinking Machine's CM-2 with 64K single–bit processors was considered by many as the epitome of "massively parallel." Manufacturers of multi transputer systems have announced that they will develop T9000–based platforms with 64K transputers. A Connection Machine with 256K processors has been announced. Another recent development has been the "MIMD-ization" of the Connection Machine as manifested by the CM5. The Japanese *Real World Computing* Study envisions MIMD systems with up to a million processors [3]. With the up-coming 100–million–transistor technology (64–Mbyte chip) in combination with waver scale integration this seems to become a feasible task.

One important, yet unanswered question is whether massively parallel systems are meant to introduce a new programming style or whether they are just a means to raise the peak performance limits of supercomputers by some orders of magnitude while adhering to a conventional programming style. In either case the success of such an endeavor will strongly depend on the solution to the question how to program efficiently a system with many thousands or even millions of processors [1]. All these are pertinent questions that as of yet have hardly been addressed. This paper tries to give an answer.

A programming paradigm for massively parallel systems should meet the following requirements:

- it should not put any restrictions on the degree of parallelism exploited by the program;
- it should provide unlimited interconnectivity of the "computing nodes" of the system;
- the user should not be aware of the idiosyncrasies of the physical processors in the system, let alone have to program them, as this very well might prove to be an unmanageable problem.

These requirements lead to the definition of an abstract machine that provides any arbitrary number of processors that can be interconnected in any arbitrary topology. We call this the *virtual processor model* (VPM).

The virtual processor model will be very suitable in programming paradigms where the problem consists of a very large number of objects, each of which is to be subjected to an elementary transformation. In this case, each object may have individually assigned one of the virtual processors to carry out the transformation.

While such a model exists for the Connection Machine [4], it does not yet exist for massively parallel MIMD architectures. In the paper, it will be shown how the virtual processor model can be implemented on general–purpose MIMD machines on the basis of object–oriented programming.

The virtualization of processors introduces additional overhead, which is the price to pay for the manageability of the system. Our goal is to minimize that overhead.

Therefore, new concepts for extremely efficient parallel operating systems [5] and run-time systems as well as supporting communication hardware [6] have been developed, cumulating in the notion of *featherweight processes* and *featherweight communication.*

The data parallel VPM programming methodology can be viewed as a *hierarchical cellular automaton* with arbitrary interconnection topology among the cells, exhibiting the following special features:

- the model is based on the notion of "procedural homogeneity" (SPMD rather than SIMD);
- a global lock–step mechanism requires synchronization to take place only with every iteration as opposed to every communication or process switch;
- the model is embedded into a configuration description ("set–up") language.

Hence, switches between different paradigms are avoided, and a strong synergism between the application, the programming model, and the system architecture is established.

2. THE VIRTUAL PROCESSOR MODEL

Largely parallel computer architectures are by nature distributed memory architectures. In such a system each processing node has access only to its local memory, while communication among the nodes takes place through message passing. This leads to the programming model of cooperating parallel processes. The processes communicate on the basis of an appropriate inter process communication protocol. Data objects are encapsulated into the process that owns them.

If the algorithmic structures and solution domains are very regular, the communication and synchronization conditions of the parallel program can be satisfied by pre-programmed communication constructs loaded from a library [7]. If the algorithmic structures and solution domains are highly irregular, this approach is prone to fail. Consequently, it is left to the programmer to explicitly perform the program partitioning into cooperating processes, the workload distribution over the nodes, and the communication and synchronization through the insertion of send and receive constructs. In massively parallel systems this may not be practically feasible [8].

One solution to this problem consists in the construction of a virtual shared memory on top of the physically distributed system [9]. The thus created global address space then allows conventional programming languages such as Fortran, Lisp, C, Ada, etc. to be used. The drawback of this approach consists in the large overhead incurred by the tremendous amount of message traffic needed to implement the virtual shared memory model in a coherent manner [10]. In massively parallel systems, the overhead may become untolerable. Therefore, we introduce an alternative programming model which, on the one hand, is message–based rather than shared memory based. On the other hand, our program model leads to very straight–forward, readily applicable programming paradigms.

As was pointed out in the introduction, by *massively parallel computing* we understand a programming model where the user can assign an individual processor to every basic computational activity in the program. Here are some representative examples.

- *Neural network computation*: Every neuron in the network—no matter how many—will have assigned its individual, dedicated processor, to compute the firing behavior of that neuron. If one has a million neurons, one defines a million processors.
- *Particle simulation (e.g., lattice gauge)*: Each molecule has its "own" processor to compute its movement and its energy, etc. If one has a billion molecules, one needs a billion processors.
- *Computational fluid dynamics (PDE solvers)*: Each grid point has a processor attached that executes the relaxation algorithm for that grid point. Typically one has in the order of magnitude of 10^7 grid points; therefore, one needs 10^7 processors.

All these examples have in common that the *elementary computational step* performed by each processor consists in approximately 30 to 1000 primitive operations such as add, subtract, multiply, etc. All examples have furthermore in common that, after an elementary computational step, data must be exchanged with other processors.

Consequently, synchronization of and communication among the communicating processors may be greatly facilitated by two major simplifications wherever suitable:

1. Synchronization may be performed in a lock–step fashion. That is, there are alternating phases of computation and communication. In the computation phase all computational steps of an iteration are performed by all processors. In the subsequent communication phase the results of the computation step are communicated throughout the system. The lock step–mechanism ensures that the receiving processors are ready to receive a message when the communication phase is entered. Therefore, the overhead of a rendezvous protocol can be avoided. The lock–step mechanism is implemented in a distributed fashion.
2. Communication is not secured by a rendezvous protocol. This leaves it to the communication hardware and the transmission protocol (e.g., error detection by checksum, etc.) to secure the correctness of message passing.
3. Exceptional conditions that may occur in an asynchronous execution environment, e.g., a send issued at a time when the receiver is not yet ready for it, will be avoided by a synchronous operation of the virtual processors achieved through the simple lock–step mechanism. The lock–step mechanism will ensure that values communicated from other nodes have been consumed before they may be overwritten.

The virtual processor model, in connection with the lock–step synchronization, is appropriate in all cases that allow for a *fine–grain* partitioning of the solution algorithm into a very large number of elementary computational steps that all have approximately the same execution time. In the examples above, such a behavior is evident.

This model is maintained regardless of the physical size of the machine, i.e., the actual number of processors. Consequently, the processors of the programming model are virtual processors that are dedicated by the compiler to the computational tasks of the program and mapped by the operating system onto the set of available physical processors. That is, a virtual processor is in reality a thread of control (a process) that is executed by one of the physical processors. In order to make this scheme as efficient as possible, we introduce in the following the notion of featherweight processes.

3. FEATHERWEIGHT PROCESSES

3.1. What Are Featherweight Processes ?

Unlike heavyweight processes, lightweight processes do not constitute a domain of protection but just some means of structuring a program [11]. Protected address spaces are usually provided only for entire groups of lightweight processes. This makes the context switches among lightweight processes of the same group much faster, as they all have the same environment.

In order to implement our virtual processor model efficiently, we need a mechanism that is yet simpler and more efficient than lightweight processes. Therefore, we introduce the notion of featherweight processes. The foundation for the implementation of featherweight processes is provided by the PEACE family of operating system kernels [12].

Featherweight processes are the mechanization of the virtual processor programming model. They provide no protection for process execution and inter process communication, leaving the physical separation of the node memories as the only means of protection in the system. Naturally, this does not protect the system against faults in inter process communication. Therefore, featherweight processes are suitable only in a single–user mode of operation that can tolerate sporadic communication faults. The thus reduced functionality of featherweight processes reduces their run–time overhead to a bare minimum.

All the virtual processor activities which are mapped into the same node will be executed there as a featherweight process, that is, a single thread of code executed in a coroutine fashion. The collapsing of several virtual processor activities into a single thread of code is strictly a measure of optimization that may not always be feasible. In the worst case there may be several featherweight processes running on the node.

3.2. Semantics of Inter Process Communication

Featherweight processes are somewhat comparable to *occam* processes [13]. Since no protected communication domains for the featherweight processes are provided, there are no constraints as to when communication can take place. Moreover, there are no restrictions in connectivity. Consequently, every process can communicate with any other process.

Unlike in conventional systems, where it is the task of the operating system kernel to provide domains of protection, the correctness of the program execution is ensured by the execution model of a single–user, single–task operation in a lock–step fashion. The global lock–step synchronization scheme excludes the possibility that messages may be sent at a time when the recipient is not in the receiving state. Synchronization is needed only with every iteration as opposed to every communication or process switch.

Hence, featherweight processes are combined with *featherweight communication*, in which data transfers are secured only by the hardware and the transmission protocol but not by the operating system kernel. In this kind of communication the sender must not first seek a rendezvous with the receiver to find out whether the latter is ready for the communication, before a message can be sent. However, even in that scenario some minimum of supervisory functions must be exercised by the operating system kernel, because it must still be guaranteed that the physical communication channel does exist; e.g., that the interconnect is not blocked.

Note, this simple model does not handle problems of data loss, node crashes, etc. Data losses will lead to deadlock situations. Therefore, the operating system should comprise lightweight processes for diagnosis purposes, to detect and handle such exceptions. Furthermore, the operating system mechanisms should allow for more sophisticated communication mechanisms, e.g., buffered–asynchronous communication, when so desired. The price to pay in that case is an increase in overhead.

3.3. Featherweight Process Implementation

The implementation of featherweight processes is based upon a coroutine mechanism, executed under supervision by the operating system. This reduces context switches to the simple task of saving some registers. Therefore, the operating system kernel executes a function `toc_resume()` (toc: thread of control). The implementation of `toc_resume()` and the number of registers to be saved depends in the first place on the node processor architecture. In our implementation of the PEACE kernel, which is written in C++, one must make sure that all the registers used by C++ are saved too. Therefore, the number of registers to be saved depends also on the implementation. The overhead caused by register saving is minimized by the following mechanism.

The compiler partitions the register set of the physical processor into two banks: volatile and non–volatile registers. The volatile registers are used only for holding local parameters and intermediate results. Therefore, they need not be kept consistent between procedure calls (assuming an interrupt–free operation). Only the non–volatile register bank is used for storing global variables and, thus, need be exchanged on a coroutine switch. The reader will notice that this model corresponds with a modern trend in computer architecture, namely the trend towards the development of a new generation of processors for multi–threaded architectures. These processors are designed to mimimize the penalty for the environment switch.

The functionality of the operating system kernel that supports featherweight processes is simple: all that is required is the handling of TOCs and the (unprotected) communication among them. This is performed at the time a communication port is opened. The availability of the communication hardware is checked by an appropriate driver. This operating system kernel is the simplest member of the PEACE family of operating system kernels [12]. It can be bound to the application program as a library routine.

3.4. Communication

In the view of the user, communication between featherweight processes is mapped onto communication between virtual processors. To this end, the user can define for each virtual processor an arbitrary number of input/output ports. A *port* is a logical connection set–up at the receiving end to buffer exactly one message object of fixed length. We call this mode of communication *single–buffered asynchronous* [14]. During the communication phase, the virtual processor will read data from its ports and write data into the ports of other processors.

The buffer space for the ports are allocated in advance by the pre–compiler for the configuration language in cooperation with the operating system. A port can communicate its state (full, empty) to the sender of a message. This information is used for point–to–point communications coupled through a produce–consume mechanism. We recognize the similarity with *systolic communication* [15].

Such a simple communication model has the following properties:

- it is asynchronous, single–buffered
- it is routed via ports
- it is strongly supported by hardware.

Other communication policies can be realized on top of this simple mechanism. For example, asynchronous, buffered communication can be realized by a thread of control dedicated to that task. In our terminology, we may also say that other forms of communication can be realized by implementing a virtual communication processor associated with every virtual worker processor. The same holds true for the implementation of dynamic restructuring methods, which may be based upon our simple communication model as well. What must be implemented in that case are mechanisms for an n–to–1 correspondence between ports and threads and for forwarding identifiers.

Ports have system–wide, unique names [16]. To make the system better manageable, the virtual processors of the massively parallel programming model may be grouped hierarchically into *groups, clusters, processor farms,* etc. This will lead to an equally hierarchical, indexed naming scheme of the ports.

The behavior of ports can be summarized as follows:

- end–to–end communication between virtual processors
- routing capabilities with system–wide unique identifiers
- buffering of single messages of fixed length
- one–to–one correspondence with threads (processors)
- **overhead only in exceptional cases.**

3.5. Coroutine Performance

In a first implementation of `toc_resume()` on a system based on the Intel i860 processor [17], the cost of a coroutine switch amounts to 2 instructions for the call, 1 instruction for the return, and $2n$ instructions for exchanging the non–volatile registers. Hence, a coroutine switch takes a total of $3 + 2n$ cycles.

Our C and C++ compilers assign 15 integer and 6 floating–point registers to the non–volatile bank, thus requiring the exchange of 21 registers. In contrast, the Fortran compiler may utilize the full set of registers for optimizations and thus declare all 32 floating–point registers of the i860 as non–volatile. Hence, the coroutine switch overhead on the next generation of RISC processors or superscalar processors will be in the order of magnitude of 1 microsecond or less. Assuming for such a processor a sustained performance of 50 MFLOPS, this is the equivalent of 50 numerical operations. One can assume that the primitive operation performed by the virtual processor in each computational step encompasses approximately ten times that many instructions, which means that the process switch overhead for the featherweight processes becomes negligible.

The estimate above scales with technology; i.e., as the MFLOPS rate goes up, so will the MIPS rate. This reconfirms our belief that the virtual processor paradigm will become a viable, highly appropriate programming model for massively parallel computer systems.

4. OPERATING SYSTEM AND PROGRAMMING ENVIRONMENT

4.1. Operating System

The operating system kernel needed to support the virtual processor model can be extremely simple [5]. Only three basic types of services are needed per physical processor, viz.:

- Creation/destruction of thread objects. Because of the one–to–one correspondence between threads and virtual processors, this means creation/destruction of virtual processors as well.

- Creation/destruction of port objects (with the creation/destruction of virtual processors).

- Execution of threads and communication between threads.

Except for communication, all other services are invoked by remote procedure calls. This is mandated by the fact that threads must be manageable remotely and I/O and file handling must be performed remotely either by the frontend operating system (e.g., UNIX) or by system threads running on some physical processors dedicated to the handling of peripherals. These services are performed by the PEACE operating system.

The PEACE operating system consists of three building blocks:

Nucleus: The nucleus performs communication and thread execution as the most basic operating system functions. The nucleus must exist in every node (physical processor) of the system.

Kernel: The kernel serves as a *hardware abstraction*. Among other problem–oriented activities, the kernel creates and destroys thread objects and port objects and associates these objects with address spaces. In addition, it encapsulates device drivers and enables high–level system threads to be attached to the trap/interrupt vector of the executing physical processor. Thus, the kernel converts traps and interrupts into messages to higher–level threads.

System: This is the distributed operating system proper, whose major purpose is to provide application–oriented system services. The services are executed by the underlying physical processor in non–privileged user mode. In addition, the services are site–independent, i.e., can be remotely performed in any node of the system. Both properties let the operating system appear as a readily configurable building block.

Figure 1 illustrates the PEACE system organization as described above, including a building block of distributed applications. Kernel and system proper are minimal extensions of the nucleus.

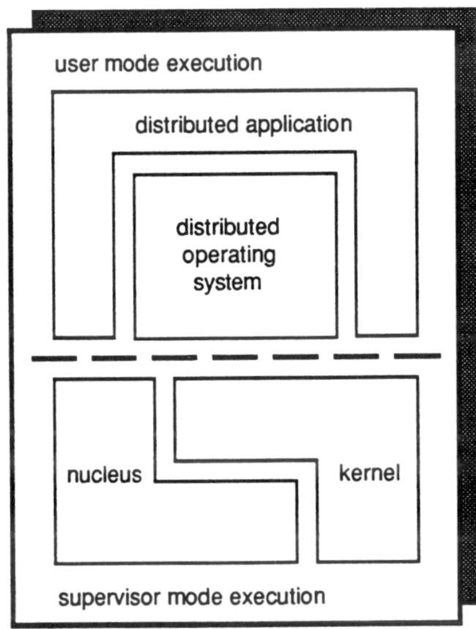

Figure 1. PEACE system organization

4.2. Programming Environment

The programming model will materialize in a number of language concepts:

- Declaration of virtual data topologies similar to those in [18]. They will be used to describe the component replication and inter–component communication patterns of distributed objects. The type–wise homogeneity of the distributed objects mirrors the procedural homogeneity of the SPMD model.
- Parallel procedure calls on distributed objects, usually with communication between their components, according to the topology declarations.
  Reduce and accumulate constructs.
- Additional iterative constructs to allow the description of convergent iterations and asynchronous methods. These are the high–level constructs that describe delayed termination of iterations and delayed communication, which are useful ingredients for massively parallel computations.

These abstract language concepts may constitute either a separate set–up language or a generic extension scheme for existing languages. In a simple setting the programming environment for the virtual processor model consists of:

- the Set–up Language (SL)
- the Application Language (C++).

The Set–up Language allows the user to declare the virtual processors and their ports. A configuration description may be textual, or it may be graphical. We are planning to implement both versions in order to allow for some experimentation. The set–up language is translated by the SL compiler described below. The Application Language is used to program the threads, i.e., the algorithms executed by the virtual processors. In principle, this can be any existing programming language. The language of our choice is C++.

5. THE SL COMPILER

5.1. The Set–up

The set–up describes the topology of virtual processors and their interconnection as dictated by the application algorithms. That is, it specifies virtual processors together with their input and output ports and the interconnection of the ports. The arrangement of virtual processors may be highly hierarchical, consisting of cluster, groups, and subgroups, etc.

The translation of the set–up description into an executable program is performed primarily by two sophisticated units of the SL compiler:

- the aggregator and
- the mapper.

Figure 2 shows the layers of the virtual processor programming system.

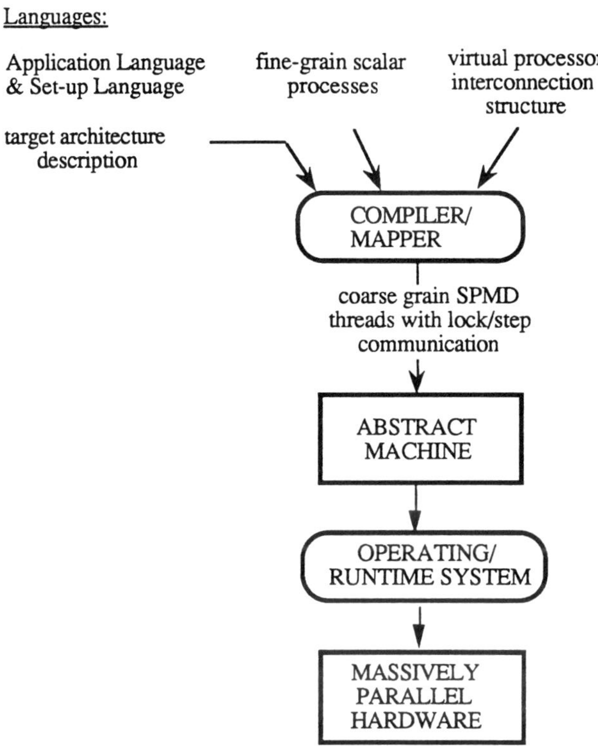

Figure 2. The layers of the virtual processor programming system

5.2. The Aggregator

The aggregator has the task to collapse a number of fine–grain virtual processes into a coarse grain process that will be executed by a physical processor. Theoretically, this boils down to the task of mapping a computational graph with many nodes onto a coarser graph with a lesser number of nodes by collapsing several fine–grain nodes that are directly interconnected into one coarse–grain node. There exist solutions to this problem [19].

5.3. The Mapper

The task of the mapper is to assign the processes generated by the aggregator to the resources of the physical machine. To this end, the *mapper* must map the symbolic addresses of virtual processors and ports onto system–wide physical addresses, replace the read–from–port and write–to–port instructions by the appropriate send and receive constructs, and invoke the code blocks constituting the threads for the virtual processor.

The programming interface (textual or graphical) is object–oriented. Therefore, two kinds of abstractions are needed:

- PEACE specific abstractions such as thread objects, port objects, communication objects;
- UNIX–like abstractions for I/O, file handling, and host access (networking).

5.4. Object–Oriented Implementation

The object paradigm is highly appropriate for the programming of massively parallel systems based on the virtual processor model. The virtual processor may be represented as a class type, and a set of individual virtual processors can then be created by instantiating objects of this class. This procedure strongly supports compiler optimizations. Classes, as well as class hierarchies built by means of inheritance, allow for an application–driven customization of the parallel application with respect to the given target architecture. In order to express locality, thus giving a compiler some hints as to how to map the virtual processors, a class–based approach as exemplified with C++ can be used to group a number of related objects by associating them with a new class. A cluster of virtual processors can be declared by using standard C++ features. Clusters of clusters can be built in the same fashion.

5.5. The Use of C++ as Programming Language

C++ is the most widely used object–oriented programming language; therefore, using C++ as the basis for the application language as well as the target language of the SL compiler seems to be the best choice from the viewpoint of user acceptance. Moreover, C++ has a number of features that strongly support object–oriented programming and, thus, is quite suitable as implementation language.

With each class, constructor and destructor methods can be defined that are automatically invoked when objects of the class are created and destroyed. With objects being virtual processors, this supports the task of a runtime system to keep track of the (static/dynamic) assignment of virtual processors to either processes (passive approach) or physical processors (active approach). Load balancing—at least in a static sense—can be readily introduced in a transparent manner. Furthermore, class–related load balancing strategies are made feasible, implementing different strategies with the different constructor methods.

Port classes are the vehicles communication between virtual processors. A port is a passive object with read and write methods defined on it. Different port types may be meaningful for different application requirements. Non–, single–, or multi–buffering ports may be introduced as needed. All port types will provide the same read and write methods yet will exhibit the different buffering capabilities. Inheritance is the key for deriving more specialized versions from a port base class which, for example, may provide only non–buffered communication.

The principle of inheritance should in general be applied to derive the object classes of the virtual processor model from the more primitive classes used to construct the parallel computing surface of the operating system, thus achieving the closest possible link between application level and operating system and runtime level.

A similar abstraction can be made with respect to synchronization. For example, a barrier class may be defined that meets the synchronization needs of the lock–step execution inherent in our virtual processor model. The declaration of a barrier object could be given the semantics of introducing a specific synchronization point. The constructor for this object then will execute the proper synchronization protocol. Again, one can start with the most simple and common synchronization strategy and end up with a derived class that incorporates a more complex strategy.

Finally, the inlining feature of C++ helps to develop the most efficient parallel programs without sacrificing a clean and well–structured program organization. Class methods can be declared as inline. Invocations of these methods then will involve neither a function call nor the passing of arguments. Program development based on the abstract data type concept is strongly supported without the risk of yielding inefficient code.

6. CONCLUSION

We believe that massively parallel computing is not just another word for *very large scale multiprocessor architecture* but, first of all, a programming style. To this end, we introduce in the paper a novel programming model for MIMD architectures, called the *virtual processor model.* We see the virtualization of processors as a *means of abstraction* that furthers the wide–range scalability of message–passing systems, providing a viable and, in many applications, more appropriate alternative to the *virtual shared memory approach.* In the paper, some first implementational concepts for the virtual processor paradigm are discussed and it is shown that such a model can be implemented with negligible overhead.

The RWC Report [3] attests the conventional programming models a "lack of capabilities to describe and process problems in which myriad of elements are complicatedly and dynamically involved with each other." We claim that the programming model for massively parallel systems presented in this paper provides exactly the lacking capabilities.

1 Amari S. et al.: *The Master Plan for the Real World Computing Program*, Draft of March 2, 1992, Feasibility Study Committee of the Real World Computing Program, MITI, Tokyo 1992

2 Giloi W.K., Montenegro S.: *Choosing the Interconnect of Distributed Memory Systems by Cost and Blocking Behavior*, Proc. 5th Internat. Parallel Processing Symposium, IEEE Computer Society Press Order no. 2167, 438–444

3 Ishi T.: *Report of the Research Committee on New Information Processing Technology*, Ministry of International Trade and Industry (MITI), Tokyo, March 1991

4 Hillis W.D.: *The Connection Machine*, MIT Press 1965

5 Berg et al.: *The PEACE Family of Distributed Operating Systems*, paper accepted for publication by J. of Distributed and Parallel Computing

6 Giloi W.K., Schröder–Preikschat W.: *Very High–speed Communication in Large MIMD Supercomputers*, Proc. ICS +89, ACM Order no. 415891, 313–321

7 Thole C.A.: *Application Software and Its Support by the Abstract SUPRENUM Machine*, in Jesshope C.R., Reinartz K.D.(eds.): CONPAR 88, Cambridge University Press 1989, 35–43

8 M. Malek (organizer): *Joint Workshop of INRIA and the US Office of Naval Research*, Roquencourt, France, Dec. 1990,

9 Li K.: *Shared Virtual Memory on Loosely Coupled Multiprocessors*, Ph.D. thesis, Yale University 1986

10 Giloi W.K. et al.: *A Distributed Implementation of Shared Virtual Memory With Strong and Weak Coherence*, Proc. EDMCC2: Distributed Memory Computing, Lecture Notes on Computer Science 487, Springer 1991, 23–31

11 Cheriton D.R.: *Multi-Process Structuring and the Thoth Operating System*, Ph.D. thesis, University of Waterloo, UBC Tech. Report 79–5, 1979

12 Schröder–Preikschat W.: *Overcoming the Startup Time Problem in Distributed Memory Architectures*, Proc. 24th Hawaii Internat. Conf. on System Sciences (1991), IEEE catalog no. 91TH0350–9, 551–559

13 Pountain D., May D.: *A Tutorial Introduction to OCCAM Programming*, INMOS, BSP Professional Books (1987)

14 Behr P.M., Giloi W.K., Schröder–Preikschat W.: *Synchronous Versus Asynchronous Communication in High–Performance Multicomputer Systems*, in M. Wright(ed.): Proc. IFIP WG 2.5 Working Conf. on Aspects of Computation in Asynchronous Parallel Processors, North–Holland, Amsterdam 1989, 239–249

15 Gross T.: *Communication in iWarp Systems*, Proc. Supercomputing +89, ACM order no. 415892, 436–445

16 Sander M., Schmidt H., Schröder–Preikschat W.: *Naming in the PEACE Distributed Operating System*, Proc. Int. Workshop on Communication Networks and Distributed Operating Systems Within the Space Environment, North–Holland (Oct. 1989)

17 Brüning U., Giloi W.K., Schröder–Preikschat W.: *The Architecture of the European MIMD Supercomputer GENESIS*, Proc. EDMCC2: Distributed Memory Computing, Lecture Notes on Computer Science 487, Springer 1991, 450–462

18 T. Bräunl, *Massiv parallele Programmierung mit dem Parallaxis–Modell*, Springer 1990.

19 Ben–Natan R., Barak A.: *Parallel Contractions of Grids for Task Assignment to Processor Networks*, Tech Report 91–01, The Hebrew University of Jerusalem, Department of Computer Science(Feb. 1991)

IFIP

The INTERNATIONAL FEDERATION FOR INFORMATION PROCESSING is a multinational federation of professional and technical organisations (or national groupings of such organisations) concerned with information processing. From any one country, only one such organisation – which must be representative of the national activities in the field of information processing – can be admitted as a Full Member. In addition a regional group of developing countries can be admitted as a Full Member. On 1 October 1991, 46 organisations were Full Members of the Federation, representing 70 countries.

The aims of IFIP are to promote information science and technology by:

- fostering international co-operation in the field of information processing;
- stimulating research, development and the application of information processing in science and human activity;
- furthering the dissemination and exchange of information about the subject;
- encouraging education in information processing.

IFIP is dedicated to improving worldwide communication and increased understanding among practitioners of all nations about the role information processing can play in all walks of life.

Information technology is a potent instrument in today's world, affecting people in everything from their education and work to their leisure and in their homes. It is a powerful tool in science and engineering, in commerce and industry, in education and adminstration. It is truly international in its scope and offers a significant opportunity for developing countries. IFIP helps to bring together workers at the leading edge of the technology to share their knowledge and experience, and acts as a catalyst to advance the state of the art.

IFIP came into official existence in January, 1960. It was established to meet a need identified at the first International Conference on Information Processing which was held in Paris in June, 1959, under the sponsorship of UNESCO.

Organisational Structure
The Federation is governed by a GENERAL ASSEMBLY, which meets once every year and consists of one representative from each Member organisation. The General Assembly decides on all important matters, such as general policy, the programme of activities, admissions, elections and budget.

IFIP ORGANISATION CHART

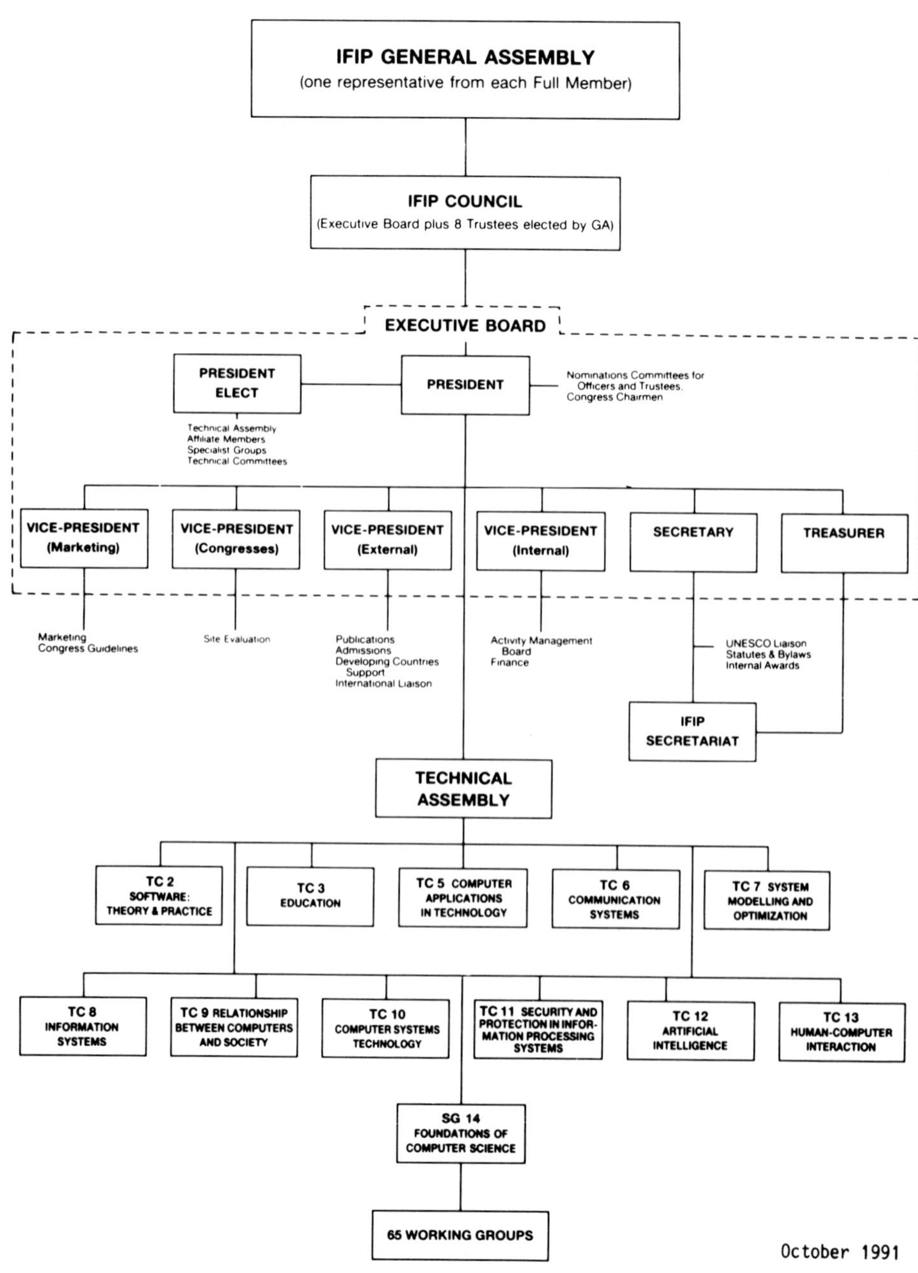

October 1991

The day-to-day work of IFIP is directed by its Officers: the President, Vice-Presidents, Secretary and Treasurer, who are elected by the General Assembly and together constitute the EXECUTIVE BOARD.

The COUNCIL, consisting of the Officers and up to eight Trustees elected from the General Assembly, meets twice a year and takes decisions which become necessary between General Assembly meetings.

The headquarters of the Federation are in Geneva, Switzerland where the IFIP Secretariat administers its affairs.

For further information please contact:

IFIP Secretariat
attn. Mme. GWYNETH ROBERTS
16 Place Longemalle
CH-1204 Geneva, Switzerland
telephone: 41 (22) 28 26 49
facsimile: 41 (22) 781 23 22
Bitnet: ifip@cgeuge51

IFIP's MISSION STATEMENT

IFIP's mission is to be the leading, truly international, apolitical organisation which encourages and assists in the development, exploitation and application of Information Technology for the benefit of all people.

Principal Elements

1. To stimulate, encourage and participate in research, development and application of Information Technology (IT) and to foster international co-operation in these activities.
2. To provide a meeting place where national IT Societies can discuss and plan courses of action on issues in our field which are of international significance and thereby to forge increasingly strong links between them and with IFIP.
3. To promote internation co-operation directly and through national IT Societies in a free environment between individuals, national and international governmental bodies and kindred scientific and professional organisations.
4. To pay special attention to the needs of developing countries and to assist them in appropriate ways to secure the optimum benefit from the application of IT.
5. To promote professionalism, incorporating high standards of ethics and conduct, among all IT practitioners.
6. To provide a forum for assessing the social consequences of IT applications; to campaign for the safe and beneficial development and use of IT and the protection of people from abuse through its improper application.

7. To foster and facilitate co-operation between academics, the IT industry and governmental bodies and to seek to represent the interest of users.
8. To provide a vehicle for work on the international aspects of IT development and application including the necessary preparatory work for the generation of international standards.
9. To contribute to the formulation of the education and training needed by IT practitioners, users and the public at large.

Note to Conference Organizers
Organizers of upcoming IFIP Working Conferences are urged to contact the Publisher. Please send full details of the Conference to:

Mrs. STEPHANIE SMIT
Administrative Editor – IFIP Publications
ELSEVIER SCIENCE PUBLISHERS
P.O. Box 103, 1000 AC Amsterdam
The Netherlands
telephone: 31 (20) 5862481
facsimile: 31 (20) 5862616
email: s.smit@elsevier.nl

IFIP TRANSACTIONS

IFIP TRANSACTIONS is a serial consisting of 15,000 pages of valuable scientific information from leading researchers, published in 35 volumes per year. The serial includes contributed volumes, proceedings of the IFIP World Conferences, and conferences at Technical Committee and Working Group level. Mainstream areas in the IFIP TRANSACTIONS can be found in Computer Science and Technology, Computer Applications in Technology, and Communication Systems.

Please find below a detailed list of topics covered.

IFIP TRANSACTIONS A:
Computer Science and Technology
1992: 19 Volumes, US $ 1181.00/Dfl. 2185.00
ISSN 0926-5473

IFIP Technical Committees
Software: Theory and Practice (TC2)
Education (TC3)
System Modelling and Optimization (TC7)
Information Systems (TC8)
Relationship Between Computers and Society (TC9)

Computer Systems Technology (TC10)
Security and Protection in Information Processing Systems (TC11)
Artificial Intelligence (TC12)
Human-Computer Interaction (TC13)
Foundations of Computer Science (SG14)

IFIP TRANSACTIONS B:
Applications in Technology
1992: 8 Volumes. US $ 497.00/Dfl. 920.00
ISSN 0926-5481

IFIP Technical Committee
Computer Applications in Technology (TC5)

IFIP TRANSACTIONS C:
Communication Systems
1992: 8 Volumes. US 497.00/Dfl. 920.00
ISSN 0926-549X

IFIP Technical Committee
Communication Systems (TC6)

IFIP TRANSACTIONS FULL SET: A, B & C
1992: 35 Volumes. US $ 1892.00/Dfl. 3500.00

The Dutch Guilder prices (Dfl.) are definitive. The US $ prices mentioned above are for your guidance only and are subject to exchange rate fluctuations. Prices include postage and handling charges.

The volumes are also available separately in book form.

Please address all orders and correspondence to:

ELSEVIER SCIENCE PUBLISHERS
attn. PETRA VAN DER MEER
P.O. Box 103, 1000 AC Amsterdam
The Netherlands
telephone: 31 (20) 5862602
facsimile: 31 (20) 5862616
email: m.haccou@elsevier.nl